Macmillan
English
Grammar
In Context

Advanced

Macmillan Education
Between Towns Road, Oxford OX4 3PP
A division of Macmillan Publishers Limited
Companies and representatives throughout the world

ISBN 978-1-4050-7052-2 (with key edition)
ISBN 978-1-4050-7147-5 (without key edition)

First published 2008

Designed by Giles Davies
Illustrated by Fred Blunt; Chris Ede; Andy Hammond; Joanna Kerr; Darren Lingard; Julian Mosedale; Sarah Nayler
Cover design by Katie Stephens
Cover photographs by Alamy/Bailey-Cooper Photography, Image Source, Photodisc, Stockbyte

I would like to thank Carl Robinson, Amanda Holmbrook and Sarah Curtis for their support and help during this project. Special thanks are due to my editor Clare Shaw. I would also like to thank the many teachers whose classes I have visited, and who have commented on versions of this book.

The authors and publishers are grateful for permission to reprint the following copyright material: The BBC for an extract from 'Bond film stage "will be rebuilt"' published on www.news.bbc.co.uk 31 July 2006, copyright © www.bbc.co.uk 2006. Guardian News & Media Ltd for an extract from 'The appliance of Science' by Mike Hulme published in The Guardian 14 March 2007, copyright © Guardian 2007. BritainUSA.com for an extract from 'Which cheeses are produced in Britain?' published on www.britainusa.com. The Scotsmans Publication Limited for an extract from 'Blocked drains shut gallery' by Joanna Vallely published in The Scotsman February 2006. Telegraph Media Group Limited for an extract from 'Cure for blindness within five years' by Roger Highfield published in The Telegraph 6 June 2007, copyright © The Telegraph 2007.

These materials may contain links for third party websites. We have no control over, and are not responsible for, the contents of such third party websites. Please use care when accessing them.

Although we have tried to trace and contact copyright holders before publication, in some cases this has not been possible. If contacted we will be pleased to rectify any errors or omissions at the earliest opportunity.

The authors and publishers would like to thank the following for permission to reproduce their photographic material: Alamy/ Robert Stainforth p 77, Andrew Fox p 131, Bailey-Cooper Photography p 140; Ancient Art & Architecture Collection/ p 145; Anthony Blake Picture Library/ p 36; Art Directors & Trip/ David Clegg p 33, Helene Rogers p 141t, Mark Maclaren p 201; Bananastock/ pp 28ct, 28cb, 28b, 123, 209; Brand X/ pp 23, 53, 99, 153; Cartoon Stock/ p 26; ComStock/ p 32; Corbis/ Eberhard Streichan/ zefa p 31, Richard Cummins p 55, Bettmann p 87, John Springe Collection p 117, W. Perry Conway p 168, The Gallery Collection p 219; Digital Stock/ Corbis p 102; Digital Vision/ p 81; Eyewire/ p 28t; Getty Images/ Holly Harris p 15, Hulton Archive pp 18,108, 149, Petrified Collection p 85l, AFP 141b, Kazumi Nagaswawa p 157, Altrendo images p 207, Frank Whitney p 211; Haddon Davies/ p 107; Image 100/ p 109; Image Source/ pp 160, 210, 213, 214; Jupiter/ Michel Fainsilber/ Photononstop p 63, Mary Evans Picture Library/ pp 113, 161; Photodisc/ p 59, 67, 187, 191, 212; Rex Features / pp 85r, 98; Science Picture Library/ NASA p 165, Ed Young p 186, Still Pictures/ William Campbell p 38; Stockbyte/ pp 9, 22, 95, 135; Superstock/ pp 45, 85c, 103.

Printed and bound in Thailand

2013 2012 2011 2010 2009
7   6   5   4   3

Introduction

This book is designed to revise and consolidate grammar points at the level of Council of Europe Framework (CEF) C1 and C2. It assumes that the basic points have been covered. These can be practised in Macmillan English Grammar In Context Essential and Macmillan English Grammar In Context Intermediate.

The practice material includes a wide range of topics to reflect both everyday language use and the kinds of subjects learners might be studying in schools or colleges. Many learners are likely to use English to learn another subject during their education and the choice of text tries to reflect this fact. Some texts contain information which learners should find interesting or challenging. The intention in general is that language should have a familiar context and that learners should have something to use language for.

Within each unit, exercises range in difficulty. This allows learners to build up their confidence with the simpler, more familiar tasks before moving onto the more challenging ones later in the unit. The longer, topic-based texts include highlighted words whose definitions can be found on the accompanying CD-ROM. This is a good opportunity for learners to widen their vocabulary and see grammar used in realistic contexts.

The Review section at the back of the book offers more activities for students who have finished the other exercises. It is also for students who feel that they haven't fully grasped the grammar point and need some further practice. In addition, it can be used as a means of testing or revising previous study, either in class or at home.

The CD-ROM
This includes two further exercises for each unit in this book, and a test section. Plus, where you see highlighted words like this, you will find the definitions in the glossary section. Just follow the link from the homepage.

To the student
Macmillan English Grammar In Context has been written to make grammar more interesting than other books on the market. We hope you find it enjoyable as well as useful. If you are studying at home, the units can be covered in any order but the exercises within each unit have been graded. If you find some exercises difficult, read the presentation page again. The extension activities and Review offer the opportunity of further practice.

To the teacher
Unlike many other grammar books, *Macmillan English Grammar In Context* puts grammar into context. The aim is to encourage students to see grammar used more realistically and in more interesting ways. The topics covered in the exercises can be used as a starting point for a lesson, as a subject for discussion, and as a means of helping to build students' vocabulary in useful areas. There is opportunity for individual study, group work and homework, plus testing, in the different sections of the book.

Contents

1 present simple, present continuous (1)

basic uses of present simple and present continuous

- Use present simple for facts, or things that always happen.
  *Water **freezes** at 32 degrees Fahrenheit and 0 degrees Celsius.*
  *Sea water **contains** on average 2.7% salt by weight.*

- Use present simple for routines and habits.
  *The birds **return** to the island every spring.*
  *Fiddler crabs **turn** red when they become angry.*

- Use present continuous for actions happening at the moment of speaking, and not finished.
  *Sorry, I'm busy at the moment. **I'm doing** my homework.*

- Present continuous is also used for actions happening generally around the time of speaking, rather than exactly at the same time.
  ***I'm reading** a really interesting book.*

state and action verbs

Some verbs have meanings which refer to states or conditions, and others have meanings which refer to actions. State verbs are either only used in simple form, or have a different meaning when used in continuous form.

state verbs normally in present simple

- *belong, consist of, contain, cost, depend on, deserve, matter, own, possess, resemble*
  *Does this **belong** to you?*
  *Fresh fruit **contains** a range of vitamins.*

- *believe, imagine, know, prefer, realize, understand, mean*
  *Some people still **believe** that the Earth is flat.*

- *seem*
  *This **seems** to be what we're looking for.*

- *cost* is sometimes used in continuous to describe a process that is still going on.
  *We're having a house built, and **it's costing** a fortune!*

- *realize, regret, understand*
  These are normally used with state meanings in present simple, but can be used in continuous to show a changing situation, usually with an adverbial which shows that change is happening.
  *Some people **don't realize** how dangerous cars can be.*
  *People **are slowly realizing** the cost of global warming.*
  ***Do** you **understand** this point?*
  *We**'re understanding** more and more about the universe.*

verbs with state and action meanings

state	action
● *do*	
*What **do** you do?* (= what's your job)	*What **are you doing**?* (= explain your actions)
● *be, have*	
*This house **is** over 100 years old.*	*He **is being** very silly!*
*Do you **have** a car?*	*I**'m having a great time** here.*
● *imagine, suppose, think, expect*	
*I **suppose** this is Jim.*	*You**'re supposing** he is guilty.* (= make an assumption)
*I **imagine** you feel the same.*	*Ghosts! No, you**'re imagining** things!*
*What **do you think**?* (= have an opinion)	*What are **you thinking**?*
	*I**'m thinking** of changing jobs.* (= considering)
*I **don't expect** him to understand.*	*Are you **expecting** someone?*

- **hope, wonder**

  *I **hope** you haven't been waiting long.*　　　*We're **hoping** to continue the talks next week.* **(less definite)**

- **enjoy, like, love**

  Normally state verbs, but often used in continuous for actions going on at the moment

  *I **enjoy / love** going for long walks.*　　　*Are you **enjoying** the party?*

  　　　　　　　　　　　　　　　　　　　　*I**'m loving** every minute of my new job!*

- **appear**

  *Your visa **appears** to be out of date.*　　　*Tom is **appearing** in Hamlet at the Grand Theatre.*

- **look**

  With the state meaning of 'seem', *look* can be used in present simple only.

  *This book **looks** interesting.*

  In descriptions of appearance, *look* can be used in both simple and continuous.

  *Jim **looks** ill.*　　　　　　　　　　　　*Helen **is looking** well.*

- **see, hear**

  *I **see / hear** you've had your hair cut.*　　　*Jane **is seeing** Harry. (= spending time with)*

  *I didn't **hear** any noises.*　　　　　　　*You'**re hearing** things! (= imagining)*

- **feel, see, smell, taste**

  *The room **smells** awful!*　　　　　　　*I**'m smelling** the flowers! (an active choice)*

- **ache, feel, hurt**

  Verbs that describe how the body feels can use either simple or continuous forms with little change in meaning.

  *My foot **hurts**.*　　　　　　　　　　*My foot **is hurting**.*

  *I **feel** sick.*　　　　　　　　　　　　*I**'m feeling** sick*

- **weigh, measure**

  *This bag **weighs** more than 25 kilos.*　　　*I**'m weighing** the parcel before I post it.*

Note that what is said here about present simple and present continuous is generally true for simple and continuous use in other tenses.

1 Underline the correct form.

a Some kinds of fish <u>contain</u> / *are containing* high levels of dangerous metals.

b Scientists nowadays *slowly begin to understand* / <u>are slowly beginning to understand</u> more about how the brain works.

c What <u>do you think</u> / *are you thinking* of Kate's new hairstyle? It's unusual, isn't it?

d Loud music can be really annoying. Some people <u>don't realize</u> / *aren't realizing* what a nuisance it can be.

e You can't really have seen a UFO! You *imagine* / <u>are imagining</u> things!

f Technicians report that they *have* / <u>are having</u> difficulty installing the new computer system.

g No wine for me! *I take* / <u>I'm taking</u> antibiotics for an ear infection.

h In career terms, having a good degree <u>appears</u> / *is appearing* to make little difference.

i The National Theatre *considers* / <u>is considering</u> putting on a new production of *Uncle Vanya*.

j <u>Does this wallet belong</u> / *Is this wallet belonging* to you?

2 Underline the present simple / continuous verb errors in the text. Write a correction at the end of the line where necessary.

15 Tiptree Rd
Warwick
CV29 7AL

friday, 15th October

Hi everyone,

I <u>have</u> problems getting a new phone connection here, so instead
of sending e-mails as usual, I'm actually <u>sitting down</u> to write a
letter.

   <u>I'm imagining</u> you'll be surprised to get this as I've never been
much of a letter-writer. <u>I'm putting</u> the return address in big
letters at the top, because to tell you the truth I'm beginning to feel
quite lonely here.

   well, perhaps <u>I'm not meaning</u> that exactly. There are plenty of
people for me to talk to. In fact <u>I settle</u> in to the student life quite
well, but I don't really know anyone yet. I've got a room in a house
a long way from college, and <u>I'm seeming</u> to spend a long time on
the bus. A lot of students here cycle, so I'm trying to find a cheap
bike, and I <u>also think</u> of moving nearer to college when I can find
somewhere. Sorry – an interruption, someone <u>knocks</u> at the door. More
later. Later. One of the girls downstairs <u>has a party</u>, and I'm invited.
And the phone line has been fixed, so <u>I'm expecting</u> you'll get an e-
mail from me very soon! In fact, <u>I consider</u> tearing up this letter, so
just ignore everything I've said ...

a   I'm having

b

c   I imagine

d

e

f   don't mean

g   I'm settling

h

i   I seem

j

k   I'm also thinking

l   is knocking

m   is having

n   I expect

o   I'm considering

3 Complete the text with the present simple or present continuous form of the verb in brackets.

European traffic accident rates fail to meet targets

Although the number of deaths caused in traffic accidents in the EU **a** (go down) *is going down*, experts **b** (still try) *are still trying* to find ways of reducing the number throughout the EU to around 25,000 fatalities per year by 2010. Traffic safety **c** (improve) *is improving* but experts **d** (believe) *believe* that achieving the 2010 goal will prove difficult. Recent statistics **e** (show) *show* that in 2005 in the EU 41,600 people were killed in road accidents. Although progress has been made, most experts **f** (agree) *agree* that this figure will have fallen to only around 32,000 by 2010, which **g** (means) *means* that the EU target will be missed by about 7,000. On the other hand, as the amount of traffic **h** (increase), *is increasing* it is possible to argue that the situation is not really as bad as it **i** (look) *looks*. However one **j** (interpret) *interprets* the statistics, it **k** (remain) *remains* true that as time goes on, it **l** (become) *is becoming* harder and harder to reduce the figures, especially since accident-reduction schemes **m** (cost) *cost* a lot of money. Many countries have tried and failed to reduce the number of accidents, and in the EU as a whole, only Sweden **n** (pursue) *is persuing* the goal of zero accidents. Accident reduction is more difficult for newer EU members who **o** (currently face) *are currently facing* very rapid growth in traffic and **p** (have) *are having* difficulty in building new roads and in introducing safety measures at a fast enough rate. To complicate matters, most new members **q** (have) *have* very little experience in dealing with the demands of heavy traffic. Experts **r** (suggest) *?* that any safety programme must also set about changing the way drivers **s** (behave) *?*. Despite what people often **t** (say) *?* it **u** (seem) *seems* to be the younger generation that **v** (cause) *cause* most accidents. In line with this research, many countries **w** (introduce) *are introducing* tougher driving tests, and **x** (concentrate) *are concentrating* on the main causes of accidents: speed, reckless overtaking, alcohol, and over-confidence.

GLOSSARY

present simple, present continuous (1)

2 present simple, present continuous (2)

more uses of present simple

Present simple is also used

- in informal spoken instructions, with *you*.
  You open this part of the camera here. Then you take out the battery.

  Formal written instructions such as recipes use the imperative form.
  Take 300g of flour. Add three eggs.

- in newspaper headlines to describe events. There are other conventions for writing headlines, such as leaving out articles, using active verbs, and preferring short words.

> Three **die** in plane crash.

> MPs **say** no to green laws.

- for performative verbs *accept, apologize, dare, deny, understand, see* (with a meaning of 'understand') *etc*. These are verbs which, when used in present simple, describe an action as the word is spoken.
  *I **agree** with you.   I **accept** your offer.*
  *I **understand**.   I **see**.*

> *Thank you,*
> *I accept your offer.*

- for verbs reporting news: *gather, hear, see, tell, say, understand.*
  *I **hear** you've got a new job.*
  ***People tell me** she's difficult to work with.*
  ***We understand** that the house is now for sale.*
  (See Unit 19, reporting verbs)

- in *here comes, there goes, here lies.*
  These expressions include inversion of verb and subject.
  ***Here comes** trouble!   **There goes** a brave man!*
  ***Here lies** John Smith.* **(written on a tomb)**

colloquial narrative and commentary

Although narrative generally uses past tenses, there are uses of present simple and present continuous in everyday speech.

- In jokes, present simple can be used instead of past simple for narrative events, and present continuous instead of past continuous.
  *A man **goes** to see his psychiatrist. He **says** he **is having** problems because he imagines **he's** a pair of curtains. The psychiatrist **tells** him to pull himself together.*

- In sports commentaries, present simple is often used to describe events happening as the commentator speaks.
  *And now Rooney **crosses** the half-way line and **passes** to Giggs.*

  Present continuous is also used in commentaries for continuous and changing events.
  *And the two Italians **are moving up** in the outside lane.*

- Plot summaries in films and books are generally in present simple.

  *Tom and Daisy **are** an old couple who **live** a dull life in a suburb of Birmingham. But everything **changes** when their granddaughter Karen **comes** to stay.*

summary of meaning in the continuous

- verbs that describe activities which continue for some time, eg *play, rain, read, work, write* etc

  It's raining.   *The children **are playing** upstairs.*

  Note that the activity may not be going on at the exact moment of speaking.
  ***I'm reading** Harry Potter and the Goblet of Fire.*   (I haven't finished it yet, but I'm not reading at this moment)

- verbs that describe a changing situation, eg *change, get* + adjective, *grow, increase* etc

  ***It's getting** dark.*   *Computers **are changing** all the time.*

repeated actions with *continually* etc

In everyday speech we can use present continuous with an adverb such as *continually, forever, constantly, always* to criticize actions that we feel are irritating or annoying, or which we wish to exaggerate. The adverb is usually stressed in speech.

  *You are **continually** interrupting!*
  *He's **forever** getting into trouble!*

Is that my jacket? Give it back, you're always wearing my clothes!

simple or continuous?

In some cases, the choice between simple and continuous is part of the attitude of the writer or speaker, especially in explanations and descriptions of situations.

  *Professor Thorne explains that some patients **eat** too much because they **grow up** in families with poor eating habits.*
  *Professor Thorne explains that some patients **are eating** too much because they **are growing up** in families with poor eating habits.*

  The first example (present simple) describes something that is generally true, the second (present continuous) describes something more temporary or something not always the case.

These exercises include material from Unit One.

1 <u>Underline</u> the correct verb form. Tick the sentence if both forms are possible.

a I can't walk any more. My knee *is really hurting* / *really hurts*.　✓

b This cheese *is smelling* / <u>*smells*</u> terrible!

c Thanks for your e-mail. *I'm hoping* / *I hope* to get back to you very soon.　✓

d 'What *are you doing* / *do you do*?' 'I'm a musician.'

e We're having our house completely redecorated. <u>*It's costing*</u> / *It costs* a lot.

f In this country, more than a million people *are living* / *live* in poverty.　✓

g Can you stop the car? *I'm feeling* / *I feel* a bit sick.　✓

h 'What's the answer?' 'Wait a moment, <u>*I'm thinking*</u> / *I think*.'　✓

i I think <u>*we're beginning*</u> / *we begin* to understand this problem.　✓

j Nice to see you again! *You're looking* / *You look* really great!　✓

3/9

2 Put the verb in brackets into present simple or present continuous.

a Somebody (knock) ___is knocking___ at the door. Can you see who it is?

b First you (cook) ___cook___ the onions in a little oil until they are golden brown.

c Carlos (forever lose) ___is forever losing___ his temper with people! He must learn to calm down.

d Here (come) ___comes___ the bus! You'd better hurry!

e 'Where's Jack? ' 'He (read) ___is reading___ the paper in the kitchen.'

f Whenever I put up my hand, Harry (kick) ___kicks___ me under the desk.

g I'm sorry, but I (not understand) ___don't understand___ you.

h Maria (leave) ___is leaving___ now, so could you get her coat?

i Come and eat your dinner. It (get) ___is getting___ cold.

j I (hear) ___hear___ you did really well in your exams. Well done!

7/9

3 Complete each sentence with the present simple or present continuous form of the verb in brackets.

a (you do) ___Are you doing___ anything at the moment? I need some help with the computer.

b This product (contain) ___contains___ no added chemicals of any kind.

c Nobody (visit) ___visits___ Rome without going to see the ruins of the Roman Forum.

d Sarah (begin) ___is begining___ to regret not taking the job in France she was offered.

e Martin (see) ___is seeing___ Tina at the moment. They've been going out together for the past month.

f I'm sorry, but I (not know) ___don't know___ where George is at the moment.

g 'Is Helen ready yet?' 'She (take) ___is taking___ her time, but she says she'll be ready soon.'

The larger of the two rooms (measure) ___measures___ 8 m by 4 m.

What (happen) ___is happening___ in the street now? I can't see anything from ...re.

...re's nobody else to do the job, so I (suppose) ___suppose___ I'll have to do it.

9/9

4 Complete the two texts with the present simple or present continuous form of the verb in brackets. If both forms are possible, write both.

Doctors express concern over heavy school bags

Every year thousands of children **a** (go) _go_ to the doctor because of back pain, and in fact, this kind of problem **b** (rapidly become) _is rapidly becoming_ one of the most common childhood complaints. And what exactly **c** (cause) _causes_ this outbreak of back strain and muscle fatigue? It **d** (seem) _seems_ that even quite young children **e** (take) _are taking_ more and more to school – not just books, but also clothes and games players – and their backpacks **f** (simply weigh) _simply weigh_ too much. 'Some kids **g** (carry) _carry/are carrying_ more than 25% of their bodyweight in a bag that has a nice cartoon character on the bag, but which **h** (actually give) _is actually giving /gives_ them serious backache,' reported Dr Elaine Sachs, a GP in North London. 'Most parents **i** (simply not realize) _simply don't realize_ what **j** (happen) _is happening_ to their children.'

Investigators to report on train crash

Accident investigators **k** (still examine) _are still examining_ the wreckage of the high-speed train which left the rails and overturned in northwest England last week. According to reports, they **l** (not believe) _don't believe_ the accident **m** (involve) _involves_ driver error. 'We **n** (expect) _are expecting/expect_ to publish a inquiry into this accident quite soon,' a spokesman announced yesterday. 'Engineers **o** (work) _are working_ round the clock to replace the track, and we **p** (hope) _hope /are hoping_ to restore a normal service within two weeks. We **q** (realize) _realize_ that people **r** (depend) _depend_ on the railway, and we **s** (understand) _understand_ how much everyone has been shocked by this accident. However, we **t** (check) _are checking_ thousands of sections of track all over the country to make sure that nothing like this can ever happen again.'

5 Rewrite the sentence so that it contains a word from the list and has same meaning.

belong contain cost look matter see seem smell think weigh

a Is this car yours, sir? _Does this car belong to you, sir?_
b This perfume has a nice smell. _this perfume smells so nice_
c I think there's a mistake. _there seems to be a mistake_
d I don't understand what you mean. _I don't see what you mean_
e What's your opinion? _What do you think?_
f At birth a baby elephant is about 90 kg in weight. _At birth a baby elephant weights arround 90 kg_
g Is the price important? _the price doesn't matter_
h What's the price of this model? _How much does this model cost?_
i This book could be interesting. _This book looks interesting_
j What's in the box? _what does the box contains_

6 Write a new sentence with the same meaning containing a form of the word in capitals.

a Apparently, Harry is a very good card player. SAY
  They say Harry is a very good card player.

b This maths problem is incomprehensible to me! UNDERSTAND
  I don't understand this maths problem

c I have the same opinion as you. AGREE
  I agree with you

d 'Where's Anna?' 'At work in the garden.' WORK
  Ana is working in the garden

e Stop shouting, the teacher's in the corridor. COME
  Stop shouting, the teacher's coming

f Somebody is at the door. KNOCK
  Somebody is knocking at the door

g According to some people, UFOs have landed on Earth. BELIEVE
  Some people belive (that) UFOs have landed on Earth

h It's hotter all the time in here. GET
  It's getting hotter all the time in here

i Skiing is my favourite sport. LOVE
  I love skiing

j Peter keeps losing his homework! ALWAYS
  Peter is alway losing his homework

9/9

7 Complete the text with the present simple or present continuous form of the verb in brackets.

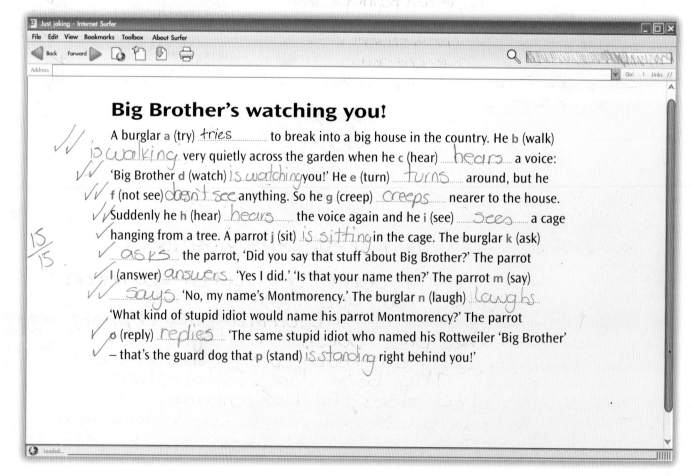

Big Brother's watching you!

A burglar **a** (try) *tries* to break into a big house in the country. He **b** (walk) *is walking* very quietly across the garden when he **c** (hear) *hears* a voice: 'Big Brother **d** (watch) *is watching* you!' He **e** (turn) *turns* around, but he **f** (not see) *doesn't see* anything. So he **g** (creep) *creeps* nearer to the house. Suddenly he **h** (hear) *hears* the voice again and he **i** (see) *sees* a cage hanging from a tree. A parrot **j** (sit) *is sitting* in the cage. The burglar **k** (ask) *asks* the parrot, 'Did you say that stuff about Big Brother?' The parrot **l** (answer) *answers* 'Yes I did.' 'Is that your name then?' The parrot **m** (say) *says* 'No, my name's Montmorency.' The burglar **n** (laugh) *laughs* 'What kind of stupid idiot would name his parrot Montmorency?' The parrot **o** (reply) *replies* 'The same stupid idiot who named his Rottweiler 'Big Brother' – that's the guard dog that **p** (stand) *is standing* right behind you!'

15/15

8 Complete the text with the present simple or present continuous form of the verb in brackets. Where both are possible, write both.

19/25

Students now taking longer to finish studies

In the USA some university students nowadays **a** (spend) _are spending_ more and more time in university before graduating. In American universities, many students **b** (pay) _pay_ their own fees, and this **c** (mean) _means_ more time working and less studying. Alan Chester is a 25-year-old journalism student from Ohio who **d** (take) _is taking_ six years to complete his undergraduate degree. In order to pay tuition fees and other expenses he **e** (work) _works_ four days a week in the university kitchen, while in the university holidays he **f** (do) _does / is doing_ a full-time job. 'I **g** (find) _am finding_ it difficult at the moment to study and pay my bills at the same time,' he **h** (admit) _admits_. 'But I **i** (try) _'m trying_ my best and I **j** (manage) _'m managing_ to keep the wolf from the door.' Alan's parents **k** (understand) _understand_ his decision to take longer to graduate. 'They **l** (know) _know_ what I **m** (go) _'m going_ through, and they **n** (help) _help / are helping_ me as much as they can. It's hard, but I **o** (learn) _'m learning_ to look after myself, and I **p** (experience) _am experiencing_ stuff that might be useful one day when I'm a journalist.' He **q** (point out) _points out_ that some students **r** (take) _are taking / take_ more time to graduate because they **s** (not really know) _don't really know_ what they **t** (want) _want_ to study. 'New courses of study **u** (develop) _are developing_ all the time, new subjects **v** (appear) _are appearing_ on the curriculum. Some students **w** (spend) _are spending_ time experimenting with different courses before choosing their major. So it's not all about money. I **x** (think) _think_ universities **y** (go) _are going_ through a period of change like everything else, and students have to adapt to this changing situation.'

GLOSSARY

EXTENSION ACTIVITY

A Use these verbs in present simple or present continuous to make more interview questions like these below: *do own believe in have like weigh*.
Use the questions to interview a partner.

What do you think of ... ? (name a film book etc)
What are you reading at the moment?

B Look these words up in a dictionary and find example sentences which use the present simple form: *gather, hear, see, tell, understand*

3 past time

past simple basic use

Use past simple
- for finished events in the past which have a definite time.
  *In 1969 the first men **landed** on the Moon.*

- in narrative.
  *The door **opened** and two boys **came** into the room.*

- for past habits and routines, usually with a time expression.
  *Few people in Victorian times **took** a bath **every day**.*

Many common verbs have irregular past forms which have to be learnt. Always check in a dictionary if you are not sure of the past form.

other uses of past simple

- Past simple can also be used for very recent events, without a time expression.
  *What **happened** to you?   Someone **hit** me!*

- Past simple is also used in conditional sentences and with *it's time* (see **Units 12, 13, 14**).
  *It's time **we left**.*

past continuous basic use

Use past continuous
- to describe a continuing unfinished action in the past.
  *I looked out of the window and saw that **it was raining**.*
  *Whenever I visited him, **he was working** in his garden.*

- for a continuing unfinished action interrupted by a sudden past action.
  *While we **were getting** ready to go out, the rain suddenly **stopped**.*
  *While I **was getting** ready for bed, the doorbell **rang**.*

- for activities as background description.
  *Helen looked down into the busy street. Crowds of people **were pushing** along the pavements, and cars **were hooting**.*

- for two continuing events happening at the same time.
  *While Jim **was painting** the outside of the house, Sarah **was decorating** the bedrooms.*

other uses of past continuous

Past continuous can also be used
- to emphasize that an action was still continuing.
  *They started producing the car in 1946 and **were still producing** it thirty years later.*

- to describe a changing situation (see **Unit 2**).
  ***It was becoming** more and more difficult to find work.*
  *Her performances **were getting** better and better.*

- with *forever, continually, always* etc (see **Unit 2**) to criticize actions we feel are annoying, or which we wish to exaggerate.
  *At school, **he was always getting** into trouble.*
  ***She was forever falling** in love with the wrong kind of man.*

We do not generally use past continuous to describe habitual actions in the past.
  *That summer **we were going** swimming nearly every day.*
  *That summer **we went** swimming nearly every day.*

past perfect simple and continuous  *study Hard*

- are used to refer to events in the past which happened before other events in the past, usually when there is no time expression to make this clear. Past perfect simple refers to finished events and past perfect continuous to unfinished, recently completed or continuing events.
  *By the time we got to the cinema, the film **had started**.*
  ***He'd been working** hard all morning, and he felt really tired.*
  In both examples, the past perfect happens before the past simple.

- are common after verbs such as *realize, remember, know, understand* etc.
  *When I got on the bus, **I realized I had left** my wallet at home.*

- are common in reported speech (see **Unit 17**).

- are **not** used to emphasize that an event happened a long time ago.

Compare the use of past simple and past continuous with past perfect tenses.
  *While we **were watching** a film, the fire alarm **went off**.*   (past events)
  *I remembered the events of the day before. At 11.00 while **we had been watching** a film, the fire alarm **had gone** off.*   (past seen from the past)

Only use past perfect tenses when absolutely necessary to show that one event in the past happened before another event in the past. Often the meaning is clear without using past perfect. When we describe a series of short actions, we usually use past simple.

used to do

- Use *used to* to describe habits and states in the past, especially when we make contrasts with the present. Any time reference tends to be general. The pronunciation is /juːst tuː/
  ***I used to play** chess quite often, but I haven't played for ages.*
  *In those days people **used to wash** all their clothes by hand.*
  ***I used to like** tennis, but I don't play much now.*

- *Used to* refers only to the past. There are no other tense forms in modern English, though they can be found in older literary texts.

- The question is normally *Did you use to?*
  ***Did you use to** play hide-and-seek when you were a child?*

- The negative is normally *didn't use to*.
  *In those days, people **didn't use to** travel abroad so much*

- Past simple is also used to describe past habits, with other details added to make a contrast between past and present.
  ***When I was younger I played** chess quite often, but I haven't played for ages.*

- *Be used to something* has no connection with *be used to,* and means *be accustomed to* something. *To* in this case is a preposition, so it is followed by a noun or *-ing*.
  *I can't eat any more. **I'm not used to** such big meals.*
  *She can't climb all those steps! **She's not used to taking** so much exercise!*

would

- can be used to describe a person's habitual activity. It cannot be used with state verbs.
  *Every summer **we would stay** in a small village in the mountains.*
  It is not possible to say ~~I would like tennis, but I don't play much now.~~

- *Would* is more common in more literary texts, reminiscences etc

past tenses used as polite forms

- Past simple and past continuous are often used when the speaker is being more polite or less direct. The time reference is to present time.
  ***Did you want** to see me about anything?*
  ***I was wondering** what you wanted.*

1 Complete the sentence using the verb in brackets and *would* or *used to*. If both are possible, write both.

a Every day the young prince (go) _would go / used to go_ hunting in the forest.

b Wild animals (sometimes come) _sometimes would come / used to come_ into the garden at night.

c I (enjoy) _used to enjoy_ computer games, but I've grown tired of them.

d Brian (speak) _used to speak_ Italian quite well, but he's forgotten it all.

e Every day Anna (wake up) _would wake up / used to_ at 4.00 am and go to work at the bakery.

f My mother (often play) _often used to play / would play_ the piano and sing after dinner.

g I (own) _used to own_ a racing bike but I sold it and bought a scooter.

h Tony (believe) _used to believe_ that one day he would be famous.

i When I was a student I (usually go) _usually used to go / would usually go_ to bed about 1.00 am.

j Helen (live) *_used to live_ in an old boat on the canal.

9/9

history

2 Complete the two texts about World War 1 with the correct form of the verb in brackets. Use past simple, past continuous, past perfect simple or past perfect continuous. Only use a past perfect form if it is necessary to make the meaning clear.

The condition of Britain in 1917

The government also **a** (need) _needed_ to ensure that Britain was fed. Under the Defence of the Realm Act it was able to take over land and turn it over to food production. In February 1917 it **b** (set up) (PS) _set up_ the Women's Land Army to recruit women as farm workers. By then, however, the food supply in Britain **c** (became) _had become_ desperate. German U-boats **d** (sink) _were sinking_ one in every four British merchant ships and Britain had only six weeks' supply of wheat left. As food supplies **e** (run) _had run_ short, so prices **f** (rise) _rose_ . Wages **g** (hardly rise) _had hardly rising_ during the war because people were mostly prepared to sacrifice better pay to support the war effort, but prices were now almost double what they **h** (be) _had been_ in 1914. Poorer people could not even afford basic supplies such as bread. Shops **i** (close) _closed_ were closing early each afternoon as they **j** (run out) _had run out_ of goods to sell.

MUST BE FED

GLOSSARY

German reactions to the Treaty of Versailles 1919

The overall reaction of Germans was horror and outrage. They certainly **k** (not believe) _didn't believe_ they **l** (start) _had started_ the war. They **m** (not even think) _didn't even think_ they **n** (lose) _had lost_ the war. In 1919 many Germans **o** (not really understand) _didn't really understand_ how bad Germany's military situation **p** (be) _had been_ at the end of the war in 1918. They believed that the German government **q** (simply agree) _had simply agreed_ to a ceasefire, and that therefore Germany should have been at the Paris Peace Conference to negotiate peace. They were angry that their government was not represented at the talks and that the Allies **r** (force) _had forced_ them to accept a harsh treaty without any choice or even a comment. At first, the new government **s** (refuse) _refused_ to sign the treaty and at one point it **t** (look) _looked_ as though war might break out again. However, Ebert, the new German leader, was in an impossible position. Reluctantly, he agreed to accept the terms of the treaty and it was signed on 28 June 1919.

GLOSSARY

3 Underline the correct form. Only use the past perfect form when other forms are not possible.

9/10

a When Dora _went_ / had gone to pay for the petrol she was putting / _had put_ in her car, she _realized_ / was realizing that she lost / _had lost_ her credit card.

b While I _was waiting_ / had waited for my meal to arrive, I _saw_ / was seeing that the two men who had followed me into the restaurant _were staring_ / had been staring at me from a nearby table.

c When I _heard_ / was hearing the noise at the window, I _knew_ / had known that someone tried / _was trying_ to break into the house.

d Maria _didn't remember_ / wasn't remembering anything about the accident, except that she didn't drive / _had not been driving_ too fast and in fact _had almost stopped_ / was almost stopping before she reached the crossroads.

e By the time the fire engines _arrived_ / was arriving at the cottage, Tom and his neighbours already put out / _had already put out_ the fire and _were carrying_ / had been carrying furniture out of the blackened building.

f 'What did you do / _were you doing_ in the High Street at that time of night, and why _did you run away_ / had you run away when the officer _told_ / was telling you to stop?' asked the lawyer.

g While Sally painted / _was painting_ the ceiling, she _fell off_ / was falling off the ladder but luckily she _didn't break_ / wasn't breaking any bones.

h Our taxi to the airport _didn't turn up_ / wasn't turning up on time, and so by the time _we got_ / were getting to the check-in desk, the flight already closed / _had already closed_.

i Marlowe walked slowly into the room. He didn't forget / _hadn't forgotten_ his last visit to the house, when Miss LaPorte _had fired_ / was firing two shots at him, so he _had taken_ / was taking no chances this time.

j Alice could see that the tall boy _had_ / was having difficulty making himself understood, but she _decided_ / was deciding not to help him. After all, nobody _had helped_ / was helping her during her first days in this country!

EXTENSION ACTIVITY

A Choose a novel or story, and select one or two pages. Make a list of the past tenses used on these pages. Are these the only tenses possible, or are others also acceptable?

B Translate some of the sentences in Exercise 2 into your language. Does your language have a similar set of tenses, or is it different?

past time

4 present perfect

present perfect simple

Use present perfect simple

- to refer to events connected to the present, without a definite past time, often with *just*.
  *Someone **has stolen** my bike!*   ***I've just had** an idea.*

- to refer to indefinite events that happened at an unknown time in the past. This time is often recent, and is often used in news items when the information is 'current'.
  *Archaeologists **have discovered** an Anglo-Saxon palace in London.*
  *Police **have recaptured** two escaped prisoners.*

  The time can also be all time up to the present.
  *No-one **has (ever) proved** that aliens exist.*

- to refer to indefinite events with a result in the present.
  *My car **has broken down**.*   (That's why I want a lift from you)

- to describe what has been done or how many things completed in a period of time.
  *The building **has been completed** on time.*
  *United **have scored** three goals, and there's still half an hour left.*

- to describe a living person's experiences, what he or she has done in life so far.
  *She **has painted** some of the best portraits of recent years.*

- to describe a state that lasts up to the present, with state verbs.
  ***I've worked** in this department for the past six months.*

- to refer to a repeated action in a period of time up to the present.
  ***I've cooked** dinner every night for ten years!*

- with some time expressions.
  *I've worked here **since** 2002.*
  This is the first time I've eaten squid!
  *We've **already** seen this film.*

  Note that most time expressions can be used with various tenses.
  ***I've lived** here **for** ten years. (present perfect simple: I'm still here)*
  ***I lived** there **for** three years. (past simple: I'm not there now)*

present perfect simple or past simple

- Use present perfect simple for unfinished time and past simple for finished time.
  *She **has painted** some of the best portraits of recent years.*
  *She **painted** some of the best portraits of recent years.*
  In the first sentence the action has happened in a period up to the present, and may well continue. In the second sentence the action is finished. The artist may be dead. The events are in a period of time not connected to the present.

- Use to show speaker attitude.
  Speakers may decide whether they see an event as connected to the present (present perfect simple) or not (past simple). This may be a matter of time or place. Tense use is here a matter of choice, rather than of grammatical 'right' or 'wrong'.
  ***I've left** my books at home. (The speaker feels the event is recent, or is still near home.)*
  ***I left** my books at home (The speaker feels the event is distant in time and place.)*

- Use with different time expressions.
  ***I haven't been** to the cinema for ages / a long time.*
  Present perfect refers to an action over a period of time and *for* describes how long the period is.

  *It's ages / a long time **since I went** to the cinema.*
  It's ages describes a period of time since an event and past simple describes when that event happened.

present perfect continuous

Use present perfect continuous
- for recent continuing activities, continuing up to the present.
  I've been waiting here for half an hour!
  I haven't been taking a lot of exercise lately.

I've been working
out a lot lately.

- to explain a present situation.
  I've been washing the dog – that's why my clothes are wet.

- to emphasize the length of a continuing activity.
  I've been working on my project all morning.

- for a repeated activity, to emphasize the repetition of the activity.
  He's been phoning me every day since the party.

- with *how long* questions.
  How long have you been having these disturbing dreams? (this is a continuing process, and isn't finished)

- with *mean, think, consider*.
  I've been thinking of changing my job.
  I've been meaning to get in touch with Helen.

- with time words *lately, recently, all* (day), *every* (morning), *for, since*.
  What have you been doing lately / recently?
  I've been working on these accounts all day / since 9.00 / for hours.

present perfect continuous or present perfect simple

- With state verbs such as *live, work*, there is little contrast.
  How long have you lived here? How long have you been living here?

- Verbs such as *sit, stay, wait* prefer the continuous form.

- With event verbs, present perfect simple emphasizes completion.
  I've written my letters. (finished)
  I've been writing letters. (describes my activity during a recent period)

1 Complete the sentence with the present perfect simple or past simple form of the verb in brackets.

a Ian McEwan is a British writer who, according to many critics, (write) _has written_ some of the best novels of recent years.

b Born in 1948, he (spend) _has spent_ much of his childhood abroad as his father was an army officer.

c He (study) _has studied_ English literature and creative writing at the universities of Sussex and East Anglia.

d He (write) _has written_ a number of successful collections of short stories and novels.

e His novel *The Child in Time* (win) _won_ the Whitbread Novel Award in 1987.

f His later novels, including *Amsterdam*, *Atonement* and *Saturday*, (be) _have been_ very successful.

g *Amsterdam* (receive) _received_ the Booker Prize for Fiction in 1998.

h *Atonement* and *Saturday* (also win) _also won_ literary prizes.

i However, McEwan (always be) _has always been_ a controversial writer.

j Some writers (accuse) _have accused_ him of stealing details in *Atonement* from the work of another author, Lucilla Andrews.

k However, he (point out) _has pointed out_ the acknowledgement made to Lucilla Andrews in an author's note in the book.

l During this controversy, the American author Thomas Pynchon (write) _wrote_ a defence of McEwan in a British newspaper.

---

science

2 Underline the correct form.

The nature of intelligence

For many years scientists **a** *tried* / <u>*have been trying*</u> to define the nature of human intelligence. However, they **b** *were* / <u>*have been*</u> unable to agree on whether there is one kind of intelligence, or several kinds. In the early 20th century, psychologist Charles Spearman **c** *came up* / *has come up* with the concept of 'g' or 'general intelligence'. He **d** <u>*gave*</u> / *had given* subjects a variety of different tests and **e** <u>*found*</u> / *has found* that the people who **f** <u>*performed*</u> / *have performed* well in the tests **g** <u>*used*</u> / *have used* one part of the brain, which he **h** <u>*called*</u> / *has called* 'g', for all the tests. More recently, research **i** *found* / <u>*has found*</u> that this idea may well be true, as one part of the brain (the lateral prefrontal cortex) shows increased blood flow during testing. However, some scientists believe that intelligence is a matter of how much people **j** *learned* / <u>*have learned*</u> rather than some ability they are born with. They believe that environment also matters.

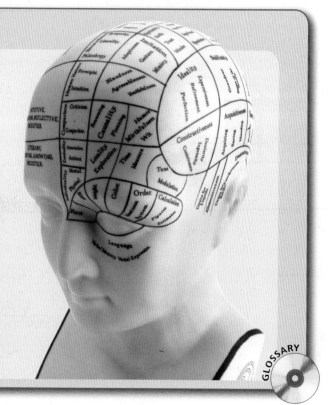

GLOSSARY

3 Rewrite the sentence so that it means the same as the first sentence. Use present perfect simple or continuous.

a I came here at 3.00 and now it's 5.00.   I have been here for _two hours._

b I haven't seen this film before.   This is _the first time I've seen this_ film.

c Mark is asleep.   Mark _has gone_ to bed.

d I began work here in 1999.   I've _working here_ since 1999.

e Anna isn't here yet.   Anna _hasn't arrived_ yet.

f We don't know each other.   We _have not met_ before.

g There isn't any food left.   Someone _has eaten_ all the food.

h We started waiting in this queue half an hour ago!   We _'ve been waiting_ for half an hour.

i It's a long time since I was last here.   I _'ve been here for_ a long time.

j This is our seventh wedding anniversary.   We _'ve been married_ seven years.

---

4 Complete the text using the present perfect simple, present perfect continuous or past simple form of the verb in brackets.

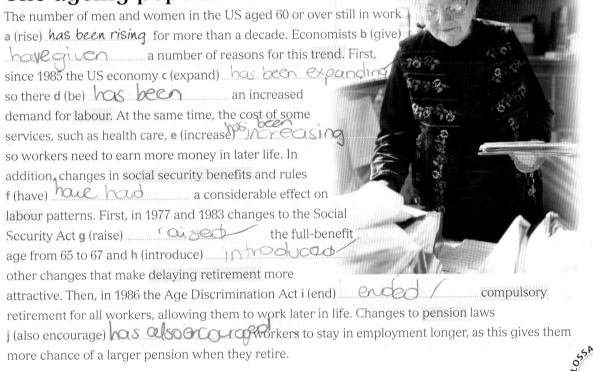

The ageing population

The number of men and women in the US aged 60 or over still in work **a** (rise) _has been rising_ for more than a decade. Economists **b** (give) _have given_ a number of reasons for this trend. First, since 1985 the US economy **c** (expand) _has been expanding_ so there **d** (be) _has been_ an increased demand for labour. At the same time, the cost of some services, such as health care, **e** (increase) _has been increasing_ so workers need to earn more money in later life. In addition, changes in social security benefits and rules **f** (have) _have had_ a considerable effect on labour patterns. First, in 1977 and 1983 changes to the Social Security Act **g** (raise) _raised_ the full-benefit age from 65 to 67 and **h** (introduce) _introduced_ other changes that make delaying retirement more attractive. Then, in 1986 the Age Discrimination Act **i** (end) _ended_ compulsory retirement for all workers, allowing them to work later in life. Changes to pension laws **j** (also encourage) _has also encouraged_ workers to stay in employment longer, as this gives them more chance of a larger pension when they retire.

GLOSSARY

EXTENSION ACTIVITY

A Choose one of these topics and say what has happened, what has been happening or what has happened. These can be fictional if you prefer.

news of family and friends   climate change   the political situation in your country

B Use your knowledge of the news to make lists of:

things that have happened recently   things that have been happening
things that happened

*Need more practice? Go to the **Review** on page 208.*

5 future time

will and won't

Use *will* and *won't*
- for factual predictions.
  Inflation will increase by 1% over the next twelve months.
  Inflation will almost certainly increase by 1% over the next twelve months.
  Other qualifying adverbials include *definitely, probably, no doubt*

- for habits of which the speaker disapproves.
  He will keep opening the window.
  Jack is so lazy. He'll spend the whole day lying in bed reading the papers.

- for an assumption taken from the facts.
  'The phone's ringing.' 'That'll be Sue. I'm expecting her to phone.'

- for an immediate decision.
  'Anything to drink, sir?' 'I'll just have a glass of water, please.'

- *Will* is used to express many other meanings connected with the future (see **Unit 15**).
  Offer   *I'll carry that for you.*
  Refusal   *They won't give me my ball back!*

In speech, contractions are frequently used, so *I'll, you'll, he'll* etc are the usual spoken forms.

shall and shan't

- *Shall* and *shan't* are forms of *will* used in first person singular and plural in formal and deliberate speech, and in many modal uses (see **Unit 16**).
  We shall inform you, upon admission, of the rules of the Library.
  'I'll give you my work on Friday.' 'I shall look forward to receiving it!'

be going to

Use *be going to*
- for personal plans and intentions.
  I'm going to stay in this evening and watch an old film.
  What are you going to do now? I don't know!

- when the cause of a possible event is present.
  Look at the colour of the sky! It's going to snow.

- for decisions about the future.
  I've decided what I'm going to do. I'm going to phone the police.

will or going to?

- In many cases, *will* as prediction can be replaced by *going to*, especially in everyday speech. This is not true for other meanings of *will*.
  Inflation will increase by 1% over the next twelve months.
  As I see it, inflation is going to increase by 1% over the next twelve months.

- Normally *going to* cannot be replaced by *will* without changing the meaning.

- *Was going to* describes events which were supposed to happen, but did not.
  I was going to come over and see you, but I left it too late.

be to, be about to, be on the point of, be due to

- *Be to* is used to describe arrangements with future reference.
  The conference is to take place in July.

- The past arrangement form is *was / were to have done.*
  There was to have been a second match but it was cancelled.

- *Be (just) about to* describes what is going to happen very soon.
  *I can't talk now. **I'm just about to go** out.*

- The past form describes an event in the past which was going to happen soon.
  ***I was about to go** to bed when the phone rang.*

- *Be on the point of* has a more formal meaning than *about to*.
  *David **is on the point of** leaving the company.*

- *Be due to do, be due* describe what is expected to happen.
  *The train is **due to arrive** at any moment.   The train is **due**.*

present simple and continuous

- Present continuous can be used for a fixed arrangement (one already definitely made).
  ***We're having** a party on Saturday. Do you want to come?*

  Using *going to* in this example gives the same information.
  ***We're going to have** a party on Saturday. Do you want to come?*

- Present simple can be used for a fixed future event. There is no personal choice here.
  *Next year Christmas **is** on a Tuesday.*

future time clauses

- After time expressions *as soon as, after, before, by the time, immediately, the moment, until, when* etc we use present simple although there is a future reference.
  ***As soon as we make** a decision, we'll let you know.*

- Present perfect is also used instead of present simple to show completion.
  ***As soon as I've finished** this letter, I'll help you.*

- *Going to* is also possible instead of *will* to show a future plan.
  *As soon as I've saved up enough money, **I'm going to buy** a car.*

future continuous

Use future continuous for
- an event or a state at a future point.
  *This time next week, **they'll be lying** on the beach in the Seychelles!*

- events that have already been arranged for a future date.
  *The Rolling Stones **will be performing** in Moscow in June.*

- very formal requests.
  ***Will you be wanting** anything else, sir?*

future perfect simple and continuous

- Use for time looked back on from a future point.
  *By the time the exam begins, **I'll have forgotten** everything!*
  *By the end of the month, **I'll have been working** at this company for ten years!*
  These examples look into the future to 'when the exam begins' and 'the end of the month', and then back from there. At that future point, the speaker can say 'I have forgotten' or 'I have been working'.

- Use to express an assumption.
  ***You'll have heard** the news about Anna, I suppose?*

hope, expect, think, believe, doubt whether

- These verbs introduce and show our attitude to future actions.

- With *think, expect, believe* we show negative meaning by using *don't think / expect / believe*.
  ***I don't think** you'll like this.   **I don't believe** I'll be late.*

- *Hope* can be followed by *will* or a present tense. The other verbs are followed by *will*.
  ***I hope you have / will have** a good time.   **I expect you'll** want some tea.*
  ***I doubt whether they'll** be here before six.*

1 Underline the best verb form.

a 'Have you decided yet?' 'Yes, _I'll have_ / _I have_ the roast beef, please.'

b Q: How _will I have known_ / _will I know_ that I have won a prize?

A: You _are receiving_ / _will receive_ an email giving full details.

c Quick get out of the car! _It's going to burst_ / _It's bursting_ into flames at any minute!

d Don't come round before midday, because _I'll be cleaning_ / _I clean_ the house until then.

e Sorry I can't come on Thursday evening. _I'm going to work_ / _I'm working_ late on an important project.

f The cost of construction _is almost certainly rising_ / _will almost certainly rise_ before the end of the year as wage increases begin to take effect.

g The conference _is going to begin_ / _begins_ next Friday morning at 9.00.

h Here's the money you asked for – €1000. What _will you_ / _are you going to_ do with it?

i Why don't you give Helen this cheap perfume instead of the expensive one! She _won't have known_ / _won't know_ the difference!

j I just want to remind everyone that _we'll be holding_ / _we hold_ a Latin-American evening at the town hall this Friday.

2 Choose all possible forms, A, B or C, to complete the sentence.

I've just received some new sales figures ...

a 'The fish is very fresh. And the beef is very good too.' 'I think A, B the fish.'

b 'There's someone knocking at the door! Who can it be at this time of night?'
'B, ✓ Helen. She said she might come round to watch the midnight movie on TV.'

c 'I've just received some new sales figures. A, B them very much, I'm afraid.'

d Over the next six months, the company B, C, ten new supermarkets in France.

e C with this kind of problem before, I expect, so I'll leave you to get on with it.

f According to sources close to the prime minister's office, the foreign minister C, A.

g Well, that's all for today. B, C you next week at the same time, if that's all right.

h Next year C, B some time travelling, and then look for a teaching job.

i The problem we have with Jack is that he C insist on opening all the windows in the cold weather.

j There's not much bread, I'm afraid. I hope A, B, C eat it all before the others arrive!

k At this rate, by the time we get to the party, most people B ✓

l The riot police are running into the square. There A trouble!

a	A _I'm going to have_	B _I'll have_	C _I'm about to have_
b	A _That's going to be_	B _That'll be_	C _It's due to be_
c	A _You're not going to like_	B _You won't like_	C _You're not liking_
d	A _is going to open_	B _will be opening_	C _is opening_
e	A _You are going to deal_	B _You are dealing_	C _You'll have dealt_
f	A _is on the point of resigning_	B _is due to resign_	C _is about to resign_
g	A _I'm going to see_	B _I'm seeing_	C _I'll see_
h	A _I'm spending_	B _I'm going to spend_	C _I'll spend_
i	A _is going to_	B _is about to_	C _will_
j	A _you won't_	B _you aren't about to_	C _you're not going to_
k	A _will leave_	B _will have left_	C _are on the point of leaving_
l	A _is going to be_	B _will be_	C _is due to be_

3 Complete the sentence with the present simple or *will*-future form of the verb in brackets.

a We will usually respond to enquiries immediately we (receive) _receive_ them.

b When we (reach) _reach_ an agreement, we'll ask our legal department to draft a contract.

c Work on the second stage of the project (begin) _will begin_ as soon as the first stage (prove) _proves_ successful.

d Until the economic situation (improve) _improves_ , the company (not risk) _won't risk_ any further investment in this field.

e A detailed break-down of the figures (appear) _will appear_ on our web site as soon as both companies (sign) _sign_ the agreement.

f Our office (contact) _will contact_ you the moment we (have) _have_ any news.

g Our human resources team (then assess) _will then assess_ your application before we (decide) _decide_ whether you can go forward to the next stage.

h By the time the banks (reach) _reach_ an agreement on this issue, the amount of debt (be) _will be_ out of control.

4 Write a new sentence with the same meaning containing the word in capitals.

a The 12th English Teaching Conference takes place on 5–12 June. TO
  The 12th English Teaching Conference is to take place on 5-12 June.

b The president is expected to arrive here at 9.30. DUE
  The president is due to arrive here at 9:30

c Everyone was on the point of leaving when the fire alarm went off. ABOUT
  Everyone was about to leave when the fire alarm went off

d He's got the bad habit of playing very loud music late at night. WILL
  He will play very loud music late night

e The car has broken down, we're miles from anywhere, and we haven't got a phone. So, what's our plan? TO
  So, what're we going to do

f Good news! Jane is expecting a baby! HAVE
  Good news Jane will have a baby!

g I intended to phone you last night, but it slipped my mind. GOING
  I was going to phone you last night, but...

h I'm driving to Leeds anyway on Tuesday, so why don't I give you a lift? I'LL
  I'll driving to Leeds anyway on tuesday...

i 'There's a letter for you.' 'I'm sure that's my new credit card.' WILL
  That'll be my new credit card

j I expect the police have caught the thief by now. WILL
  the police'll have caught the thief by now

[handwritten margin note: Point to of + ing ver about and due no ing verb]

5 Complete the text with *will be*, *will have* or *will have been* + the correct form of the verb in brackets.

What are your hopes for the future?

Anna

It's hard to make predictions too far into the future, but I think I can say quite a lot about my life in about ten years' time. I think I
a (still live) _will still be living_ in the same city. By that time I **b** (finish) _ʼll have finished_ my studies, and, who knows, perhaps I **c** (find) _will_ a good job. And I **d** (probably go out) _have been probably going out._ with the same friends too!

Bernard

I'm optimistic about the future, so I think that by the time I'm 35, say, **e** (make) _I will have make_ my fortune. By then I **f** (run) _will be running_ my own company for about ten years, and I **g** (almost certainly become) _will have almost c become_ a millionaire! So I **h** (drive) _will be driving_ an expensive sports car, I hope!

Catherine

I think we should all be worried about what the world **i** (be) _will be_ like in fifty years' time. By then, I hope that the world's governments **j** (find) _will have find_ an answer to the problem of global warming, but perhaps scientists **k** (still search) _will still searching_ for technological solutions. It's quite possible that we **l** (still talk) _will still talking_ about the problem, as we are now!

David

By the time I'm fifty, I expect that nearly everything **m** (change) _will have changed_ and everyone **n** (try) _will try_ their best to adapt to new circumstances. For example, I can't imagine that we **o** (use) _won't be using_ cars, because by then most of the oil in the world **p** (run out) _will have run out_. People **q** (travel) _will travel_ in electric cars, or perhaps we **r** (walk) _will walk_ everywhere. I hope that scientists **s** (solve) _will solve_ the pollution problem, but who knows! Perhaps some other worse problem **t** (come) _will come_ along by then!

GLOSSARY

6 Choose the correct form, A, B or C, to complete the sentence.

a 'Can I talk to you for a moment?' ' Sorry, _B_ .'

b Actually, _A_ Sue's house tomorrow, so if you like I could leave the books for her.

c David and Susan _B_ in May, but they've had to change their plans.

d We _A_ a party for Professor Allan on Friday evening, and we'd like you to come.

e I've done a lot of revision, but I'm sure that when I sit down to do the exam _B_ .

f Chris doesn't do much work. _C_ the whole day drinking coffee and looking out of the window.

g Come back about 4.30. _B_ the report by then, and you can take a copy.

h I _C_ , but I'll let you know if I get delayed.

i 'What time is the plane supposed to get here?' 'It _A C_ any minute now.'

j Quick, run! The bomb _B_ !

a A *I'm just going to leave.*   B *I'm just leaving.*   C *I'll just leave.*

b A *I'll pass*   B *I'm going to pass*   C *I'll be passing*

c A *will be getting married*   B *were going to get married*   C *expect they will get married*

d A *are giving*   B *are about to give*   C *will give*

e A *I'm forgetting everything*   B *I'll forget everything*   C *I'll be forgetting everything*

f A *He's going to spend*   B *He'll spend*   C *He will have spent*

g A *I've finished*   B *I'll have finished*   C *I'm finishing*

h A *am not due to be late*   B *am not going to be late*   C *don't think I'll be late*

i A *will come*   B *was going to arrive*   C *is due*

j A *is exploding*   B *will explode*   C *is going to explode*

EXTENSION ACTIVITY

A   Make some personal predictions about ten years' time (or choose another length of time).

what you will / won't be doing   where you will / won't be
what you will / won't have done by then

B   'According to the 2006 Revision, the world population will probably increase by 2.5 billion over the next 43 years, passing from the current 6.7 billion to 9.2 billion in 2050.' Use research in a library or on the Internet to find more predictions about the next fifty years.

6 tense contrasts

1 Complete the sentence using a suitable form of the verb in brackets.

a 'What exactly _did you do_ when you saw the smoke?' 'I pressed the fire alarm.' (do)

b By the time we get to the stadium, the match _will have been started_ (start)

c 'How long _are you going to stay_ here for?' 'I don't know. I haven't decided yet.' (stay)

d Jackson _has won_ the Nobel Prize, but says she is still hoping for recognition. (win)

e If you happen to see any one in the garden, don't worry. It _will be_ the gardener. (be)

f 'I'm sorry to be late. I hope you _haven't await too_ long./ _I've been waiting 4_ (wait)

g Anna didn't understand why the mysterious stranger _sent_ her such a letter. (send)

h Tom sends his apologies but he _will be_ a few minutes late. (be)

i I don't like this bed. It _feels_ uncomfortable. (feel)

j There _was going to be_ a strike this morning, but it has been cancelled. (be)

k It's really unfair! You (always) _always criticize_ me! (criticize)

l I'm glad I've run into you. I _____ to get in touch with you for ages. (mean)

2 <u>Underline</u> the best verb form.

The arguments about climate change

According to all the measurements, climate change **a** *happens* / <u>*is happening*</u>, but science **b** *appears* / *is appearing* to be split on what to do about it. Unfortunately, scientists **c** <u>*do not all agree*</u> / *are not all agreeing* about the causes of global warming. In a recent book, two scientists – Fred Singer, a climate physicist, and Dennis Avery, a biologist – **d** *argue* / *are arguing* that the warming currently observed around the world is part of a 1,500-year cycle in solar energy. Singer, an outspoken critic of the idea that humans **e** *warm* / <u>*are warming*</u> the planet, and Avery, **f** *believe* / *are believing* that a well-established, 1,500-year cycle in the Earth's climate can explain most of the global warming that **g** *takes place* / <u>*has taken place*</u> in the last 100 years. We are currently on an upswing, getting warmer after the Little Ice Age, but in a few hundred years **h** *will be* / *are* back on the downswing, and getting colder again. They **i** *say* / *are saying* that efforts to slow down the current warming by reducing emissions of greenhouse gases are at best pointless, or at worst economically damaging. This, of course, is not what the fourth assessment report of the UN Intergovernmental Panel on Climate Change (IPCC) **j** *has said* / *said* a few weeks ago. That report from the UN climate science working group **k** *has concluded* / <u>*concluded*</u> that it **l** *is* / <u>*has been*</u> likely that rising greenhouse gas concentrations **m** <u>*have caused*</u> / *caused* most recent warming and that, depending on our actions now to slow the growth of emissions, warming by 2100 **n** <u>*will probably be*</u> / *is probably* between about 1.5°C and 6°C. So, which scientists **o** *tell* / <u>*are telling*</u> us the truth?

science

30

GLOSSARY

3 Choose the correct phrase 1 to 15 for each gap.

New tunnel planned beneath the Alps

For centuries, the Alps **a** __10__ as a natural trade barrier between northern and southern Europe. Sending Italian wine to the Netherlands, or German washing machines to Greece, **b** __7__ a long, slow journey along narrow Alpine valleys, through tunnels and over passes.

The amount of freight crossing the Alps in heavy goods vehicles **c** __8__ sharply over the last two decades. In 1990 an estimated 40 million tonnes **d** __15__ by road; in 2001 that **e** __9__ to 90 million tonnes, with further big increases expected by 2010. But concerns for the Alpine environment and fears over safety **f** __6__ to big pressure to move freight off the roads and onto the railways. Both Switzerland's Gotthard road tunnel and France's Mont Blanc road tunnel **g** __11__ major fires in the last ten years in which many **h** __3__ .

As long ago as 1994, the Swiss **i** __14__ in a nationwide referendum to put all freight crossing their country

onto the railways. Naturally, such an ambitious plan **j** __4__ overnight, but now the project dubbed the engineering feat of the 21st Century **k** __12__ . Deep beneath the Alps, the Swiss **l** __2__ a high-speed rail link between Zurich and Milan. It **m** __5__ , at 57 kilometres (35 miles), the world's longest tunnel. A key feature of the project, which is new to Alpine transport, is the fact that the entire railway line **n** __13__ at the same altitude of 500 metres (1,650 ft) above sea level. This **o** __1__ trains using the line to reach speeds of 240 km/h (149 mph), reducing the travel time between Zurich and Milan from today's four hours to just two and a half.

1 will allow	8 has risen
2 are building	9 had risen
3 died	10 have served
4 was not going to happen	11 have suffered
5 will include	12 is slowly taking shape
6 have led	13 will stay
7 means	14 voted
	15 went

GLOSSARY

4 Complete the text with the appropriate form of the verb in brackets.

POLICE SEEK MISSING SHED

A 32-year-old man **a** (get) __got__ home from work on Friday to find that someone **b** (steal) __has stolen__ the shed from his back garden. Martin Graham, who **c** (live) __lives__ in Francis Road, Darnely, **d** (tell) __told__ us he couldn't believe his eyes. 'There was simply nothing there. I thought I **e** (go) __went__ into the wrong garden.' A neighbour who **f** (notice) __noticed__ the men while they **g** (disassemble) __were disassemble__ the shed, **h** (assume) __assumed__ that Mr Graham **i** (ask) __has asked__ them to do it. The two men **j** (drive off) __drove off__ in a white van. Police **k** (investigate) __investigated__ and **l** (issue) __issued__ a description of the two men.

5 Complete the text with the appropriate form of the verb in brackets.

Life expectancy

Our country **a** (go) _is going_ through a period of accelerating change. Today, there **b** (be) _are_ around 3.7 million people aged over 60 in this country but the large numbers of people who **c** (belong) _belong_ to the baby-boom generation **d** (produce) _produce / will produce_ an explosion in the number of elderly people from around 2011. By 2030, there **e** (be) _will be_ some 8.8 million and because the birth-rate in the period after the post-war baby boom **f** (decline) _has declined_ sharply, these elderly people **g** (represent) _'ve represented_ a much larger share of the country's population than ever before in our history. In 1966, when we **h** (introduce) _introduced_ our national pension scheme, there **i** (be) _were_ about eight working-age people for every retired person, whereas today, there **j** (be) _are_ about five, and in 2030, there **k** (be) _is going to be_ only three. There **l** (be) _will be_ another dramatic change which also **m** (affect) _affects_ this situation, as thanks to medical advances and higher living standards, life expectancy **n** (increase) _has increased_ and **o** (continue) _will continue_ to increase in future years. Today people can expect to live three years longer than in 1966. By 2030, they **p** (live) _will live_ an average of 4.5 years longer.

GLOSSARY

6 Write a new sentence with the same meaning containing the word in capitals.

a There's a party at our house on Friday. — **WE**
   We are having a party on Friday.

b This is my first trip to Siberia. — **BEFORE**
   I haven't been to Siberia before

c What's your job, exactly? — **DO**
   What do you do exactly?

d Karen's hair was short once. — **HAVE**
   Karen used to Have you ever had short hair / short hair ✓

e I'm leaving in a minute, so I can't talk now. — **JUST**
   I can't talk right now cos I'm leaving in just a minute

f It's a long time since I last went to the theatre. — **FOR**
   I haven't been to the theatre for a long time

g When was the invasion of Britain by the Romans? — **INVADE**
   When did the Romans invade Britain?

h I'm sure it won't rain tomorrow. — **DON'T**
   I don't think it will rain tomorrow

i Is this your suitcase? — **DOES**
   Does this suitcase belong to you?

j When I have enough money, I'm going to buy a new computer. — **SAVED**
   When I have saved enough money I'll buy a new computer.

7 Complete the text with the appropriate form of the verb in brackets.

Child employment in Victorian Britain

In Victorian London, mud larks were children who **a** (search for) _searched for_ valuable bits and pieces on the shores of the River Thames. They **b** (not do) _did not do_ this from boats, but **c** (wait) _waited_ until the tide **d** (go) _went_ out, and then **e** (crawl) _crawled_ about in the river mud looking for anything valuable. Henry Mayhew, a Victorian writer, **f** (interview) _____ a 'mud lark' in his book about poor working people in London in the 1850's.

'My family is Irish though I was born in London. My father **g** (work) _works_ at London Docks. He is a strong-bodied man of 34. I **h** (go) _went_ to school with my brothers for about three years and **i** (learn) _learnt_ reading and writing and arithmetic. One of my brothers **j** (be) _was_ at sea for the past five years. I **k** (work) _____ in the neighbourhood of Millwall picking up pieces of coal and iron, copper and bits of canvas on the surface. When bargemen **l** (carry) _____ coal to the shore some of it **m** (fall) _____ in the mud and we **n** (pick it up) _____. The most I **o** (ever see) _____ my companions find is one shilling's worth a day. There are usually thirteen or fourteen mud larks, boys and girls, around Limehouse in the summer and six boys steadily in the winter. When a bargeman **p** (gets hold) _____ of one, he generally **q** (throw) _____ them into the river. The police boat **r** (chase) _____ me two or three times. One night I **s** (see) _____ a large piece of copper drop down where they **t** (repair) _____ a ship. That evening as a ship **u** (come) _____ out of the docks, I **v** (strip off) _____ my clothes and **w** (dive) _____ down several feet, **x** (seize) _____ the piece of copper and later **y** (sell) _____ it to a marine dealer.'

GLOSSARY

EXTENSION ACTIVITY

A   Write a short news report, like the one in Exercise 4. If you prefer, find a report in your own language and translate it.

B   Write a report about yourself for an online dating service. Include information about what you do, what you are doing, and things you have done recently. Make yourself sound as interesting as possible!

7 passive

passive forms

The basic formation is *be* + past participle. All tenses and simple or continuous forms are possible, but some are much more common than others.

be + past participle	
present simple passive	The machines **are controlled** by computer.
present continuous passive	The crime **is being investigated**.
will passive	The building **will be completed** next year.
past simple passive	The new school **was opened** by the Mayor.
past continuous passive	The man died while **he was being taken** to hospital.
present perfect passive	A thousand new books **have been published** this month.

Only transitive verbs (verbs with an object) can be made passive. Some transitive verbs cannot be made passive: *become, fit, get, have, lack, let, like, resemble, suit*

why use passive?

- to move important information to the beginning of the sentence
  The new swimming pool has just been opened.

- to be impersonal in a scientific or technical process
  *The plastic casings **are produced** in China.*

- when the performer of the action is general (eg *people*) or obvious from the context, or unimportant, or is intentionally not named
  *All pupils **are taught** computer skills.*
  *The match **has been** cancelled.*
  *The workers **have been told** that the factory will close next week.*

  We can also use *it* + passive *decide* to show an impersonal decision.
  ***It has been decided** to close the factory.*

- Use of the passive is partly a matter of choice, though some verbs may be used more often in passive than active.

agent and instrument

- We can mention who or what performed the action using *by* and a word or phrase.
  *The new swimming pool **has just been opened by** the Mayor.*
  *The parked car **was hit by** a lorry.*

- The agent is not mentioned if it is unknown, general, obvious or unimportant etc, but is mentioned if the speaker wants to draw attention to it.
  ***I was told** I wouldn't need a visa.*
  ***I was told by the Embassy** that I wouldn't need a visa.*

- We use *with* when something is used deliberately for a purpose.
  *During the robbery, the manager was hit **with a baseball bat**.*
  Compare: *Two passengers were hit **by flying glass**.*
  ***By** shows that the action was accidental, not deliberate.*

verbs with two objects

Verbs such as *bring, give, lend, pass, pay, promise, sell, send, show, tell* can be made passive in two ways:

They gave Sarah a prize.   *They sent me a letter.*
***Sarah was given** a prize.*   ***I was sent** a letter.*
***A prize was given to** Sarah.*   ***A letter was sent to** me.*

verbs with object and complement

Some verbs have an adjective or noun phrase as a complement. When they are made passive, the complement still follows the verb.

People consider her attractive.   They elected Jim class representative.
She is considered attractive.   **Jim was elected class representative.**

verbs and prepositions

When a prepositional verb is made passive, the preposition goes at the end of the sentence and has no object.

Someone is looking after the children.   **The children are being looked after.**
Someone shot at them.   **They were shot at.**

make

The passive forms of *make* are followed by *to*-infinitive.

They made Helen write the test again.   Helen **was made to write** the test again.

Helen was made to write the test again.

see, hear, feel

Verbs *see, hear, feel, watch, notice* etc have different meanings when followed by bare infinitive, or *-ing*.

I saw him **leave.** (completed)   I saw him **leaving.** (incomplete)

When *see* and *hear* + bare infinitive are changed to a passive, the verb is followed by *to*-infinitive.

He was seen **to leave.** (complete)   He was seen **leaving.** (incomplete)

1 Rewrite the sentence using a passive form so that it does not contain the words <u>underlined</u>.

a <u>They</u> are collecting the rubbish on Tuesday this week.
The rubbish is being collected on Tuesday this week.

b <u>The police</u> have already arrested both of the suspects.
....

c <u>We</u> have decided that your contract will not be renewed.
....

d <u>Someone</u> stole my bike last week.
....

e <u>The chef</u> cooked the fish perfectly.
....

f <u>We'll</u> reach a decision next week.
....

g <u>The builders</u> completed the building at the end of last month.
....

h <u>People</u> deliver all our products to your door.
....

i <u>We</u> have asked Pauline to take over the job until the end of June.
....

j While <u>they</u> were making the film, the money ran out.
....

2 Complete the text with a passive or active form of the verb in brackets, in a suitable tense according to the context.

Local cheeses

Traditional cheeses **a** (produce) ___*are produced*___ in many regions of the UK and **b** (name)
.... after the area in which they **c** (first develop) .... Cheddar, a hard cheese
with a strong, nutty taste, is the most popular and **d** (now make) .... all over the world. A 'true'
Cheddar must come from the counties of Somerset, Dorset or Devon in southwest England or specifically from the
Somerset village from which it **e** (take) .... its name.
Wensleydale **f** (come) .... from the Yorkshire Dales (valleys)
in northern England. Originally made from sheep's milk, it **g** (base)
.... on a recipe introduced by the Cistercian
monks in the 11th century and has a mild refreshing flavour.
Traditional Lancashire, from northwest England, has a light, salty
flavour. During the Industrial Revolution (around 1760–1830),
Lancashire cheese **h** (become) .... the staple
food of the mill workers. Caerphilly, a crumbly cheese,
i (first produce) .... in the Welsh town of
that name in about 1831. The cheese **j** (soak) ....
overnight in salt water to seal in the moisture. It was popular with
the local coalminers who **k** (lose) .... a lot of
salt during their work underground. Blue Stilton, made only in the
counties of Leicestershire, Nottinghamshire and Derbyshire,
l (prize) .... as the 'king' of British cheeses.

3 Complete the text with a suitable passive form of the verb in brackets.

Blocked drains shut gallery link

A multi-million pound underground tunnel connecting two of Edinburgh's art galleries
a (close) _has been closed_ for two weeks so that blocked drains which have dogged
the building from the outset can be fixed. The repair work b (estimate) ....
to cost around £100,000 but it is unclear who will foot the bill. Major losses
c (expect) .... at the museum and at the gallery restaurant, which
d (house) .... in the link and e (force) ....
to shut whilst the work f (carry out) .... The head of buildings said it
was likely that the fault had occurred while the tunnel g (construct) ....
'It probably happened while it h (build) .... because we have had
blockage problems since it opened. We i (tell) .... it will cost around
£100,000 – who will pay for it will be the issue.' A spokeswoman for the National Galleries said:
'Everything j (do) .... to ensure minimal disruption to visitors. Many of
the educational workshops and events k (accommodate) .... elsewhere
in the galleries. The National Gallery of Scotland and the Royal Scottish Academy Building
l (not affect) .... by the work, and will open as normal throughout.'
The work to the faulty drainage system at the Weston Link, which m (only complete)
.... in August 2004, will take eight weeks from mid-February until the
start of March.

4 Rewrite each sentence so that it contains a passive verb and *by* + an agent or *with* + an instrument.

a A number of trainee doctors examined Dora.
  Dora was examined by a number of trainee doctors.

b The extent of the flood-damage has surprised everyone.
  ....

c Someone used a counterfeit key to open the security door.
  ....

d The freezing conditions put off many would-be shoppers.
  ....

e Someone used a brick to smash the window.
  ....

f The high cost of gas and electricity is hitting some families hard.
  ....

g The force of the explosion blew in the windows on nearby buildings.
  ....

h The high winds damaged several buildings.
  ....

i Somebody used a blunt instrument to hit the security guard on the head.
  ....

j The unusually high tide completely washed away the sea wall.
  ....

5 Complete the text with a suitable passive form of the verb in brackets.

Wangari Maathai

Wangari Maathai **a** (award) _was awarded_ the Nobel Peace Prize in 2004. She **b** (praise) .... by the Nobel committee as 'a source of inspiration for everyone in Africa fighting for sustainable development, democracy and peace'. When she started her Green Belt movement in 1977, Kenya was suffering from deforestation and desertification. Thousands of trees **c** (cut down) .... and many families **d** (leave) .... in poverty as a result. Since then, her successful campaign to mobilize women to plant some 30 million trees **e** (copy) .... by other countries. During that time the movement **f** (transform) .... into a campaign on education, nutrition and other issues. Her campaign has not always been popular. Mrs Maathai **g** (arrest) .... several times for campaigning against deforestation in Africa, and once she **h** (beat) .... unconscious by heavy handed police. But in elections in 2002, she **i** (elect) .... as an MP as part of an opposition coalition which swept to power, and she **j** (appoint) .... as a deputy environment minister in 2003.

GLOSSARY

6 Complete the sentence using a passive, so that it means the same as the first sentence.

a The managing director promised me a pay-rise.
.... _I was promised a pay-rise_ .... by the managing director.

b They sent me the contract by courier the next day.
The contract ....

c A multi-national company is taking over our firm.
Our firm ....

d Several people noticed the man trying to climb in the window.
.... by several people.

e They awarded David a medal for bravery.
David ....

f They made Sylvia take the exam again.
Sylvia ....

g An elderly aunt gave Paul the paintings.
Paul ....

h The police are going to look into the case.
.... by the police.

i They considered any further rescue attempts pointless.
Any further ....

j They elected George president for a second term.
George ....

7 Rewrite each sentence about the James Bond film stage, using a passive form where possible.

a Pinewood Studios will rebuild the James Bond stage which fire destroyed at the weekend, according to a statement from the studios.

  According to a statement from Pinewood Studios, the James Bond stage, which was destroyed by fire at the weekend, will be rebuilt.

b Nobody has yet confirmed the cause of the blaze at Iver Heath, Buckinghamshire, which left the celebrated stage completely gutted.

c They had completed shooting of the latest production and were removing the film sets, a spokesperson explained.

d 'We have not yet assessed the full effects of this incident, but it won't affect the financial performance of the company.'

e Someone called Buckinghamshire Fire Brigade at 1118 BST on Sunday.

f Eight fire engines tackled the blaze, and the smoke was visible from ten miles away.

g The roof covering the stage caved in through fire damage and they required special equipment to reach it.

h It is the second time fire has destroyed the stage, originally built for the 1977 Bond film *The Spy Who Loved Me*.

i They previously rebuilt the building following a fire in 1984 after which they treated six people for burns, smoke inhalation, and shock.

j Since its reopening, when they christened it *The Albert R Broccoli 007 Stage* after the long-time producer of the series, they have used it in five James Bond films.

EXTENSION ACTIVITY

A Choose a page from a book or magazine, and count the number of passive tenses. Do this with several different kinds of texts. Do some have more passives than others?

B Translate the answers to Exercises 2 and 4 into your language. How is the passive used differently in your language?

8 hearsay reporting

Hearsay reports describe what people say, report, believe, think, consider, know, etc, and are often used in news reporting. They are introduced by a passive form of the report verb, either in present simple or past simple form with a *to*-infinitive. The report can refer to the present, or past, or a time before the time of reporting.

present verb, present reference

We use a present reporting verb and refer to a state or action in the present.

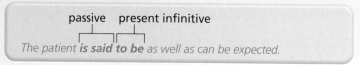

passive   present infinitive

The patient **is said to be** as well as can be expected.

(That's what people say now about the present situation.)

present verb, past reference

We use a present reporting verb and refer to a state or action in the past.

passive   past infinitive

The robbers **are thought to have stolen** more than £3 million.

(That's what people say now about the past situation.)

past verb, reference to time of reporting

We use a past reporting verb and refer to a state or action at the time the report was made.

past simple passive   present infinitive

Last week, the Prime Minister **was said to be** undecided.

(That's what people said then about the situation then.)

past verb, reference before time of reporting

We use a past reporting verb and refer to a state or action at the time before the report was made.

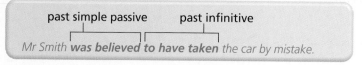

past simple passive   past infinitive

Mr Smith **was believed to have taken** the car by mistake.

(That's what people said then about something that had happened earlier.)

continuous forms

Continuous infinitive forms are also possible.

*The escaped men **are believed to be wearing** prison clothes.*
*The injured man **is thought to have been trying** to climb the cliff.*

present continuous infinitive	*wear*	**to be** *wearing*
past continuous infinitive	*wear*	**to have been** *wearing*

BREAKING NEWS - PRISONERS ESCAPE   09:30

passive infinitives

Hearsay report expressions can also be followed by passive infinitives.

*There are a number of diseases which **are known to be caused** by poor hygiene.*
*The men **are said to have been recaptured**.*
*At the time of the wreck, the diamonds **were thought to have been lost**.*

present passive infinitive	*eat*	**to be** *eaten*
past passive infinitive	*eat*	**to have been** *eaten*

passive participles

- These can be used with report verbs like *appreciate, deny, enjoy, remember* etc.
  *I appreciated **being met** at the airport.*
  *Mr Archwood denied **having been convicted** of any crime.*

- Note that there may be no difference between using past and present participles.
  *He denied **being** there.   He denied **having been** there.*

present passive continuous	*eat*	**being** *eaten*
past passive continuous	*eat*	**having been** *eaten*

1   Rewrite each sentence about ancient beliefs so that it does not contain the words underlined.

   a   In Irish mythology, people said a meteor was a soul passing from purgatory to heaven.
       In Irish mythology, a meteor was said to be a soul passing from purgatory to heaven.

   b   In Greek mythology, people believed the beech tree was able to carry messages from a worshipper to Zeus, the father of the gods.

   c   In ancient Egypt people thought bats' blood cured blindness.

   d   In Aztec mythology, people believed the Sun was the home of the god Quetzalcoatl.

   e   In Norse mythology, people thought the bravest warriors lived after death in the hall of Valhalla.

   f   In ancient Egypt, people believed the scarab, or beetle, carried the Sun across the sky.

2   Rewrite each sentence so that it begins with the words underlined.

   a   People say that the company's European division is having a good year.
       The company's European division *is said to be having a good year.*

   b   In contrast, they say that the Far East division has been suffering from rising costs.

   c   People believe that the company has been talking to a competitor about a possible merger.

   d   People know some directors have been thinking on these lines for some time.

   e   People believe the CEO, Carl Graham, is making an attempt to focus the business more sharply in some areas.

   f   People say he is also looking at the possibility of job cuts.

   g   People think the company is holding a top-level meeting about these matters next week.

3 Complete the sentence so that it means the same as the first sentence.

a Oak Island in Canada is one of many places in the world which people think is the site of buried treasure.

Oak Island in Canada is one of many places in the world which is _thought to be the site of buried treasure._

b People say that the treasure is in a place called 'the money pit'.

The treasure is _____ .

c People think that pirates buried the treasure centuries ago.

Pirates are _____ .

d The money pit story dates back to 1795, when people report that a local youth fell into a hole at the foot of a large tree.

The money pit story dates back to 1795, when a local youth is _____
_____ .

e People believe that he and a friend discovered traces of treasure in the hole

He and a friend are _____ .

f People say that the two men found a treasure chest in later excavations.

The two men are _____ .

g However, before they could open the chest, people say that water flooded in.

However, before they could open the chest, water is _____ .

h Since then, people believe that more than a dozen groups of treasure hunters have searched for the treasure.

Since then, more than a dozen groups of treasure hunters are _____
_____ .

i People think that some explorers found old pieces of metal in the hole.

Some explorers are _____ .

j However, people now report that the pit is a natural phenomenon, or the remains of old colonial fortifications.

However, the pit is now _____ .

4 Rewrite each sentence using *appreciate, deny, enjoy, like* or *remember* and the word in capitals.

a Thanks for taking me to the station.   TAKEN

   I appreciate being taken to the station.

b I was shown around the school, and I enjoyed it.   BEING

   _____

c I don't remember when they arrested me!   BEING

   _____

d He said he liked it when people took him seriously.   TAKEN

   _____

e Tina said she hadn't been paid to appear in the play.   HAVING

   _____

f I don't remember when they gave me the anaesthetic.   BEING

   _____

g Thanks for giving me another chance.   GIVEN

   _____

5 Write a new sentence with the same meaning containing the word in capitals.

a People say that the hat sold yesterday at the auction was worn by Napoleon during the invasion of Russia in 1812.   SAID
The hat sold yesterday at the auction is said to have been worn by Napoleon during the invasion of Russia in 1812.

b People think that the earthquake in the North Sea was caused by a release in pressure after oil and gas extraction.   THOUGHT

c People believe that Harriet the tortoise, who has just died aged 176, was owned by Charles Darwin.   BELIEVED

d People now know that three patients were infected with the disease through blood transfusions.   KNOWN

e People think that more than a hundred football supporters were involved in the riot after the match.   THOUGHT

f People believe that the recent forest fires in California were started deliberately.   BELIEVED

g People now know that three other religious leaders were arrested at the same time.   BEEN

h People believe that the helicopter which crashed yesterday killing 18 service personnel was shot down.   BELIEVED

6 Rewrite each sentence so that it is a hearsay report, using a form of the verb in capitals.

a Two suspects have been arrested.   THINK
Two suspects are thought to have been arrested.

b The plane crashed into the sea near a small island.   BELIEVE

c The minister is considering changing the laws on smoking in public. SAY

d Yesterday the situation had improved.   REPORT

e Whales have been seen in the area for the first time.   SAY

f The fire broke out at 3 am.   BELIEVE

g Last year the company recorded rising profits.   REPORT

h The number of unemployed has fallen by 10%.   THINK

7 Read the information about the life of Shakespeare and the example hearsay sentence. Then write seven more hearsay sentences about events in his life, beginning 'he is believed' or 'he is thought'.

The life of Shakespeare

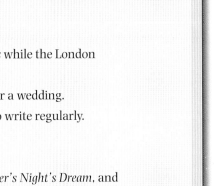

We know some definite facts about Shakespeare's life, but we can only make informed guesses about many other details.

- His actual birthday is unknown but is celebrated today on 23 April, just three days before his baptism was recorded in the parish register of the Holy Trinity Church on 26 April, 1564.
- He probably started his education at the age of seven in 1571.
- In 1582, aged 18, he married Anne Hathaway, aged 26.
- Twins, Judith and Hamnet, were born in 1585.
- Between 1585 and 1592 Shakespeare probably left his family in Stratford to join a company of actors. He was probably both a playwright and a performer.
- In 1589–1590 he may have written his first play, *Henry VI, Part One*.
- By 1592 he was well known in London as a writer.
- In 1592–93 Shakespeare may have written the poem *Venus and Adonis* while the London theatres were closed because of the plague.
- In 1595 he may have written *A Midsummer Night's Dream*, probably for a wedding. *Romeo and Juliet* was probably also written in this year. He continued to write regularly.
- In 1597 he bought an expensive house in Stratford on Avon.
- 1600–1601 is when he probably wrote *Hamlet*.
- In 1603 Queen Elizabeth was present at a performance of *A Midsummer's Night's Dream*, and after her death that year, the new king, James I, watched a performance of *As You Like It*.
- In 1616 William Shakespeare died on 23 April. He is buried in Stratford on Avon.

GLOSSARY

He is thought to have been born on 23 April, 1564.

EXTENSION ACTIVITY

A Make some comments upon these topics, using hearsay reporting.

  aliens   global warming   historical situations

B Comment on situations in the news, using hearsay reporting.

*Need more practice? Go to the **Review** on page 208.*

hearsay reporting

45

9 have and *get something done*, other uses of *get*

causative *have*

- For a service someone does for us we use *to have something done*. There is a full range of tenses but the most common are present continuous, *going to*, present perfect and past simple. The infinitive is also used.

We're having our flat decorated.

have + object + past participle	
present continuous	*We're **having** our flat **decorated**.*
going to	*She's **going to have** a tooth **taken out**.*
present perfect	*He **has had** his nose **altered**.*
past simple	*I **had** my hair **cut** a week ago.*
infinitive	*We want to **have** our car **repainted**.*

- We do not mention the agent (the person who performed the action) unless this is important.
  *I'm going to have my photograph taken **by a top fashion photographer**.*

- We may also mention the place where we have things done.
  *I have my hair cut **at my local hairdresser's**.*

- We also use causative *have* to describe unfortunate events that have happened to people.
  *Maria **had her car stolen** last night.*
  *He **had his nose broken** while he was playing rugby.*
  *They **had their house broken into** recently.*

get something *done*

In everyday speech we often use *get* instead of *have* for present continuous and past simple, but not for present perfect.
  *We're **getting our flat decorated**.*
  *He's **getting his nose altered**.*
  He's got his nose altered. (not possible)
  *He **got** his nose **broken** in a fight.*
  Maria has got her car stolen. (not possible)

get meaning *manage*

We also use *get something done* to mean 'manage to do it', with a sense of achieving something. This does not mean that somebody else did the work.

I got my work finished in the end.

*I **got** my work **finished** in the end.*   (= I managed to do it in the end.)
*Jack is difficult to work with, but **he gets the job done**.*   (= He manages to do the job.)
***Have you got the computer to work** yet?*   (= Have you managed to make it work?)

get with *-ing*

Get is also used to mean 'start to do something', when we give someone an order.
    Get moving!   (= start)

get someone *to do* something / *have* someone *do* something

This means that we make them do it.
    *I **got him to check the figures** a second time just to make sure.*

We can also say:
    *I **had him check the figures** a second time just to make sure.*

get *married* etc

Get also forms expressions with *married, arrested, accepted, chosen* etc.
    *He **got arrested** on the way out of the stadium.*
    *They're **getting married** in Paris next month.*
    *I **got accepted** for the job!*

have and get something done, other uses of get

1 Rewrite each sentence without the words <u>underlined</u>, using a causative *have* construction. Make any other necessary changes.

a <u>Some painters</u> have painted the outside of our house.
We have had the outside of our house painted.

b <u>A hairdresser</u> cut Martin's hair yesterday.

c <u>Some plumbers</u> are installing a new central heating system at our house tomorrow.

d <u>An optician</u> is going to examine my eyes this afternoon.

e <u>A surgeon</u> altered Tom's nose last year.

f <u>The dry-cleaners</u> cleaned my leather coat specially.

g <u>An art specialist</u> has valued our paintings.

h <u>A mechanic</u> looked at the car before Maria bought it.

i <u>A carpenter</u> replaced the windows in our house last year.

j <u>A dentist</u> is going to take out two of Julia's teeth.

2 Rewrite each sentence with a causative *have* construction, beginning as shown. Include the agent (the person who performed the action) if this is important.

a Katie's car was stolen by one of her friends.
Katie *had her car stolen by one of her friends* .

b A photographer is going to take a photo of us.
We _____ .

c Can you come quickly? Someone has broken into my house.
Can you come quickly? I _____ .

d Tracey Emin, the well-known British artist, is going to paint Laura's portrait.
Laura _____ .

e A well-known architect designed their house.
They _____ .

f A local tailor makes all my suits.
I _____ .

g Someone repaired Dave's bike at a shop in the High Street.
Dave _____ .

h A surgeon is replacing my hip next week.
I _____ .

i Someone broke one of Tony's fingers while he was playing cricket.
Tony _____ .

j A local firm is going to redecorate Maria's flat.
Maria _____ .

3 Write a new sentence with the same meaning containing the word in capitals. Leave out any unnecessary agents.

a Someone broke the leg of one of the players.   GOT

   One of the players got his leg broken.

b Andy wants a doctor to alter his nose.   HAVE

c The police arrested Anna as she was leaving the shop.   GOT

d Doctors amputated the patient's leg after the accident.   HAD

e The shop on the corner usually repairs my shoes.   HAVE

f I made sure that Tom checked all the windows before he left.   GOT

g Jim says he'll be late because he is at the hairdresser's.   GETTING

h Have you managed to start your work yet?   GOT

i Someone has stolen Sue's car.   HAD

4 Complete the text with one word in each gap.

A few weeks ago, while we were out at the cinema, we **a** _had_ our house broken into. We'd been meaning to **b** .... locks fitted on the windows, but we hadn't **c** .... the work **d** ...., and so the burglars found it easy to get in. Luckily we **e** .... have many things taken. When the police arrived, they **f** .... us to go through the house and check what was missing. We were actually **g** .... a new kitchen fitted at that time, and some power tools had been stolen. One of the burglars was seen acting suspiciously near another house a few days later, and **h** .... himself arrested. When he had **i** .... his fingerprints taken at the police station, the police were able to prove he was the one who had burgled us. Since then we **j** .... had new locks fitted and a new alarm installed. Next week we're **k** .... bars put on the ground floor windows, so we're hoping not to **l** .... burgled again.

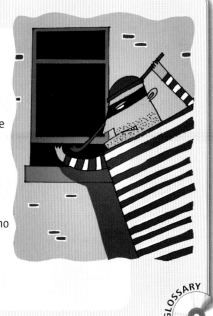

GLOSSARY

EXTENSION ACTIVITY

A Make a list of things you *have done, are having done, have had done, are going to have done, had done.*

B Some people use cosmetic surgery to have their appearance changed. Do some research in a library or on the Internet, and make a list of things people can have done.

*Need more practice? Go to the **Review** on page 208.*

have and get something done, other uses of get

10 conditional and *if*-sentences (1)

real conditions (first conditional)

- *if* + present simple + *will / won't* (*do*)
  This shows the results in the future of a real situation, with possible or likely results.
  If you eat all the ice-cream, you'll be sick!

- other variants
  If can also be followed by *can / can't*, present perfect (to emphasize completion),
  going to, present continuous with future meaning.
  If you can't answer Exercise 1, you won't be able to do Exercise 2.
  If you've finished washing the floor, I'll help you clean the kitchen.
  If you're going to buy a car, I'll lend you some of the money.
  If you're going to the shops, I'll come with you!

  The second clause can contain *could* requests, *be able to*, *can*, *going to*, imperative, *had better*,
  could and *might* etc.
  If I give you the money, could you get me some stamps?
  If you've finished washing the floor, you can start cleaning the kitchen.
  If it rains this afternoon, we're going to stay in and watch some DVDs.
  If you're going to buy a car, make sure you get it checked by a garage.
  If you're going to the shops, you'd better take some money!
  If Cole scores now, that could be the end of the match!

future results: *if* clauses with *will*

- There are some *if*-sentences that describe the possible results of an offer. In these sentences, *will* is
  used in the *if*-clause.
  I'll talk to your teacher, if that will stop you worrying so much.

- In some *if*-sentences, *if* is followed by emphasized *will*, meaning 'insist on', or *won't* meaning
  'refuse to'.
  If you will wear such thin clothes, of course you'll feel cold!
  If you won't listen to common sense, there's no point my talking to you.

- *If* can be followed by *will* and *would* as polite request forms.
  If you'll just wait here, I'll tell Mr Brown that you've arrived.
  If you'd just fill in this form, I'll check the details.

unreal conditions (second conditional)

- *if* + past simple + *would* (*do*)
  This shows the results which would follow from an imaginary situation, with impossible or unlikely
  results.
  If the Earth didn't have a Moon, there wouldn't be any tides.

- *Could* and *might* are often used instead of *would*, as are other modals.
  If we all worked together, we could solve the problem faster.

- The difference between real and unreal may be a matter of speaker choice and context.
  If you buy a bike, *you'll* get a lot fitter.
  (You are really thinking of buying one – perhaps we are in the bike shop.)
  If you bought a bike, *you'd* get a lot fitter. (We are only discussing possibilities.)

impossible past conditions (third conditional)

- *if* + past perfect + *would have (done)* / (passive *would have been done*)
  Used for the results which would follow from an imaginary past situation. As we cannot change the past, this is an impossible condition. Passive forms are common.
  If the ship had had more lifeboats, more passengers *would have been* saved.
  If the ship hadn't hit an iceberg, *it wouldn't have* sunk.
  If another ship hadn't arrived soon afterwards, none of the passengers *would have been saved*.

- *Could have* and *might have* are often used instead of *would have*, as are other modals.
  If the ship had been travelling more slowly, *it might have avoided* the iceberg.

mixed conditions

- *if* + past perfect + *would (do)*
  Used for an imagined or actual event in the past with a result in the present.
  If she had worn her seat-belt, *she would still be* alive.
  If you hadn't given me a lift, *I'd probably still be* at the station!

- *if* + past simple + *would have (done)*
  Used for a present state which has influenced past events.
  If you weren't so lazy, *you'd have finished* your work by now.
  If she was better-qualified, *she would have got* the job.

1 Complete each sentence giving computer advice using an *if*-condition, so that it has the same meaning as the first sentence.

  a Don't press that button on the keyboard, or you'll lose what you've written.
    If _you press that button on the keyboard, you'll lose what you've written_ .

  b Make a back-up copy of your work or you'll lose it.
    You won't _____ .

  c You need virus protection to avoid having problems with your computer.
    If you don't _____ .

  d Sitting too long at the computer will make your back and arms ache.
    Your _____ .

  e Don't turn off the computer before closing all programs, or you could have problems.
    You _____ .

  f You'll lose your work unless you save it before closing the word-processing program.
    If _____ .

  g You can save a lot of time by learning the keyboard short cuts.
    If _____ .

  h Running too many programs at the same time will probably make the computer crash.
    The computer will _____ .

2 Choose the correct option, A, B or C, to complete the sentence.

  a Why don't you use the Internet? If you had looked up the information on the net, you __A__ .
  b If Alice _____ a cycle helmet, she might have been seriously injured.
  c If there wasn't any water on the Earth, life _____ .
  d Luckily I checked my diary. If I _____ that, I would have completely forgotten her birthday.
  e You don't believe in yourself. That's why you failed your driving test. If you were more self-confident, I'm sure you _____ .
  f If you travelled to the Sun at the speed of light, you _____ there in about eight and a half minutes.
  g If you're thinking of having a sun-and-sea holiday, _____ yourself from the sun.
  h You can start looking at the next unit if you _____ Exercise 5.
  i It's a lot quicker going by train than by car. And even if you _____ by car, it's impossible to find anywhere to park.
  j If we _____ an hour extra every day, we could finish the project a week early.

	A	B	C
a	A would know the answer	B knew the answer	C will know the answer
b	A wasn't wearing	B hadn't been wearing	C isn't wearing
c	A wouldn't have begun	B will not begin	C wouldn't begin
d	A hadn't done	B didn't do	C would do
e	A passed	B would have passed	C will pass
f	A arrive	B would have arrived	C would arrive
g	A you have protected	B you should protect	C you will protect
h	A would have finished	B finished	C have finished
i	A went	B had gone	C go
j	A work	B have worked	C had worked

3 Choose the correct option, A, B or C, to complete the sentence.

a You can start doing Section 2 if you _____C_____ Section 1.

b If you've become completely confused, you _____ start again.

c Could you get me a book from the library, if I _____ the details.

d If _____ a moment, I'll see if I can find another question paper for you.

e I'll go over the figures again, if you _____ .

f If you _____ the instructions, then of course you'll get the answers wrong!

g If you _____ a dictionary, then make sure you know how to use it!

h If I finish my project on time, I _____ a couple of days off!

a A *will finish*	B *are going to finish*	C *have finished*
b A *will*	B *had better*	C *are going to*
c A *give you*	B *will give you*	C *have given you*
d A *you'll wait*	B *you have waited*	C *you are waiting*
e A *will think that helps.*	B *think that will help.*	C *will think that will help.*
f A *aren't reading*	B *read*	C *won't read*
g A *will use*	B *have used*	C *are going to use*
h A *had better take*	B *am able to take*	C *am going to take*

science

4 Complete the sentence with a suitable form of the verb in brackets.

The Earth after humans

If all the people on Earth **a** (disappear) _disappeared_ tomorrow, nature **b** (begin) _____ to reclaim the planet. For a start, if people no longer **c** (pollute) _____ the atmosphere, the air **d** (soon become) _____ clean again. If there **e** (be) _____ no people to maintain buildings, they **f** (soon begin) _____ to decay, but more solid parts **g** (take) _____ thousands of years to disappear. In general, if the 6.5 billion humans no longer **h** (compete) _____ with other species on Earth, most species **i** (benefit) _____ . For example, if humans no longer **j** (catch) _____ fish, the numbers of fish worldwide **k** (eventually increase) _____ . However, if humans **l** (vanish) _____ from the Earth, endangered species of animals **m** (not necessarily recover) _____ , as some are already too few in number. Some endangered species **n** (have) _____ greater difficulty surviving if no humans **o** (take) _____ the trouble to protect them from other species. Even if we no longer **p** (poison) _____ the planet, several decades **q** (go by) _____ before all dangerous chemicals **r** (disappear) _____ . And even if the burning of fossil fuels **s** (cease) _____ tomorrow, the oceans **t** (not absorb) _____ all the CO_2 in the atmosphere for thousands of years. In the end, though, if alien visitors **u** (land) _____ on the Earth in 100,000 years time, they **v** (find) _____ no signs that an advanced civilization had ever lived here.

conditional and *if*-sentences (1)

5 Complete the sentences about the possible future for our world, using a suitable form of the verb in brackets, depending on whether you think the sentence describes something real / possible or unreal / impossible.

a If the Earth (stop) _stopped_ spinning, one side (always be) _____ in darkness.

b If the polar ice-caps (melt) _____ completely, sea-levels worldwide (rise) _____ by about 60 metres.

c If we (recycle) _____ more household waste, there (be) _____ less damage to the environment.

d If an astronaut (fall) _____ into a black hole in space, what (happen) _____ ?

e If people (not stop) _____ using cars so much, the country's roads (eventually grind) _____ to a standstill.

f What (happen) _____ when the world's supplies of oil (run out) _____ ?

g If human beings (finally start) _____ living on the Moon, they (need) _____ to produce water artificially.

h If there (not be) _____ any money (the world be) _____ a better place?

i If we (not stop) _____ over-fishing the world's oceans, many species (become) _____ extinct.

j If everyone in the world (jump) _____ up and down at the same time, there (be) _____ no measurable effect (apart from 6.5 billion footprints).

6 Comment on each sentence beginning as shown. Some forms may be passive.

a Mrs Allen's neighbour searched his garden shed, and found the missing cat inside.
   If _Mrs Allen's neighbour hadn't searched his garden shed, he wouldn't have found the missing cat inside_ .

b The hikers were rescued quickly from the storm on the mountain because one of them had her mobile phone with her.
   If _____ .

c The boy who fell into the sea from the boat was wearing a life jacket, so he survived.
   If _____ .

d Mr Anderson woke up because he heard the smoke alarm, and the family managed to escape the fire.
   If _____ .

e Rescue workers didn't search the car properly and didn't notice the injured man.
   If _____ .

f Luckily most of the staff had left the room to attend a meeting, so only one person was injured by flying glass from the broken window.
   If _____ .

g United didn't win because the goalkeeper made a mistake in the last minute of the match.
   If _____ .

h A police officer stopped Pratt for drink-driving, and took a DNA sample, which led to his being charged with the previously unsolved murder of Mrs Jones.
   If _____ .

7 Put the verb in brackets in a suitable form, using a negative where necessary.

The extinction of the dinosaurs

The dinosaurs probably became extinct after a giant asteroid hit the Earth about 65 million years ago. But what **a** (happen) _would have happened_ if this asteroid **b** (miss) ....? Scientists believe that in this case, dinosaurs **c** (continue) .... to dominate the Earth, and that modern animals **d** (probably exist) .... Instead of elephants and lions and so on, there **e** (be) .... different types of dinosaurs, because the animals we have now simply **f** (be able) .... to evolve. Some scientists have even suggested that dinosaurs **g** (develop) .... along the same lines as human beings, but this is a minority view. The general view is that perhaps dinosaur brains **h** (grow) .... larger, but if they **i** (exist) .... today, dinosaurs **j** (change) .... very much in general, and **k** (look) .... much the same. The prospects for human beings would not be so good, however. If the asteroid **l** (collide) .... with the Earth, there **m** (probably be) .... any humans alive today. When the asteroid disaster wiped out the dinosaurs, it gave mammals the advantage. Without that space collision, mammals **n** (stand) .... much chance against the dominant dinosaur species.

EXTENSION ACTIVITY

A Write some endings for these *if*-sentences.

    a If the weather gets hotter / colder, ...
    b If I was able to live anywhere in the world, ...
    c If scientists hadn't discovered how electricity works, ...
    d If you want to learn a foreign language, ...

B Choose an example from each section on pages 50–51 and translate these examples into your language.

conditional and *if*-sentences (1)

11 conditional and *if*-sentences (2)

unless

Unless is used when we say that if something does not happen, something else will happen (or be true) as a result.

If you don't help me, I won't be able to lift this.
*I won't be able to lift this **unless** you help me.*

otherwise

Otherwise is another way of saying *if not*. It can also come at the end of a separate sentence.

*Help me with this, **otherwise** I won't be able to lift it.*
*Help me with this. I won't be able to lift it **otherwise**.*

if only

- *If only* can be used as a way of emphasizing *if*.
  If only you'd told me, I could have helped you.

- The *if only* clause can also be used alone as an exclamation.
  If only you'd told me!

provided / providing (that), as long as, on condition (that)

These are more emphatic ways of saying *only ... if*.

*You can **only** go to the party, **if you are home** before 12.00.*
*You can go to the party, **provided you are home** before 12.00.*
*You can go to the party, **as long as you are home** before 12.00.*
*You can go to the party, **on condition that you are home** before 12.00.*

even if

- *Even if* can also be used in conditional sentences to emphasize *if*.
  ***Even if you begged him** to take the money, he wouldn't accept.*

if (you) should ..., if you happen to ...

- *If + should* emphasizes that an event is not very likely, or to make a request seem more indirect or polite.
  ***If you should see him** tomorrow, could you give him my message?*

- *If + happen to* has a similar effect, and can be used with *should* to emphasize unlikelihood or distance. Phrases such as *by any chance* are also used in the same way.
  ***If you happen to be** in the neighbourhood, do drop in and see us.*
  ***If you should happen by any chance** to find the money, can you send it back?*

if (I) were to ...,

- This is often used in writing which speculates about the future.
  *If the government **were to lower** taxes, they would certainly win votes.*

- This can also make an event seem less likely.
  ***If I were to offer you** more money, would you stay in the job?*

if (it) were / was not for / hadn't been for ...

This describes how one event depends on another.

***If it were not for Helen**, our team would be the worst in the area!*
(If Helen wasn't a really good player...)
***If it hadn't been for Jim**, the child would have drowned.*
(If Jim hadn't jumped in to rescue the child ...)

but for

We can use *but for* to mean 'if it were not for'.

> **But for** your assistance, we would not have succeeded.

supposing, suppose, imagine

These are ways of expressing conditions without *if*.

> **Supposing you had** £5 million. What would you spend it on?
> **Imagine you were** president. How would you change the country?

if so / if not

These can refer to a previous sentence and form a condition.

> If Jean is too ill to play, Mary can play instead.
> Jean may be too ill to play. **If so, Mary can play** instead.
> Jean may still be able to play. **If not, Mary can play** instead.

leaving out *if*

In everyday speech, we can use an imperative phrase + *and* + *will* clause instead of an *if*-conditional sentence.

> If you come over here, I'll show you what I mean.
> **Come over here and** I'll show you what I mean.

if + adjective

In informal instructions, we can leave out the verb *to be* in phrases with adjectives such as *interested, necessary* etc.

> If you are interested, phone this number.
> **If interested**, phone this number.

if I might, if I can / could ...

Might and *can / could* are used in an *if*-clause which stands alone as a very polite request.

> **If I could just have** another look. (=Could I have another look?)
> If **I might help** you with your coat.

had (I) ..., were (I) ..., should (I) ...

It is possible to begin formal conditional sentences by inverting *had* or *were* or *should* and the subject, leaving out *if* (see **Unit 40**).

1 Underline the correct form.

a Small dogs can be carried on a passenger's knee *if only / <u>provided</u>* they do not cause inconvenience to passengers.

b *Even if / Supposing* you could visit any country in the world. Where would you go?

c I would like to thank the many colleagues who have made invaluable contributions: *unless / but for* their help, this project would not have been possible.

d You must register your copy of the CD-ROM online, *otherwise / unless* it will not work.

e If the government *were to / should* balance the budget, it would be able to increase spending.

f You can easily get into trouble *if you happen to be / on condition that you are* in the wrong place at the wrong time.

g We will give you a guaranteed price of €150 for your old computer, *even if / otherwise* it doesn't work.

h According to the survey, most people are happy to welcome foreigners to their country, *as long as / otherwise* they don't start behaving like foreigners.

i Please don't interrupt the lesson *as long as / unless* you have an important point to make.

j *If he should happen to have / If it hadn't been for* a leg injury, Adams would probably have won the race.

2 Choose the correct option, A, B or C, to complete each sentence about security issues.

a ___C___ leaving valuable property in parked cars, their cars wouldn't be broken into.

b _____ a serious crime, what exactly should you do?

c Please do not use the 999 emergency number _____ you are reporting a genuine emergency.

d _____ you were travelling abroad, what could you do to improve your personal safety?

e _____ the information provided by members of the public, the police would have a much more difficult job.

f Police often conduct security checks in this area so they may stop you, and _____ you might be asked for your identity card or passport.

g _____ any objectionable items on the website, let us know and we will have them removed.

h _____ CCTV cameras installed in the store, many shoplifters would escape detection.

i _____ people locked all their doors and windows, there would be fewer break-ins.

j _____ your computer has a virus protection program, you might still fall victim to e-mail scams or malicious software.

a A *Unless people stopped*   B *Imagine*   C *If only people stopped*
b A *Unless you witness*   B *If you were to witness*   C *C If only you witness*
c A *if*   B *provided*   C *unless*
d A *Supposing*   B *If so*   C *As long as*
e A *Supposing*   B *Provided that*   C *If it were not for*
f A *otherwise*   B *if so*   C *even if*
g A *Unless you notice*   B *If you happen to notice*   C *If you were to notice*
h A *If there were to be*   B *If only there were*   C *If it weren't for*
i A *If only*   B *Otherwise*   C *Even if*
j A *Unless*   B *Even if*   C *On condition that*

3 Write a new sentence with the same meaning, beginning as shown.

a We will refund your booking fee, provided you cancel 48 hours in advance.
   We will only _refund your booking fee if you cancel 48 hours in advance_ .

b I wish you'd told me about the cheap flights to Italy.
   If _____ !

c Thanks to the skill of the surgeon, the child survived.
   If it _____ .

d Let us know if you have second thoughts.
   If you should _____ .

e If you hadn't helped me, I would have made a complete mess of this.
   But _____ .

f Please come this way, sir. Could I take your coat?
   Please come this way, sir. If _____ .

g You can offer me more money, but I still won't sell the house to you!
   Even _____ .

h If you let me get a word in edgeways, I'll tell you what I discovered.
   Let _____ .

i If you changed your mind about the job, we'd be interested in hearing from you.
   If you were _____ .

j As long as there are no delays, we'll be there by six.
   Unless _____ .

geography

4 Complete the text with one word in each gap.

Environmental issues

Everyone agrees that a __unless__ the world's tiger population is
protected, tigers b _____ eventually become extinct. If it
c _____ not for the efforts made by international campaigns
over past decades, the extinction d _____ already have become
a fact. Tigers can coexist with human beings, e _____ local
people are involved in conservation. However, f _____ if tiger
habitats are redeveloped there is no guarantee of success. Government
agencies must be involved, and there must be adequate finance:
g _____ conservation projects are neglected. An organized
programme with safeguards must be introduced. If h _____ ,
the illegal hunters quickly move back in. i _____ there were no
tigers left in the world: how j _____ we all feel? According to
some environmentalists, that day may be coming sooner rather than later.

GLOSSARY

conditional and *if*-sentences (2)

EXTENSION ACTIVITY

A Make a list of instructions a teacher might give to a class, including:
   unless   otherwise   provided / as long as / on condition

B Make true examples which include:
   even if   if you should   if it hadn't been for   supposing   if so   imperative + *and* + *will* clause

*Need more practice? Go to the **Review** on page 208.*

12 unreal past tense

wishes about the present

Like a second conditional sentence, these wishes use a past tense form to express a feeling about the present.

> *I wish I knew* the answer.   (= If I knew the answer, it would be better.)
> *I wish it wasn't* raining!   (= If it wasn't raining, it would be better.)
> *I wish they were* arriving earlier.
> *I wish I was / were lying* on the beach at this moment!

I wish I was lying on a beach.

Wishes with *could* also express a feeling about the present.
> *I wish I could* get a better job.   (now)

wishes about the past

Wishes about the past use past perfect in the same way as a third conditional sentence.
> *I wish I had brought* an umbrella with me.
> (= If I had brought an umbrella with me, it would have been better.)
> *I wish we'd left* earlier.
> (= If we had left earlier it would have been better.)

hope

Wishes about the future are expressed with *hope*.
> *I hope you enjoy* your trip.   (future)
> *I hope I can / will be able* to get a better job.   (future)

wishes with *would / wouldn't*

● Wishes with *would / wouldn't* are about general behaviour or habits, often bad ones which we wish would change.
> *I wish* everyone *would* leave me alone.
> *I wish you'd* stop interrupting me.   *I wish you wouldn't* do that.

● Using unreal past tense can give the same meaning in some contexts.
> *I wish it didn't rain* so much.   (it may or may not be raining now)
> *I wish it wouldn't rain* so much.   (it's probably raining now)

● To *wish someone would do something* can also mean that we would like them to do it.
> *I wish you would ask* for my advice more often.

if I were you

We use *if I were you* for giving advice. Note that *I* and *you* are stressed more heavily than *were*. The *if*-clause can come at the beginning or at the end.

> *I wouldn't touch that wire, **if I were you**.*
> ***If I were you**, I'd go to the police.*

would rather, would sooner

- We can use *would rather / would sooner* + infinitive to express choice.
  > ***Would you rather stay** at home?*
  > ***I'd rather have** tea than coffee.*

- *would rather / would sooner* + person + unreal past are used to show what we would like someone else to do or not to do.
  > ***I'd rather you didn't tell** anyone.*   (It would be better if you didn't tell)
  > ***I'd sooner she went** to university than got a job now.*

would prefer   (see Unit 16)

- We can use *would prefer* + *to*-infinitive to express a preference.
  > *Do you want to go out? No, I think **I'd prefer to stay** at home.*

  We can compare preferences with *rather than*.
  > ***I'd prefer to go** out for a meal tonight **rather than** stay in and cook.*

- *Would prefer* + *that* + unreal past or *would prefer it if* + unreal past can be used to show what we would like someone else to do or not to do.
  > ***I'd prefer that you didn't** mention this to anyone.*
  > ***I'd prefer it if you didn't** mention this to anyone.*

- We can also use *would prefer* + person + *to*-infinitive with the same meaning.
  > ***I'd prefer you not to** mention this to anyone.*

it's time + unreal past

We use *it's time* + unreal past to express what we think we ought to do.

> *My shoes are wearing out. **It's time (that) I bought** some new ones.*
> *It's already 8.00. I think **it's time (that) we left**.*

We also often say *It's time we were going.*

as if, as though

- Real comparisons with *as if, as though* use *look, seem, appear* etc with present or future meaning.
  > ***He looks as if** he wants to leave.* (real)
  > ***It seems as though** City are going to win.* (real)
  > ***It doesn't look as if** I'll ever repay my debts.* (real)

- Unreal comparisons with *as if* and *as though* use *was / were* to refer to the present if the comparison seems unreal or imaginary.
  > *She acts **as if she was / were** queen!* (unreal – she isn't)

unreal past tense

1 Underline the correct form.

a   Parents who also work often wish they *have / had* more time to spend with their children.

b   No doubt the prime minister now wishes he *listened / had listened* to what other people were saying before he made his decision.

c   Local councillors say they wish more people *could / would* let them know what they think about the new anti-smoking laws.

d   Many people wish that fast-food companies *would stop / had stopped* targeting children with advertising.

e   Local residents generally wish that tourists *didn't leave / hadn't left* so much litter behind in the town.

f   I have had nothing but trouble with this computer, and I now wish that I *didn't buy / had not bought* it.

g   When we grow older, with hindsight we all wish that we *spent / had spent* our time at school more profitably.

h   We wish we *knew / would know* how to solve the problem of vandalism, but so far we haven't come up with a perfect solution.

i   Doctors say they wish that more people *paid / had paid* attention to the amount of salt they consume.

j   I *hope / wish* I could believe what politicians say, but I'm afraid I can't.

2 Choose the correct option, A, B or C, to complete the sentences about the generation gap.

a   It's time that older people __C__ listening to what younger people say.

b   Some older people treat teenagers as if they _____ all dangerous criminals.

c   Some older people wish there _____ more police officers on the street, and blame all bad behaviour on the young.

d   Perhaps it's time that young people _____ more responsibly towards other people.

e   Generally speaking, young people _____ spend their time with other young people.

f   Many older people _____ the world to be just the same as it was when they were young.

g   Older people also wish that young people _____ more politely.

h   Some people think _____ that 16-year-olds were given the vote.

i   Many young people, however, have no faith in politics, and just wish the world _____ different.

j   Some of them _____ if everyone just left them alone and stopped asking them for their opinions.

a	**A** *would start*	**B** *start*	**C** *started*
b	**A** *were*	**B** *would*	**C** *prefer*
c	**A** *were*	**B** *had been*	**C** *are*
d	**A** *acted*	**B** *would act*	**C** *act*
e	**A** *wish*	**B** *would rather*	**C** *hope*
f	**A** *rather*	**B** *would prefer*	**C** *as though*
g	**A** *had behaved*	**B** *didn't behave*	**C** *would behave*
h	**A** *as if*	**B** *it's time*	**C** *they wouldn't prefer*
i	**A** *is*	**B** *had been*	**C** *were*
j	**A** *would rather*	**B** *as though*	**C** *would prefer it*

3 Write a new sentence with the same meaning, beginning as shown.

a It seems that more and more young people will go into higher education in future.
It seems as _if more and more young people will go into higher education in the future._

b Most parents want their children to study a useful subject leading to a good job.
Most parents would rather ....

c Students, however, usually want their parents to let them make their own choices.
Students, however, usually wish ....

d Later on, though, some students regret not having chosen their courses more carefully.
Later on, though, some students wish ....

e University advisers don't usually want students to choose a subject simply because they think
they are good at it.
University advisers usually prefer students ....

f The usual advice is: 'Think about what kind of work you want to do in the future.'
The usual advice is: 'If I ....

g Some students seem from their behaviour to be only interested in having a good time.
Some students behave as ....

h When they leave university, many students regret not having worked harder.
When they leave university, many students wish ....

i They also think they will never repay their student loans.
It also seems to them as ....

j Universities should now pay more attention to students' financial problems.
It's ....

---

social studies

4 Complete the text using one word in each gap.

Neighbours and noise

Do you ever wish that your neighbours **a** _would_ turn down their
music? Perhaps you're trying to sleep and you wish that the people
next-door **b** .... not holding an all-night barbecue party
in their garden. Or do you feel it is **c** .... you moved to an
uninhabited island? Don't worry – you are just another victim of noise
pollution. Of course, most people would prefer **d** .... if cars
e .... no noise at all, neighbours **f** .... as quiet as
mice, and nobody **g** .... about the streets in cars with open
windows and high-powered sound systems. You may even wish you
h .... stop children from playing in the street, or planes
from passing overhead. But in the end, if I **i** .... you I **j** .... just get used to it. Close the
windows, buy some earplugs, laugh and turn up your own stereo. Just act **k** .... if the noise
l .... simply not there! Who knows, perhaps it will go away!

GLOSSARY

EXTENSION ACTIVITY

A Make a list of wishes about past, present and annoying habits.

B Choose an example from each section on page 60 and translate into your language.

*Need more practice? Go to the **Review** on page 208.*

unreal past tense

13 modals (1): obligation, recommendation, ability

must

Use *must*

- for a necessary action.
- to give someone an order.
- to describe a duty.
- to make a strong recommendation.
- to emphasize an intention.
- for formal questions (must I, you etc).

*You **must keep** this door locked.*
*You **must be** more careful!*
*Everyone **must** recycle as much as possible.*
*You really **must** go and see The History Boys.*
*I **must** lend you this book.*
Must you go?

Have to is more commonly used for questions in spoken English. ***Do you have to go?***

have to / has to

Use *have to / has to*

- for a necessary action. *We **have to be** there by six.*

- for a rule. *We **have to wear** a uniform at our school.*

- In most contexts, *must* or *have to* are both possible. Some speakers may use *have to* because it is longer and allows more emphasis.
  *You **have to be** more careful!*
  *Everyone **has to** recycle as much as possible.*

- *Have to* is the more commonly used question form. ***Do you have to go?***

- *Have / has got to* can be used informally instead of *have to*.
  *We've **got to be** there by six.*

must not, do not have to

- *Must not* describes what is not allowed.
  *You **mustn't start** until I tell you.*

- *Do not have to* or *have / has not got to* describes what is not necessary.
  *Tony **doesn't have to go** to college this afternoon.*
  *Tony **hasn't got to go** to college this afternoon.*

had to, didn't have to

- We use *had to* as a past form of *must*.
  *Sorry I'm late. **I had to stay** on at work.*
  ***I didn't have to pay** to take my bike onto the train.*

should, shouldn't (ought to, ought not to)

Use *should, shouldn't (ought to, ought not to)*

- to make a recommendation, when we say what we think is a good idea.
  ***You should come** to work on your bike. It would be much quicker.*

- to say what we think is the right thing to do.
  *I think **you ought to go** to the doctor. You look terrible.*

- to say that something is correct or incorrect.
  ***You shouldn't write** your name at the top of the letter.*
  *The answer **ought to be** a whole number.*

- in formal writing; *should* can be used with a similar meaning to *must*, but is more polite.
  *All students **should report** to the examination room by 8.30.*

should have, shouldn't have (ought to have, ought not to have)

- Use to say that we think someone has made a mistake or done something wrong.
  You shouldn't have put in so much salt.
  You ought not to have written your name at the top of the letter.

had better (not)

- Use to make a recommendation, when we say what we think is the right thing to do. Note that this is often contracted to *you'd better* etc.
  I think *you'd better* go to the doctor. You look terrible.

be to

- This is a formal way of saying *must* in instructions.
  You are to leave here at once!   All students *are to report* at 9.00.

need, need to

- *Need* is a modal verb, with no 3rd person form. It is used mainly in questions and negatives. The meaning is similar to *have to*.
  Need you ask?   The Prime Minister *need* not worry.

- *Need to* is a normal verb.
  Sarah *needs to* be more careful.   You *don't need to* worry.
  Do I need to fill in this form?

didn't need to, needn't have (done)

- *Didn't need to* describes a past situation, where something was not necessary, so it was not done.
  Kate looked after the children, so *we didn't need to take* them to the nursery.

- *Needn't have done* describes a past situation, where something happened or was done, but it was not necessary.
  I needn't have gone so early to the office. The meeting was cancelled.

be able to, can, could

- *Be able to* emphasizes that a difficulty has been overcome.
  Harry can't speak, but *he is able to communicate* with sign language.
  It is also possible to use *can* in this context.

- We use tense forms of *be able to* to make the description of ability more definite than *can*, or for time references not covered by *can / could*.
  I'll be able to finish this tomorrow. (= I can and will)
  I haven't been able to find the answer yet.

- *Could* describes a general past ability.
  Jane *could swim* 200 metres when she was nine.

- *Was / were able to* describes having the ability and doing something successfully.
  Maria *was able to swim* to the rocks and rescue the child.

  In this context, using *could* might suggest an unfulfilled possibility.
  She *could swim* to the rocks, but she decided not to.

- In negative sentences, *couldn't* has both meanings.
  However, she *couldn't / wasn't able to* rescue the pet dog.

Note that modals have more than one meaning (see **Units 14, 15**).

1 Underline the correct form.

a You *mustn't* / *don't have to* conduct any chemistry experiments unless you are wearing safety glasses.

b There are a lot of books which Anna *did not have to read* / *need not have read* as part of her university course, but which she decided to read out of interest.

c *We don't have to* / *We'd better not* talk for too long. These calls are expensive.

d I went to see the dentist yesterday, but luckily *I didn't need to have* / *I needn't have had* any painful treatment!

e You *didn't have to tell me* / *shouldn't have told me* about the party. Now it's not a surprise!

f Some people believe that the government *does not have to* / *should not* allow genetically modified crops to be grown on a large scale, as they could spread out of control.

g These books are on the wrong shelf. They *shouldn't* / *mustn't* be here.

h The report concluded that the rescuers *should not have attempted* / *didn't have to attempt* to move the injured passengers before medical help arrived.

i Please put the paper cups and plates in the bin. We *mustn't* / *don't have to* leave the room in a mess.

j There is plenty of time. We *mustn't be* / *don't have to be* at the cinema until 8.00.

2 Complete the sentence using one word in each gap.

a In the early years of motoring, drivers didn't _____have_____ to take a driving test.

b You _____ sign the application form at the end of the page, or it will not be accepted.

c Hurry up. We _____ to get to the airport by 9.30.

d I think we had _____ stop and ask someone the way.

e This bus is going to take ages. We _____ have taken a taxi.

f Important notice. All new arrivals _____ to report to the reception desk.

g Thanks for coming. I'm glad you _____ make it.

h You look really tired. You _____ take a few days off and have a holiday.

i Sorry I'm a bit late. I _____ to pick up the children from school.

j You _____ not decide immediately whether to join the class.

3 Write a new sentence with the same meaning, beginning as shown.

a If I were you, I'd take an umbrella.
I think you'd _____better take an umbrella_____ .

b Is Saturday morning school compulsory in your country?
Do students _____ .

c In the third week, students must hand in a typed copy of their first lab report.
In the third week, students are _____ .

d Sheila changed the battery in her camera, but it wasn't necessary.
Sheila _____ the battery in her camera.

e You look really ill. If I were you, I'd stay at home today.
You look really ill. I _____ to stay at home today.

f It was a bad idea to leave the windows open while it was raining.
You _____ .

g The theatre tickets were free, so there was no need for us to pay.

The theatre tickets were free, so we ....

h I can stay here until 10.00.

I .... leave until 10.00.

i Helen managed to stop the car before it crashed into a wall.

Helen was ....

j Steve's laptop had a wireless Internet connection, so there was no need for him to connect it to a phone line.

Steve's laptop had a wireless Internet connection, so he ....

social studies

4 Complete the text with one word in each gap.

Rubbish – or refuse as we **a** ....*should*........ really call it – is big news at the moment. For many years, people in Britain **b** .... had to pay a local tax (*council tax*) which includes a charge for refuse collection. In many parts of the country people have also been **c** .... to ask their local council to remove unwanted household items, such as furniture and electrical appliances. However, in recent years, as a result of EU legislation, councils have **d** .... to reconsider how they collect rubbish, and

what they do with it. In the past, householders simply **e** .... to put out their dustbins once a week, and the council collected the rubbish. Now the emphasis is on recycling, and householders **f** .... to separate recyclable waste (paper, plastic, cans and bottles) from organic waste (food and garden waste) and other items. 'Really we **g** .... have started doing this years ago,' explained Karen Graham from recycling consultants WasteNot. 'We **h** .... to stop filling up holes in the ground with rubbish and look at what other countries have **i** .... able to do.' One likely change is that soon householders **j** .... have to pay for their rubbish collections. 'People **k** .... pay according to how much rubbish they produce, and we **l** .... to reward people who recycle and consume less. People in Belgium, for example, **m** .... had to get used to this system – and it seems to have worked.' And if you think that weighing your rubbish is a strange idea, you had **n** .... get used to it. Before long, an electronic chip in your dustbin will be weighing the bin and calculating how much you **o** .... to pay.

GLOSSARY

modals (1): obligation, recommendation, ability

EXTENSION ACTIVITY

A Make a list of:

things you have to do in your job, or in your studies
things you think you ought to do
things in the past you should not have done

B Choose an example from each section on pages 64–65 and translate these examples into your language.

14 modals (2): possibility, certainty

can / could

- We use *can* to make statements about what is generally possible.
  *It **can** be very cold here in winter.* (= it is sometimes)

- We use *could* to refer to past possible situations.
  *In those days, ships **could travel** for weeks on end without seeing land.*

- We use *easily* to emphasize a possibility with *could*.
  *People **could easily fall** down these stairs in the dark.*

- We use *could always* to point out a possible choice or decision.
  *You **could always phone her** when we get to the cinema.*

- We use *can* or *could* when we ask questions about possibility.
  *Who **can / could that be** outside Mr Smith's office?*

- We use *can hardly* or *could hardly* when we think something is impossible.
  ***It can / could hardly be** Jane Thompson. She's in Berlin this week.*

- We use *can only* or *could only* when we are sure about the answer.
  ***It can / could only be** the new sales manager.*

may, might, could

- We use *may, might* or *could* to describe what is possible in particular situations. They are common with *be*.
  *This **may / might / could be** the last time I ever see you.*
  *The car won't start. The battery **may / might / could be** dead.*

- We often add *well* or *just* between *may / might / could be* and the verb to emphasize the possibility. *Just* makes the possibility less likely.
  *You **may / might / could well have** the answer!* (Perhaps it's possible)
  *Your plan **may / might / could just** work!* (It's unlikely, but possible)

- We use *may / might as well* when we say that there is no reason for not doing something, usually because we are disappointed something else has not happened.
  *There's no point waiting for the bus any longer. **We might as well start** walking.*

- We can use *may not* or *might not* for negative possibilities. We cannot use *could not* for this meaning.
  *I **may / might not be** here tomorrow. I **may / might not have** time to come.*

- We use *may have, might have*, and *could have* for possible events in the past.
  *Jack isn't here yet. He **may / might / could have missed** the train.*

- The negative forms are *may not have, might not have*. We cannot use *could not have*.
  *Perhaps he's still at home. He **may not have got** our message.*

- We use *might have* and *could have* to show annoyance, when someone fails to do something we feel they should have done.
  ***You might have told me** the match was cancelled! I went all the way there for nothing!*

- We use *might have* and *could have* when we are shocked because something nearly happened.
  *Thank heavens he's safe! He **could have drowned**!*

can't be, couldn't be

- We use *can't* or *couldn't* when we are certain that something is impossible.
  *That definitely **can't be / couldn't be** Tom over there. He's in Canada.*

must be

● We use *must* when we are certain something is true.
  *You **must be** tired after working so hard.*
  ***There must be** some mistake. I definitely booked a table for five.*

can't have done, couldn't have done

● We use *can't have* or *couldn't have* when we are certain that something in the past was impossible.
  *Helen **can't have taken** / **couldn't have taken** the car. She didn't have the keys.*

● We use *surely* to emphasize that we can't believe what has happened.
  *Surely you **can't have carried** all these bags on your own!*

● We use *can't have been* / *couldn't have been* when we are sure something wasn't true. We can also use *could* / *can* with *hardly* and *only*.
  *That **can't have been** successful. (I'm sure it wasn't)*
  *That **could hardly have been** an easy thing to do. (I'm sure it wasn't)*
  *Judging by the pawprints, it **can only have been** a very large animal.*

must have done

● We use *must have* when we are certain something in the past was true.
  *I can't find my wallet. **I must have dropped it** in the supermarket.*

I can't find my wallet. I must have dropped it in the supermarket.

be bound to, be sure to, be certain to

● When we need to describe a future event which we are sure will happen, we use *be bound to*, *be sure to* or *be certain to*.
  *We're going to the seaside tomorrow, so **it's bound to rain**.*
  *Don't worry about the exam. **You're sure to pass**!*

should, ought to

● We use *should, ought to* to describe something we think is probably true, or has failed to happen.
  ***There ought to be** a car-park at the end of this road. (I think there is)*
  ***There should be** a turning here! (but there isn't)*

should have, ought to have

● We use *should have, ought to have* when we describe what we expect has probably happened, or believe has failed to happen.
  ***They should have arrived** in London by now. (that's probable)*
  *The plane **ought to have landed**. Where is it? (it hasn't landed)*

1 Choose the correct form, A, B or C, to complete the sentence.

a Why don't you phone Katie now? She ___A___ yet.

b Take some sun-block and wear a hat, as it _____ get very hot in the middle of the day.

c There's no point waiting here any longer. We _____ go and have something to eat.

d Lucky you managed to hang on to that tree. You _____ down the cliff.

e 'What am I going to do about a present for Carol?' 'You _____ some flowers.'

f I don't know what time I'll be home. I _____ be quite late, I'm afraid.

g Don't worry about your driving test. You _____ to pass.

h There's no sign of the dog anywhere. Someone _____ it out.

i Why don't you ask Nick about it? He _____ know the answer, I suppose.

j There must be some kind of technical problem. The film _____ by now.

a **A** *can't have left*	**B** *must have left*	**C** *might have left*
b **A** *must*	**B** *can*	**C** *could have*
c **A** *can hardly*	**B** *are bound to*	**C** *might as well*
d **A** *could have fallen*	**B** *must have fallen*	**C** *may have fallen*
e **A** *might have sent her*	**B** *must have sent her*	**C** *could always send her*
f **A** *must*	**B** *can*	**C** *may*
g **A** *may*	**B** *must*	**C** *are bound to*
h **A** *is bound to have let*	**B** *must have let*	**C** *can let*
i **A** *can*	**B** *may as well*	**C** *might*
j **A** *should have started*	**B** *must have started*	**C** *might have started*

2 Choose the best continuation 1 to 10 for sentences a to j.

a I'm still waiting for the money the bank is supposed to have sent me. ___3___

b There's still no sign of Alex. _____

c It's getting rather late to deal with this now. _____

d I wish you wouldn't leave your bag near the door like that. _____

e You'd better take your umbrella with you. _____

f This piece is the right shape, but it doesn't fit. _____

g There should be a filling station here. _____

h It's a very long book. _____

i Oh sorry, yes, these are your keys. _____

j Leave yourself plenty of time for the journey. _____

1 You're bound to need it if you don't.

2 Surely you can't have finished it already!

~~3 It should have got here by now.~~

4 It can take quite a long time in the rush hour.

5 It can't be the right one after all.

6 That's strange! I can't see one anywhere!

7 You could always come back tomorrow.

8 He may have missed the train I suppose.

9 I must have picked them up by mistake.

10 Someone could easily fall over it and hurt themselves.

3 Write a new sentence with the same meaning, beginning as shown.

a Running is not allowed on the stairs. There is a danger of accidents.
Running is not allowed on the stairs. You *could / might have an accident* .

b You'd better not use this ladder. Look at it! I'm sure it's not safe.
You'd better not use this ladder. Look at it! It _____ .

c I think I know how this window got broken. I'm sure someone kicked a ball against it.
I think I know how this window got broken. Someone _____ .

d Unless you follow instructions, it's possible for a gymnasium to be a dangerous place.
Unless you follow instructions, a gymnasium _____ .

e I've turned off the electricity. I'm sure it's safe to touch these wires now.
I've turned off the electricity. It _____ .

f Ouch! Why didn't you tell me that piece of metal was hot!
Ouch! You _____ !

g Where are the fire fighters? I expected them to have arrived by now.
Where are the fire fighters? They _____ .

h I'm sure you didn't clean this bowl properly.
You _____ . I can see stains on it.

history

4 Complete the text using one of the phrases 1–10 in each gap.

> 1 can't have set off   2 could easily be   3 could expect   ~~4 must have been~~
> 5 can't have been   6 could easily sail   7 might have   8 must have made
> 9 should have reached   10 might involve

16th-century explorers

Imagine what it **a** 4 like to have sailed around the world in a small wooden ship, as Drake and his men did in 1577–1580. On a ship only some 35 metres long, it **b** _____ easy for the 80 or so crew to live comfortably. Exploration was part of war and rivalry with other nations, so these voyages **c** _____ attacks on other ships and towns, and had to make a profit. There were all the usual dangers too. A ship **d** _____ destroyed by a storm or run out of food and water, and the captain **e** _____ little idea of where the ship was or where it was going. Explorers **f** _____ many wrong decisions in an age when there were only basic maps and navigation equipment, and in unknown parts of ocean where a ship **g** _____ for weeks without reaching land. Very often places they thought they **h** _____ turned out to be much further on, or in a different direction. However, they **i** _____ on such long voyages without some general idea of the places they **j** _____ to reach along the way, and as knowledge of navigation improved, voyages became more and more successful.

GLOSSARY

modals (2): possibility, certainty

EXTENSION ACTIVITY

Write some sentences about these situations.

> You notice that a large crowd of people has gathered outside, shouting and singing.
> Who could they be?   What could have happened?   What might happen next?
> You hear a knock at the door, and when you open it there is a large parcel outside.
> Who could have sent it?   What could it contain?   What might you have to do next?

*Need more practice? Go to the **Review** on page 208.*

modals (3): other uses

can / could

Could is generally considered to be more polite than *can*.
Use *can / could*

- for requests.
  Can / Could you carry this for me?

- to ask for permission.
  Can / Could I leave early?

- to make an offer.
  Can / Could I offer you some tea?

- to make a suggestion.
  Can / Could I make a suggestion?

can't / cannot

- Use when something is not allowed.
  You can't leave your bike here.

- Use to emphasize that something is unbelievable.
  You can't be serious!

can + be + -ing

- Use when you wonder what is happening.
  Who can be knocking on the door at this time?

could

- Use to express surprise.
  How could you waste so much money!

- Use to emphasize how you feel.
  I'm so unhappy **I could cry**!

How could you be so clumsy, that vase was worth hundreds of pounds.

couldn't

- Use to mean 'it doesn't matter to me at all'.
  I **couldn't care less what** you do / when you leave / who you are / whether you go or not etc.

- Use with a comparative for emphasis.
  Things **couldn't be better**!

may

- Use for polite requests.
  May I make a suggestion?

- Use in *be that as it may* …, an idiom meaning 'perhaps that is true but …'
  Television brings the family together, even though when watching it they don't talk to each other. They are physically together, but no communication takes place. So in some respects, watching television together makes the members of a family distant from one another. **Be that as it may**, *being together as a family at least keeps the younger members at home, and away from possibly antisocial activities.*

- Use in *try as I / you* etc. *may* …, a formal phrase meaning 'Although I try I can't remember.'
  Try as I may, *I just can't remember.*

might

- Use in the formal phrase *try as I / you* etc. *might*.
  Try as I might, *I couldn't reach the shelf.* (Although I tried, I couldn't.)

- Use as emphatic form of 'perhaps I'll do that.'
  I might just do that!

- Use to express annoyance at a bad habit.
  I might have known it was you!

- Use as emphatic form of 'although you are…'
  You might be older than me, **but** …

shall

- Use for an offer.
  Shall I carry that for you?

- Use to ask for advice when uncertain.
  What shall we do?

- Use in formal legal language (all persons).
  The tenant shall be responsible for all repairs.

shouldn't have done, needn't have done

- Use to express our thanks for gifts, said in a way that expresses thanks.
  You really shouldn't have brought me flowers. That's very kind of you.

will / won't

- Use for an assertion about a result etc.
  I'll definitely win! **No, you won't!**

- Use for an offer or agreement.
  I'll do the washing-up.

- Use for a promise.
  I'll be home by eight.   **I won't be** late.

- Use for a threat.
  You'll be sorry!

won't

- Use for a present refusal.
  I won't do it! (see **Unit 16**, wouldn't)

need doing

- *The dustbin needs emptying.*   *Someone needs to empty it.*

1 Underline the best form.

a To be honest, I _couldn't_ / can't care less whether you come to my party or not!

b It's difficult to know whether to stay here, or try and walk. What *might / shall* we do?

c How kind of you to have brought such a lovely present, but you really *shouldn't / couldn't* have!

d My phone isn't working very well. The battery *needs / won't* charging.

e Look how much they have charged us for the meal! That *won't be / can't be* right!

f Excuse me, do you think you *could / shall* possibly open the window?

g Just look at this room! How *could / might* you make such a mess?

h Don't worry about the washing-up. *I'll do it / It needs doing* in the morning.

i Try as she *could / might*, Maria couldn't pull the cork out of the bottle.

j Everything is going well with my new job. In fact, things *couldn't / won't* be better.

2 Complete the sentences famous people did not say, using a modal word or phrase in each gap.

a William Shakespeare, dramatist: 'To be, or not to be ...' No, that ___can't be___ right. I'll have to think of something else.

b Neil Armstrong, first man on the moon: Well, it was a great trip! What _____ now? Any ideas?

c Genghis Khan: I'm tired of conquering the world. I think I _____ stay at home and relax for a few years.

d Isaac Newton, scientist: It was very silly of me to sit under this tree. I _____ an apple would fall on my head

e Christopher Columbus, explorer: Excuse me, _____ tell me the way to America? I seem to be lost.

f Emperor Qin Shihuang: _____ you take the wall down, and build it a few more metres in that direction?

g Ludwig Beethoven, composer: I think this music _____ changing a bit. How about adding some guitars and drums?

h Michelangelo, artist: Paint pictures all over this dome? You _____ serious! I'll fall and break my neck!

3 Read the description of each situation, and write what you would say.

a A friend comes to your house and brings you some flowers. Say something polite as you accept the gift.
   'Thanks, but you really shouldn't have brought me flowers!'

b Your teacher is carrying a pile of heavy books. Offer to help.
   _____

c A friend tells you that he / she is thinking of running away from home and joining a circus as a clown. You think this is a silly idea.
   _____

d A friend boasts that they are taller than you, so they are better at basketball.
   _____

e It is hot in the classroom, and you ask your teacher for permission to open the window.
   _____

f You are having an argument with a friend, and tell him / her that you don't care what he / she says.
   _____

4 Choose the best sentence 1 to 10 to follow sentences a to j.

a Why don't you take a day off for a change? It would do you good.   8

b So you're the one who broke the window!   ....

c This maths problem is really hard to understand.   ....

d I feel really great today!   ....

e Harry is a really irritating person.   ....

f That's funny, there's someone knocking at the door.   ....

g I'm not your little sister any more, you know!   ....

h I'll be home as soon as I can.   ....

i The last part of your answer doesn't quite make sense.   ....

j I'm sorry but I simply refuse to treat someone like that.   ....

1 In fact, he's so annoying sometimes I could scream.

2 I just won't do it.

3 Could you help me with it?

4 It needs re-writing a bit.

5 I might have known it would be you!

6 I certainly won't be very late.

7 Who can that be at this time, I wonder?

8 ~~Yes, I might just do that!~~

9 And just because you're older than me doesn't mean you're always right!

10 In fact, I'm so happy I could jump with joy!

5 Write a new sentence with the same meaning containing the word in capitals.

a Is it all right if I try that shot again?   COULD
   Could I try that shot again?

b Before we start playing, you should adjust the net.   NEEDS

   ....

c Do you want me to hold the flag while you take your shot?   SHALL

   ....

d Although I try, I can't skate properly.   MAY

   ....

e I promise not to let the team down.   WON'T

   ....

f It doesn't matter to me whether you run in this race or not.   LESS

   ....

g You never know, perhaps United will win all their matches!   JUST

   ....

h No member of the club is to use insulting language to any other member.   SHALL

   ....

i Now the weather has improved, it's an ideal situation.   COULDN'T

   ....

j That's kind of you, but there was no need for you to buy my ticket.   HAVE

   ....

modals (3): other uses

The following exercises practise grammar from units 13 and 14.

6 Choose the correct option, A, B or C, to complete the sentence.

a Well, if you always feel tired, I think you __C__ go to bed earlier!

b I'm sorry I dropped the eggs. I _____ to carry so many things at the same time.

c You _____ give a credit card number when you make your booking, or we cannot reserve your room.

d It's going to get colder later. _____ take a pullover with you.

e You _____ to begin writing until I give the instruction.

f Instruction to the author: columns in the two-column format _____ 3-1 / 4 inches wide.

g You _____ park outside the school. This is a 'no parking' area.

h I've been trying to contact Maria all day, but I _____ reach her yet.

i You _____ look up all the words you don't know. You can guess some of them from the context.

j In my country, all the young men _____ spend two years in the armed forces.

	A	B	C
a	A *don't have to*	B *must*	C *should*
b	A *don't have to try*	B *shouldn't have tried*	C *needn't have tried*
c	A *must*	B *have got to*	C *had better*
d	A *You have to*	B *You'd better*	C *You are to*
e	A *are not*	B *must not*	C *should not*
f	A *haven't got to be*	B *had better be*	C *are to be*
g	A *shouldn't*	B *don't have to*	C *need not*
h	A *couldn't*	B *haven't been able to*	C *mustn't*
i	A *mustn't*	B *needn't*	C *had better not*
j	A *should*	B *have to*	C *must*

7 Write a new sentence with the same meaning containing the word in capitals.

a Is our final test compulsory?   HAVE
   Do we have to take the final test?

b I think you were wrong to put so much lemon in the cake.   HAVE

c Tim's computer crashed, but he managed to save the pages he was working on.   WAS

d It is forbidden for passengers to pass beyond this point.   NOT

e I think you should see an eye specialist about this problem.   HAD

f Paula started the class immediately, as it wasn't necessary for her to take an entrance test.   DIDN'T

g Our tickets were free.   HAVE

h It was necessary for Dave to leave before the end of the performance.   HAD

i We bought a second tin of paint, but it wasn't necessary.   HAVE

j Kate didn't take her umbrella, which was a mistake.   HAVE

8 Write a new sentence with the same meaning containing the word in capitals.

a By the time they leave school, we expect that most students have understood the importance of regular exercise. SHOULD

By the time they leave school, most students should have understood the importance of regular exercise.

b When they start a job, or higher studies, it's possible for some people to forget that time needs to be set aside for this. CAN

....

....

c Those who don't find the time for exercise, certainly regret this in the future. BOUND

....

....

d When they feel tired or over-stressed, for example, they are sure this has happened because they have been working too hard. MUST

....

....

e They don't realize that this is possibly also the result of failing to keep fit. MIGHT

....

....

f When they do have any free time, they feel it is just as good for them to relax in front of the television, as in the gym or on the running track. AS WELL

....

....

g Perhaps they think that the people who find time for exercise are certainly taking time away from doing their job properly. MUST

....

....

h However, research shows that it's not possible for this to be further from the truth. COULDN'T

....

....

i It would be possible for most people to easily find the time to keep fit if they organized their time more effectively. COULD

....

....

j In the end, we have to remember that someone who feels fit and well is sure to be able to work more easily and with more energy. MUST

....

....

EXTENSION ACTIVITY

Write some examples using the words given.

Could I ...   I'll ...   I won't ...   ... needs ...   How could you ...   Shall I ...
You might be ...   ... I could jump for joy!   I couldn't ...

modals (3): other uses

16 *would*

habitual activity in the past

We can use *would* to describe a person's habitual activity in the past (see **Unit 4**).
*Every morning **we'd go for a walk** along the beach.*

This use is not possible with state verbs:
~~We would own a house in the mountains.~~   (Not possible)
***We used to own** a house in the mountains.*   (Possible)

annoying behaviour

We can use *would* to express annoyance or irritation at things that are happening now. There is ususally a sense that this is typical, or not very surprising.
You would say that!   (It's typical of you, and it's annoying.)
***Wouldn't you just know** it!*   (I knew that would happen – and it's annoying.)

later future events in narrative

Would is used in past narrative to refer to later future events (reported form of *will*.)
*In New York he met the woman **who would later become** his wife.*

unspoken *if*-clause

We can use *would* to talk about situations where an *if*-clause is understood but not spoken, or expressed in some other way.
***You wouldn't believe** who I've just met!* (… if I told you …)
***Why would anyone want** to live there?* (… if they could avoid it …)
***How would you feel** about going to the cinema?* (… if I asked you …)
*Why don't you take the exam? **You'd pass** easily.* (… if you took it …)
***I wouldn't do** that.* (… if I were you …)
***I wouldn't worry** about it.* (… if I were in that situation …)
***You wouldn't do that**, would you?* (… if you had the choice etc)
***It would be a good idea** to ask for some help.* (… if you want my opinion …)
*The consequences of such a storm **would be** serious* (… if it happened …)
*Under the proposals, **salaries would increase**.* (= if the proposals became fact)
***It would be great** to see you again.* (… if you wanted to.)
***It would be** good to stop and have a coffee.* (= if we stopped it would be good)

being willing

Would can be used to describe what people are willing to do. This can also be seen as including an unspoken condition.
*Tony **would lend** you his car.* (… if you asked him …)
*Only a real fan **would pay** that much for a ticket.*
(Only if someone was a fan would they pay …)

refusal

- We use *wouldn't* to describe a past refusal.
  *She was upset because **I wouldn't speak** to her.*

- Inanimate objects can also *refuse* to do things.
  ***The door refused to open.**   **My car refused to start**.*

polite requests

- Requests become more polite the more distanced they are. *Would* makes a request more distanced.
  Would you help me with my homework?
  Would you mind helping me?
  Would it be all right if I left early?

- The more tentative the request, the more distanced it becomes.
  You don't think you'd be able to help me with this, do you?

You don't think you'd be able to help me with this, do you?

- See **Unit 10** for polite requests beginning *If you would ...*
  If you would come this way, I'll take you to the director's office.

would imagine, think, hope, expect, suppose etc

- *Would imagine / think / hope / suppose + (person) + might* are used when the speaker is not completely certain what another person feels, does, etc.
  I would imagine that *you might find* John a bit difficult to work with.
  We'd hope we might complete the project before the end of the month.

- *Would hope / expect + to-*infinitive is also possible, when you hope that you would do something.
  We'd hope to complete the project before the end of the month.
  We'd expect to complete the project before the end of the month.

I'd like, I'd prefer

- *Would like* and *would prefer* refer to immediate situations.
  I'd like some coffee now.   I think *I'd prefer* tea.

- *Like* and *prefer* refer to general states.
  I don't *like* war films.   I *prefer* romantic comedies.

- We say we *would prefer it if* + unreal past when we say what we want to happen.
  I'd prefer it if you didn't wear shoes inside the house.

wouldn't you like to know

- This is an idiom we use when we refuse to give someone information.
  How much do you earn exactly?   *Wouldn't you like* to know!
  (=I'm sure you'd like to know but I'm not going to tell you!)

(For *would* in reported speech see **Unit 17**.)

1 Choose the best response 1 to 10 for comments a to j.

a   Personally, I think I should be paid more, because I'm better at the job.   6

b   Kate is going to spend her holiday painting all the inside of her house in black and gold.   ....

c   We're all going to go down to the gym to do some extra training for an hour.   ....

d   Do you fancy a nice cup of herb tea?   ....

e   I was thinking of spending my summer holiday in Slovenia.   ....

f   I think I might have given Alice the wrong directions.   ....

g   I don't know how I'm going to get home at this time of night.   ....

h   I'm still getting that pain in the leg I told you about.   ....

i   What's the matter with Sue?   ....

j   I have an appointment with Helen Adams for 10.30.   ....

1   I think I'd prefer a cup of coffee, if you don't mind.

2   If you'd just wait here, I'll see if she's free.

3   Why would anyone want to do that?

4   You'd have a great time there, it's a really fantastic place.

5   It wouldn't be a bad idea to ask the doctor about it.

6   Well, you would say that, wouldn't you!

7   I wouldn't worry about it. It's very easy to find.

8   I think she's annoyed because I wouldn't go to the shops with her.

9   Would it be all right if I stayed here and finished this work I'm doing?

10   I'm sure Mark would give you a lift.

2 Rewrite the sentence using the word in capitals.

a   Can I leave now?   BE
    Would it be all right if I left now?

b   The computer refused to work properly.   WOULDN'T

c   Trust you to say the wrong thing!   WOULD

d   I'd really like to see you again.   GREAT

e   Can you open the door for me?   MIND

f   What I did then, later turned out to be a mistake.   TURN

g   Do you want still or sparkling water?   LIKE

h   Please follow me, and I'll take you to the meeting room.   WOULD

i   Hopefully we'll deliver the finished product in six weeks' time.   TO

j   There's no need to worry about the results.   WOULDN'T

3 Underline the best verb form.

a It's a pity you haven't got a camera. Perhaps Josie _would lend_ / _lends_ you hers.

b Why _does_ / _would_ ice float on the surface of water?

c Diane was annoyed because her parents _wouldn't refuse_ / _refused_ to let her go to the club.

d Don't worry about me. I'm sure _I'll be_ / _I'd be_ all right.

e Martin _used to work_ / _would work_ as a waiter when he was student.

f 'Why don't we ask Gerry to pay?' 'No, that _would prefer_ / _wouldn't be_ a good idea.'

g Tony isn't really sure what _would_ / _will_ happen next.

h You're a good friend. What _do I do_ / _would I do_ without you?

i I'm not very keen on fantasy novels. I _would prefer_ / _prefer_ more serious ones.

j _Do you help_ / _Would you help_ me carry this case? It's rather heavy.

4 Complete the text using _would_ or _wouldn't_, or leave the gap blank.

Crime and punishment

I am one of those people who a ___would___ like to see changes made to current types of punishment in the criminal justice system. It b _____ surely be better to sentence minor offenders to community service of some kind, c _____ rather than giving them fines or prison sentences. That way they d _____ at least do something useful, and the justice system e _____ also save money. I f _____ also imagine that this g _____ work better for young offenders, as they h _____ feel 'cool' or fashionably 'bad' while they i _____ helped an old person or cleaned the streets. Of course, a system of this kind j _____ work effectively without some thought being given to the tasks which offenders were asked to perform. There k _____ obviously be more benefit to be gained from work which l _____ involved responsibility, and where offenders had to mix with others and m _____ communicate with them. Some people also n _____ think that offenders should meet and talk to their victims, and be more involved with compensating and even helping them. This o _____ certainly help to make offenders p _____ realize the consequence of their actions, and that might well stop them offending again. Whether it q _____ work for all offenders, and for all offences is another matter, but again I r _____ believe that this s _____ stop young offenders from becoming career criminals. And that t _____ be an important change for the better.

GLOSSARY

EXTENSION ACTIVITY

A Make some comments on the situations in 2 beginning with the phrase in 1.

1 _It would / wouldn't be a good idea to ... I would ... I wouldn't ..._
2 being trapped in a lift which is out of order
being lost in a foreign country without any money
being arrested by the police for a crime you didn't commit

B Choose ten examples from each section on pages 78–79 and translate them into your language.

would

17 indirect speech

present time

When we report things happening now, or general facts, or give messages, or report something we are reading, we use a present tense reporting verb, and do not backshift tenses into the past. Note that for written texts we report what the text 'says'.

'I'm going to wait for you.'   ***He says he's going to*** *wait for us.*
'Fifty people were injured.'   ***It says*** *here that fifty people **were injured**.*

past time with tense changes

When reporting what people said, we use a past tense reporting verb and we backshift the tenses following into the past.

'We're thinking it over.'   ***She said they were thinking*** *it over.*
'I had an accident.'   ***He told me he'd had*** *an accident.*
'We'll let you know.'   ***They said they would let*** *me know.*

Note that both past simple and present perfect become past perfect.

'I've had an idea.'   ***She said she'd had*** *an idea.*

facts and states

When we use a past tense reporting verb, a continuing state is not back-shifted, though if we use back-shift this is not wrong.

'Reindeer can swim really well.'   *He **told us that reindeer can swim** really well.*
*He **told us that reindeer could swim** really well.*

If we do use back-shift, it may be necessary to use a time phrase to make the time reference clear.

*She said **she was unhappy** in her job **at that time**.* (= unhappy in the past)
*She said **she was unhappy** in her job **at the moment**.* (= unhappy now)

modals and conditionals

- *Can, will / shall* (future) and *may* change to *could, would* and *might*.
  'I'll be back on Friday.'   ***He said he would be*** *back on Friday.*
  'I may be late.'   ***She said she might be*** *late.*

- *Shall* in requests etc changes to *should*. See also *wh*-questions below.
  'What shall we do?'   *They wanted to know **what they should do**.'*

- *Would, should, ought to, could, might, used to* remain unchanged. *Must* is often changed to *had to*, but can remain unchanged, or be changed to *would have to* if there is future reference.
  *'You **must be** more careful in future.'*
  *She told me I **must be** / **had to be** / **would have to be** more careful in future.*

- First conditional sentences are usually changed, but not second or third conditional.
  *'**If you're late**, they **won't let** you in.'* (first conditional)
  *He said that **if I was late**, they **wouldn't** let me in.*
  *'**If you'd brought** a map, we **wouldn't have got lost**.'* (third conditional)
  *She said that if I **had brought** a map, we **wouldn't have got lost**.'*

changes of viewpoint

- References to time, place and specific reference usually change.
  *'Bring **this** ticket with **you tomorrow**.'*
  *He told me to bring **the** ticket with **me the next day**.*
  *'Give **that to me**.'*   *He told me to give **it to him**.*
  *'I'll see you **here in the morning**.'*
  *He said he would see me **there the next morning**.*

reported *yes / no* questions

Yes / no questions are reported using *if* or *whether*. There is no inversion or auxiliary *do / did*. If the auxiliary *have* is used in the question it becomes *had*. The same backshift rules apply as for statements. There is no question mark.

'Do you like Japanese food?'   *She asked me **if / whether I liked** Japanese food.*
'Have you finished?'   *They asked me **if / whether I had finished**.*

reported *wh-*questions

● We form reported *wh*-questions without inversion or auxiliary *do / did*. Auxiliary *have* becomes *had*.
'What's the time?'   *He asked me **what the time was**.*
'Where have you been?   *She asked me **where I had been**.*

● In everyday speech, questions with very long question phrases remain inverted.
'Where is the restaurant serving the cheapest Thai food?'
*He asked me **where was the restaurant serving the cheapest Thai food**.*

● Polite requests beginning *could / would* are not back shifted into the past after a past tense reporting verb.
'Could you help me?' she asked.
*She asked me **if I could help her / to help her**.*

● It may be possible to report the request rather than the actual words of the request.
'Could you tell me where the station is?'
*He asked me **for directions to / the way to the station**.*

reporting imperatives: *tell* and *ask*

We use *tell* to report orders and *ask* to report requests.
'Stop what you are doing!'   ***She told me to stop** what I was doing.*
'Please don't go.'   ***He asked me to stay***

verbatim reporting and summary

Speakers do not always report exactly every word spoken, especially if this would make a lengthy and repetitive report. Speakers summarize and often use words that describe what was said.
'Take the first left, then go straight on, and then turn right after the church.'   ***She told me how to get there**.*
'What did you think?'   *I asked him **for his opinion**.*

think and *don't think*

When we use opinion words like *think* and *believe*, the opinion verb is negative in negative statements.
***This isn't** very tasty.*   ***I don't think** this **is** very tasty.*

(See also **Unit 18**.)

1 Underline the best option.

a When I got to the office, they told me that Mr Adams *already left / had already left.*

b My teacher warned me that if I *was / had been* late, they wouldn't let me into the examination.

c Harry told us he *is / was* catching the first bus to New York the next day.

d The students going on the trip wanted to know what time they *would / will* get back.

e Sam told the police he *didn't know / hadn't known* what had happened.

f It says here that the plane *crashed / crashes* soon after taking off.

g Alan told me he had no idea what *was / is* going on.

h The customers said angrily that they *were waiting / had been waiting* for more than two hours.

i Erica told me she *won't / wouldn't* be back until the following Thursday.

j The professor told us that the Moon *is / was* more than 380,000 km from the Earth.

2 Rewrite the sentence as reported speech, beginning as shown, and backshifting tenses.

a 'I wouldn't lend my car to just anyone,' Andy said.
Andy said that *he wouldn't lend his car to just anyone* .

b 'I'm not very satisfied with my job,' said Peter.
Peter said ....

c 'I'm not going to worry about the money until I hear from the bank,' said Elaine.
Elaine said ....

d 'I don't know where Bill is living at the moment,' said Nicky.
Nicky said ....

e 'Emma hasn't had her operation yet,' her brother told me.
Emma's brother ....

f 'If you eat too much, you'll feel ill' my mother told me.
My mother told me ....

g 'We'll be writing to you later this week,' they told Maria.
They told Maria ....

h 'The prices won't rise before the end of the year,' Mrs Devlin said.
Mrs Devlin said ....

i 'If the police had noticed Jack's car, they would have arrested him,' explained the lawyer.
The lawyer explained that if ....

j 'I'll let you know if I have any more problems,' Carol told me.
Carol told me ....

3 Read the historic predictions below. Rewrite each one as direct speech, then match it to the person who said it from the list below.

a   He said that aeroplanes were interesting toys, but did not have any military value.
   'Aeroplanes are interesting toys, but do not have any military value.'   8

b   He said that whatever young Einstein did, he would amount to nothing.

c   This person said it would be years, and not in their lifetime, before a woman would become British prime minister.

d   He said that he thought there was a world market for perhaps five computers.

e   He said that television wouldn't stay popular for more than six months, because people would soon get tired of staring at a wooden box every night.

f   They said that they didn't like their sound, and that guitar music was on the way out.

g   They said that the telephone had too many shortcomings and was of no value to them.

h   He said that the horse was here to stay, but the car was only a novelty.

1   President of Michigan Savings Bank, 1903, advising Henry Ford's lawyer not to invest in the Ford Motor Company.
2   Darryl F Zanuck, 1946, Hollywood film producer.
3   Decca Recording Co. rejecting the Beatles, 1962.
4   Albert Einstein's teacher to his father, 1895.
5   British politician Margaret Thatcher, 1974, before she became prime minister.
6   Western Union Telegraph Company, 1876.
7   Thomas Watson, chairman of IBM, 1943.
8   Marshal Ferdinand Foch, of France, in 1911.

4 Report the question beginning as shown.

a 'How long does it take to get to the city centre?' I asked her.
I asked her _how long it took to get to the city centre_.

b 'Have you visited the National Museum?' she asked me.
She asked me _____.

c 'What do you think of the hotel food?' I asked her.
I asked her _____.

d 'Will you be travelling by train?' she asked me.
She asked me _____.

e 'Do you know the way to the Opera House?' I asked her.
I asked her _____.

f 'How much did you pay to stay in the student hostel?' she asked me.
She asked me _____.

g 'Are you thinking of changing hotels?' I asked her.
I asked her _____.

h 'Do you have to leave at 10.00?' she asked me.
She asked me _____.

i 'Would you come with me to the station?' I asked her.
I asked her _____.

5 Underline the sentence, A, B or C, which best reports the statement or question.

a 'You mustn't work so hard,' he said.
b 'What did you think of the film?' she asked me.
c 'I wish you wouldn't stare at me like that,' he said.
d 'I really don't know at all where we are,' she said.
e 'Do you have any idea what time the next bus leaves,' he asked.
f 'What do you think I should do?' she asked.
g 'Whatever you do, don't touch that wire!' he said.
h 'If I ask you nicely, will you buy me an ice cream?' she asked.

a A *He told me I didn't have to work so hard.*   B *He told me not to work so hard.*
C *He told me I must not have worked so hard.*

b A *She asked me my opinion of the film.*   B *I think she asked me about the film.*
C *She asked me what did I think of the film.*

c A *He asked me if I would wish not to stare at him.*   B *He said he didn't think I was staring at him in the right way.*
C *He told me to stop staring at him.*

d A *She said they were lost.*   B *She said she didn't know they were lost.*
C *She said they didn't know where she was.*

e A *He asked me which bus came next.*   B *He asked me the time of the next bus.*
C *He asked whether there was time for the next bus.*

f A *She asked me what I should do.*   B *She asked me whether she should do it.*
C *She asked me for my advice.*

g A *He asked me whatever he should not do.*   B *He told me not to touch the wire.*
C *He told me that whatever I did, I didn't touch the wire.*

h A *She asked me to buy her an ice cream.*   B *She asked me whether I had asked her for an ice cream.*
C *She asked me to ask her for an ice cream.*

6 Complete the text with one word in each gap.

The detective story

Marlowe made some notes on a sheet of paper, and then looked across the desk at Angela. 'Go on, what did he **a** _say_ then?' Angela twisted the handkerchief around her fingers. 'He **b** .... me whether I knew what *The Enchanted Garden* **c** .... I told **d** .... I thought it was one of my uncle's paintings.' Marlowe smiled. This girl was good, very good. 'And **e** .... did he say to that?' 'He told **f** .... to stop wasting his time. He said I **g** .... very well what it was. He **h** .... it was a painting worth $10 million. And he said that my uncle **i** .... stolen it from a French art dealer.' Marlowe made more notes on the sheet of paper, but he had stopped smiling. 'Then he told **j** .... that **k** ....

Humphrey Bogart and Lauren Bacall in *The Big Sleep*

I failed to tell him where the painting was, I **l** .... never see my uncle alive again.' 'And then he left, I suppose?' He thought the girl had blushed slightly, but he wasn't sure of it. 'He told me he **m** .... call again at the end of the week – Friday, or Saturday. And he told me **n** .... to talk to anyone about it or I'd be sorry. And he gave me this.' From her bag she took something yellow and red and held it out in front of her. Marlowe told her **o** .... put it on the desk. It was a man's tie, a bloodstained man's tie. There were a few more questions he would have to ask Miss Angela Hemingthwaite.

GLOSSARY

EXTENSION ACTIVITY

A Write another paragraph of the story in 6, to include five reported questions. Use these words as a guide.

He / she asked me where ....
He / she asked me what ....
He / she asked me why ....
He / she asked me where ....
He / she asked me if ....

B Write five quiz questions, and then write them as reports beginning *They asked me…*

18 report verbs

report verbs

- Some verbs express the general meaning of what people say so we do not need to report exactly what they said.

  'I'll bring my homework tomorrow, honestly, I will, really!'
  He promised to *bring his homework the next day.*
  'Well done! You've passed the exam!'
  She congratulated me *on passing the exam.*

- Some verbs (eg *check, convince, explain, imply, point out, suggest*) express what effect someone wanted their words to have. It is not easy to show this effect in direct speech.
  She implied that *I ought to start working harder.*

- Different verbs can be followed by different constructions, and the same verb can be followed by more than one construction. Check usage in a dictionary. Note that verbs in these lists may appear in more than one section.

verb + person + *that*-clause

assure	*'I'll definitely be there.'*	**She assured me (that) she would be** *there.*
convince	*'Of course it's right.'*	**She convinced me (that) it was** *right.*
promise	*'I'll do it.'*	**He promised (him) (that) he would** *do it.*
remind	*'Remember we start at 3.00.'*	**He reminded me (that) we started** *at 3.00.*

Other verbs: *inform, tell*

verb + *that*-clause

complain	*'It's too expensive!'*	**She complained (that) it was** *too expensive.*
confess	*'I stole the money.'*	**He confessed (that) he had stolen** *the money.*
(or *confess to doing something:*		**He confessed to stealing** *the money.*)
suggest	*'Why don't you use a calculator?'*	**He suggested (that) I used** *a calculator.*

Other verbs: *accept, add, admit, agree, announce, assure, boast, conclude, decide, deny, doubt, explain, imagine, imply, insist, mention, point out, predict, promise, protest, remark, repeat, threaten, whisper*

verb + *-ing*

suggest	*'Why don't you use a calculator?'*	**He suggested** *(my)* **using** *a calculator.*
deny	*'I didn't break the jar.'*	**He denied breaking** *the jar.*

Other verbs: *admit, apologize for, mention, recommend, regret*

verb + object + preposition + *ing*

congratulate	*'Well done, you've won.'* **He congratulated her on** *winning.*

Other verbs: *accuse someone of, blame someone for, thank someone for*
We can also *blame something on someone.*

'The fire was your fault, Alan!'   They **blamed Alan for** *the fire.*
They **blamed** *the fire* **on Alan.**

verb + *to*-infinitive

offer	*'I'll help you.'*	*He* **offered to** *help her.*
promise	*'I'll bring it tomorrow.'*	*She* **promised to** *bring it the next day.*
refuse	*'I won't sit down!'*	*He* **refused to** *sit down.*
agree	*'OK, I'll pay (you) £300.'*	*He* **agreed to pay (him)** *£300.*

Other verbs: *swear, threaten, volunteer*

verb + person + *to*-infinitive

advise	'I would (wouldn't) stop, if I were you.'	She **advised me (not) to** stop.
beg	'Please stop!'	He **begged me to** stop.
remind	'Don't forget to lock the door.'	She **reminded him to** lock the door.
warn	'Don't touch that wire!'	She **warned me not to** touch the wire.

Other verbs: *challenge, command, convince (meaning persuade), encourage, expect, forbid, instruct, invite, order, permit, persuade, request, tell, warn*

She warned us not to go near the building.

verb + person + *to*-infinitive + complement

believe	'He's over 21, I believe'.	**I believe him to be** over 21.

Other verbs: *believe, consider, presume, understand*

verb + person + object

invite	'Would you like to come to dinner?'	He **invited me to dinner.**
offer	'Would you like some ice cream?'	He **offered her** some ice cream.

other patterns

explain	'This is how you do it.'	She **explained how to** do it.
agree with	'Yes, I think the same.'	She **agreed with** him.
greet	'Good morning.'	She **greeted** me.
announce	'And now the names of the winners.'	He **announced** the names of the winners.

verb + *whether / if*

doubt	'I don't think he knows.'	**I doubt whether** he knows.
wonder	'Am I right?'	**She wondered whether she was** right.

insist, demand, propose etc

- Verbs used to tell people what they should do, or to give advice or orders, are often used with *should*, or subjunctive (without 3rd person s) or unreal past. This is a more formal use.
  *They insisted that **he should hand over** the documents immediately.*
  *They insisted that **he hand over** the documents immediately.*
  *They insisted that **he handed over** the documents immediately.*

- Other verbs which can be followed by *should* or *to*-infinitive: *advise, instruct, order, persuade, recommend, remind, urge*

Always check the meaning and use of report verbs in your dictionary.

1 Underline the best verb.

a All my friends _congratulated_ / _greeted_ me on passing my driving test.

b Rachel _refused_ / _denied_ that she had used the laptop without permission.

c The two students _confessed_ / _admitted_ to setting fire to the telephone box.

d You didn't _remind_ / _suggest_ me to bring my dictionary.

e The boy said he _explained_ / _regretted_ not telling the truth from the outset.

f Paul _apologized_ / _admitted_ for being rude to his next-door neighbour.

g Sarah _volunteered_ / _insisted_ to stay behind and pick up all the litter.

h The manager _boasted_ / _pointed out_ that the prices were in fact clearly stated on the menu.

i David _assured_ / _insisted_ me that he would definitely finish all the work on time.

j Jane's doctor _warned_ / _instructed_ her that she was putting her health at risk.

2 Choose all possible answers, A, B or C, to complete the sentence.

a The bank manager reminded George _B, C_.

b To be honest, I doubt .... much difference.

c Tom's parents expected .... his pocket money by doing jobs around the house.

d The driver of the white van ....

e Dr Collins convinced his colleagues .... right.

f Jim boasted .... to the island and back.

g The travel agent recommended .... the earlier flight.

h The managing director threatened .... if his proposals were not accepted.

i Harriet refused .... with the police, and was arrested.

j Robin wondered .... the right thing to do.

	A	B	C
a	A _bringing his passport_	B _to bring his passport_	C _that he should bring his passport_
b	A _whether it will make_	B _it making_	C _it to make_
c	A _to earn_	B _earning_	C _him to earn_
d	A _blamed the collision for Helen_	B _blamed Helen for the collision_	C _blamed the collision on Helen_
e	A _that he was_	B _of being_	C _to be_
f	A _to swim_	B _his swimming_	C _that he could swim_
g	A _to take_	B _that we should take_	C _taking_
h	A _that he would resign_	B _resigning_	C _to resign_
i	A _co-operating_	B _that she would co-operate_	C _to co-operate_
j	A _whether it was_	B _about doing_	C _that it was_

3 Complete the text with one word in each gap.

The head teacher, Mrs Symes, congratulated me a ___on___ winning the science competition, and told b .... she was very pleased that I had worked so hard. I admitted c .... I hadn't expected to win first prize, and that at one point I even regretted d .... the competition. My brother had persuaded e .... that I should have a try, and I doubted f .... I could have won without his encouragement. Mrs Symes pointed g .... that my project was supposed to be all my own work, and wondered h .... perhaps my brother had helped me at all. She didn't want the organizers to accuse me i .... cheating. I assured j .... that the project was all my own work. My brother had offered k .... find some articles for me on the Internet, but I had refused l .... let him do it.

4 Tick the line if it is correct. If you find an error, underline it, and write a correction above the line.

Medical report forecasts increase in high blood pressure problems

00 A recent medical report has predicted that increasing numbers of people in developed   ✓

a   countries will suffer from high blood pressure. The authors pointed out whether many   ....

b   developing countries now have the same problems and accused governments failing   ....

c   to educate people about unhealthy lifestyles. They blamed the situation to a   ....

d   high-fat diet, long working hours and lack of exercise and announced that a quarter   ....

e   of the world's population were affected. They explained them high blood pressure is a   ....

f   major cause of heart disease and advised people that they are making changes in   ....

g   lifestyle to deal with these problems. They recommended that everyone should avoid a   ....

h   diet which contains high amounts of fat and salt, and added to smoking and alcohol   ....

i   contribute to the problem. The report concluded and by 2025 almost a third of the   ....

j   world's adults could be suffering from high blood pressure.

---

history

5 Complete the text with a verb from the list in each gap.

> agreed announced begged decided invited ordered persuaded
> pointed out reminded swore thanked volunteered

The wooden horse of Troy

Agamemnon **a** _invited_ all the Greek generals to come to his tent to discuss the situation, and
b .... that he was considering abandoning his attempt to capture Troy. He **c** ....
everyone for their efforts, but said that they had tried everything and the task seemed impossible. Then
Odysseus stepped forward and **d** .... the king to try one last idea. Agamemnon
e .... him that they had been trying to capture the city for years, and all their previous
attempts had failed. Odysseus **f** .... that the war had not succeeded, but then
g .... that his plan was different, and involved using a giant wooden horse filled with men.
After a long discussion, he **h** .... the generals that this plan would succeed and then asked
who would come with him inside the horse. Many of the best warriors **i** .... to accompany
him. They **j** .... to conquer the city of Troy from the inside, or die in the attempt. Agamemnon
thought about this, and finally **k** .... that they would try Odysseus's plan, so he
l .... his men to build the giant wooden horse.

GLOSSARY

EXTENSION ACTIVITY

A   Make a list of ten things that people told you in the recent or distant past, using different report verbs.

B   Look up the report verbs on page 88 in your dictionary, and find other ways they can be used.

*Need more practice? Go to the **Review** on page 208.*

19 questions

indirect questions

- Questions can be introduced by statements. In this case we do not use inverted word order for a question, or auxilliary words, or a question mark. These questions are generally called *indirect* or *embedded* questions.
  *I was wondering **when the train leaves**.   I'd like to know **what her name is**.*
  *It's not clear **what I write** here.   I'm not sure **who I'm talking to**.*

- Questions can be introduced by other direct questions in the same way. In this case there is a question mark.
  *Do you know **when the train leaves**?   Could I ask you **what her name is**?*
  *Would you mind telling me **what I should write here**?*

tag questions

- positive verb, negative tag
  When we use a positive verb and a negative tag, we generally expect a *yes* answer.
  ***You like** horror films, **don't you**? Yes, I do.*

- negative verb, positive tag
  When we use a negative verb and a positive tag, we generally expect a *no* answer.
  ***You haven't got** a pen, **have you**? No, I haven't.*

- positive verb, positive tag
  When we use a positive verb and a positive tag, we are showing surprise.
  *So **you're** a student, **are you**?   (You don't look like one!)*

intonation and meaning

- The meaning of the question depends on the intonation we use.
  When the intonation falls or is level, we are checking information we already know.
  ***You like** horror films, **don't you**? Yes, of course I do!*
  ***You're not** in tomorrow, **are you**? No.*

  When the intonation rises, we are asking a question.
  ***You are** a student, **aren't you**?   (I'm not sure about this)*
  ***You're not** Helen, **are you**?   (I'm surprised)*
  ***You haven't** broken the window, **have you**?   (I hope not!)*

negative questions

We use a negative question when:

- we assume someone will agree   *Don't you feel tired?*
- we are annoyed with someone   *Can't you stop talking!*
- we are surprised, or don't believe something   *Don't you remember me?*
- we want to get the answer we want   *Wasn't it you who stole the money?*

Can't you stop talking?

echo questions

- Echo questions are commonly used in informal conversation to show interest or other feelings eg surprise, disbelief.

  I've got a new job.   ***Have you****? Congratulations! That's wonderful!*

- Echo questions are made in response to statements. Normally a positive question echoes a positive statement, and a negative question echoes a negative statement.

  I don't know the answer.   ***Don't you****? It's a very easy problem!*
  There isn't any milk left.   ***Isn't there****? Are you looking in the right place?*
  I really like her new novel.   ***Do you****? I found it rather heavy going.*

echo tags

- When we agree with what the speaker says or are surprised by it we can echo the statement and add a tag.

- Echoing positive with positive with a negative tag, or negative with negative with a positive tag, suggests agreement. The intonation is level or falling.

  It's really cold today. ***It is, isn't it****?* (agreement)
  I'm not a very good golfer. *You **aren't, are** you?* (agreement)

- Echoing positive with negative with a positive tag, or negative with positive with a negative tag, suggests disbelief. The intonation is rising.

  I've just seen David Bowie! ***You haven't, have you****?* (disbelief)
  *I **don't like** ice-cream.* *You **do, don't** you?* (disbelief)

... do you think ...

In everyday speech when we ask someone's opinion it is common to put *do you think / believe / suppose* etc between a *wh*-question and the verb.

*What **do you think** the others are doing now?*
*What **do you believe** we should do?*

ellipsis

In everyday speech, questions are often shortened by using the verb stem only.

***Like** my new flat?* ***Want** a drink?* ***Had** a good time?*

end prepositions

- When we make questions with verb + preposition, the preposition generally goes at the end of the sentence, unless the preposition is part of a phrase eg *in what sense*.

  *What are we waiting **for**?* *Who am I talking **to**?*
  ***In what sense** is Jane Eyre a feminist novel?*

- With *whom*, used in formal speech and writing, the preposition comes first.

  ***With whom** do we work?*

1 Underline the best form.

a What do you think <u>they should give him</u> / should they give him for his birthday?

b I'm not absolutely sure what time *does her plane arrive* / *her plane arrives*.

c That's a really nice dress she's wearing, *isn't she* / *isn't it*?

d 'Sarah hasn't arrived yet.' '*Has she?* / *Hasn't she?* I wonder where she is.'

e 'You were right about Steve. He's a really great player.' '*He is, isn't he?* / *He isn't, is he?* And you didn't believe me.'

f Excuse me, but *for what exactly are you waiting* / *what exactly are you waiting for*?

g Do you happen to know *where the Astoria Hotel is* / *where is the Astoria Hotel*?

h 'There's a police officer waiting to see you.' '*There isn't, is there?* / *There is, isn't there?* I wonder what on earth the police want with me!'

i *You'll be long, won't you?* / *You won't be long, will you?* I need you to be back here by 11.00 at the latest.

j Would you mind telling me *when the text train leaves* / *when does the next train leave*?

2 Complete the sentence so that it contains an indirect question and means the same as the first sentence.

a How old is she? I'd really love to know. I'd <u>really love to know how old she is</u> .

b How much does this shirt cost? Can you tell me? Can .... ?

c Where's the projector? I don't suppose you know. I don't ....

d Which room is which? It's not clear. It's ....

e What time does the lecture finish? I wonder. I ....

f Where do I have to go? I'm not sure. I'm ....

g How does this work? Can you explain? Can .... ?

h How long do we have to wait? Have they told you? Have .... ?

3 Rewrite the sentence as a question, so that it contains the word in capitals and has the same meaning.

a I wish you'd finish your work on time!   CAN'T
   <u>Can't you finish your work on time?</u>

b Why are we waiting?   FOR

c What's her first name?   KNOW

d I'm sure this isn't your seat.   IS

e What's the time?   COULD

f Good heavens, is it really 8.00 already?   ISN'T

g Surely you understand the second example.   DON'T

h Have you seen Chris, by any chance?   HAVEN'T

4 Write a response to each statement or question. Check the answers on page 231.

a The Albanians don't call their country Albania, do they?
No, they don't. They call it Republika e Shqipërisë.

b Doesn't the small country of Andorra lie between France and Italy?

c Isn't the island of Trinidad just off the coast of Venezuela?

d Sydney is the capital of Australia.

e Dominica is another name for the Dominican Republic, isn't it?

f Over a third of the people on the island of Fiji originally came from India.

g Lesotho in southern Africa used to be called Liberia, didn't it?

---

science

5 Complete the text with one word in each gap. Contracted forms (eg *isn't*) count as one word.

Global warming arguments

It's easy to suppose that we all feel the same way about global warming. After all, everybody wants to save the world, **a** *don't* they? We all want to make a contribution, however small, and we all do our best. You aren't one of those people who wastes water, **b** .... you? Of course not! And I'm sure you've got low-energy light bulbs in your house, **c** .... you? You bet! Not everyone is so enthusiastic, of course. Some people wonder **d** .... they can do to help, and don't really know what to do. Until they find out by paying attention to what the world's scientists are saying. At least, we all hope this is true, **e** .... we? Still, there are quite a lot of people who just hope that the problem will go away. Why do they do this, we might ask. **f** .... they want to make a difference?

Their usual response is 'We don't really know whether the climate is changing.' **g** .... we? Well, of course we do. There is plenty of evidence of climate change, isn't **h** .... ? We know that we are wasting energy and polluting the planet, don't **i** .... ? It's all quite simple really. And if you do know anyone who is still uncertain about whether to save the world or not, your message to them should be clear. What are you waiting **j** .... ? If you think this is just somebody else's problem, it will, very soon, be your problem as well. Believe it.

GLOSSARY

EXTENSION ACTIVITY

A Write some quiz questions like the ones in Exercise 4 and ask a partner to make tag responses.

B Make a list of indirect questions which would be useful to a traveller.

*Need more practice? Go to the **Review** on page 208.*

questions

20 articles (1)

article use depending on context

- When we refer to something we have already mentioned, we use the definite article.
  *First, I grate some cheese. Then I sprinkle **the cheese** into the sauce.*

- A noun can be made definite by the details which follow it. This is called post-modification.
  *There's a tower over there.   Yes, it's **the Tower of London**.*

- Some things are definite because they are already known to the people talking about them.
  *Jim is at **the pub**.   (= The one we all usually go to.)*
  *Pass **the vegetables**, please.   (= These ones on the table.)*

groups and classes

- An example of a thing, instrument etc uses *a / an*.
  ***A barometer** is used to measure air pressure.*

- We use *a / an* for one of a class of things or people.
  *Peter is **a German**.   Maria is **a teacher**.   This is **an electric shaver**.*

- We use *a / an* for one of a set of named things.
  *They've bought **a Picasso**.   (= a work of art)*
  *This is **a Henry Moore sculpture**.*

- We use *zero article* with plurals and uncountables when they refer to a class of things or people in general.
  ***Teachers** often work very long hours.*
  ***Water** is becoming a scarce resource.*
  ***Girls** are better at learning **foreign languages** than **boys**.*

  These too can be made specific, eg by the details which follow.
  ***The water** tastes funny.   (= the water from the tap)*
  ***The girls in my class** learn fast.   (= these particular girls)*

- A singular noun to describe a class of things uses *the*.
  ***The bicycle** is becoming increasingly popular.*
  ***The whale** is in danger of extinction.*

ideas

- Abstract ideas use zero article.
  ***Health** is one of the most important things in **life**.*

  Note that an abstract noun can be made specific by what comes after it – then we use *the*.
  ***The** health **of** millions of people may be at risk.*

numbers and measurement

- With rates and speeds use *a / an*.
  *The car was going at **50km an hour**.   The rent is **£500 a month**.*

- Use *a / an* for large whole numbers, fractions with singular nouns, weights and distances.
  a hundred   a million   a third   a fifth
  *two and **a** half   **a** kilo   **a** metre and a half*
  But: *two and seven eighths   half-way*

  Half is usually used without an article.
  *He has eaten **half** of the cake.*

people

- We use zero article with names of people, unless we specify the person.
  *Tom lives in Bristol.   Is he **the Tom Davis** you went to school with?*

- We can use *a / an* with names when we mean 'a person called …'
  *Is there **a Tom Davis** staying here?*

- We can use *the* with the names of groups, when these are clearly plural.
  the Democrats

  However, if a proper name comes before the noun there will be zero article.
  Euro MPs   Manchester United supporters

- Names of music groups vary a great deal, and may not fit general rules.
  The Who   Primal Scream

  Many groups of people are described by *the* + singular adjective.
  the unemployed   the dead

cities, towns, streets, places

- Use zero article with proper names, though *the* is used when there is post modification with *of*.
  *I live in **Allan Road** in Bristol in an area called **Redland**.*
  *Oxford University   **the University of** Oxford*

- Use *the* with the names of shops and places with a general reference.
  *at **the** cinema / **the** supermarket / in **the** garden / in **the** mountains / at **the** beach etc*

- Other places vary. If they begin with the name of a place or person, then they tend to use zero article.
  London Bridge   Waterloo Station   Madame Tussaud's
  But: ***the** London Eye*

  Otherwise they use *the*.
  ***the** Golden Gate Bridge   **the** Hard Rock Café   **the** Odeon Cinema*

- Note that a place name can also be used as an adjective, in which case we could use *the*.
  The London rush hour can cause long delays.

  Some other cities have adjective forms, eg *Paris / Parisian, Rome / Roman.*

unique objects

- *The* is used with some familiar objects when we think of them as the only one.
  *The Sun was setting over **the sea**. **The moon** rose into **the sky**.*

illness etc

- *A / an* is used with a headache, a cold etc.
  *Have you got **a cold** / **a headache** / **a toothache** / **an earache**?*

  Most illness words use zero article.
  *I've got **flu**.   She's suffering from **appendicitis**.*

exclamations

- Use *a / an* in the expressions *what a …!, such a …!*
  We use *what a …* when we are surprised or impressed by something.
  ***What a** fantastic sight!   **What an** awful room!*

  We use *such a / an …* for emphasis with singular nouns.
  *This is **such a** great film!   He is **such an** interesting person.*

(See also **Unit 21**.)

1 Complete the text with *the* or zero article.

a _The_ survival of .... most large mammals is being put at risk by .... global warming.

b Is .... person you are talking about .... Jane Small you knew at .... university?

c .... foreigners often have .... trouble getting used to .... Scottish climate.

d .... decoration in .... small bedroom is really pleasing but I don't like .... colour of curtains.

e I missed .... beginning of .... film, so I didn't understand .... plot until half-way through.

f .... experts disagree as to whether .... men are .... better drivers than .... women.

g .... most of .... people I know don't always get on with .... other people .... first time they meet them.

h What exactly is .... difference between .... rhythm of a piece of .... music and .... tune?

i Helen has gone to .... library to get .... information she needs for .... project she's doing at .... school.

j I don't know why you always put .... sugar in your coffee if you're trying to lose .... weight.

the arts

2 Complete the text with *a / an* or *the*, or leave blank for zero article.

George Orwell

a _The_ author George Orwell (1903–1950: real name Eric Blair) was b .... English novelist, critic and political and cultural commentator. He is best known for c .... novels *Animal Farm* and *Nineteen Eighty-Four*, d .... both of which were written and published toward e .... end of his life. He chose f .... name George Orwell in g .... early 1930s when his first book, *Down and Out in Paris and London*, was published. This book describes what it was like to be h .... poor and i .... homeless in j .... Britain, and also described k .... time he spent in Paris working in l .... kitchen of m .... high-class hotel. n .... Orwell's father was o .... civil servant in India, and Orwell grew up in p .... middle-class family. He was q .... pupil at Eton, r .... well-known English school, and as his family could not afford to send him to university, he joined s .... Indian Imperial Police. He learnt t .... lot about u .... British Empire, but came to hate v .... job, and in 1927 he resigned and decided to become w .... writer. He worked as x .... schoolteacher, and in y .... bookshop, wrote z .... book about 1 .... poverty in 2 .... northern England (*The Road to Wigan Pier*) and also fought for 3 .... Republican side in 4 .... Spanish civil war. He developed 5 .... career as 6 .... journalist and reviewer, and during 7 .... Second World War he made 8 .... regular broadcasts on 9 .... BBC. He died of 10 .... tuberculosis in 1950 at 11 .... age of 46.

GLOSSARY

3 Complete the sentences with *a / an* or *the*.

a The tiger is .... animal which struggles to survive in .... modern world.

b I need .... kilo and .... half of minced beef, but I want all .... fat taken off please.

c .... art gallery used to own .... Picasso, but it was stolen in .... daring daylight robbery.

d .... first thing students need to appreciate is that .... laboratory can be .... dangerous place.

e We spent .... week in Paris and had .... great time going up .... Eiffel Tower, and taking .... trip along .... Seine in .... small boat.

f Tom Gibson, ... architect mainly responsible for .... design of .... new building, lives in .... farmhouse in .... country.

g .... rent is €1000 .... month because .... apartment is in .... most expensive part of .... city.

h I can never understand .... US elections, because I'm not sure I know .... difference between .... Democrats and .... Republicans.

i .... worst thing about travelling on the motorway is that if there is .... accident, there is usually .... huge traffic jam.

j My dad is down at .... pub having .... drink with .... other members of .... pub-quiz team.

science

4 Complete the text with *a / an* or *the*, or leave blank for zero article.

Bird migration

Whether **a** ....*a*.... particular species of **b** .... bird migrates depends on **c** .... number of **d** .... factors. **e** .... most important influence on **f** .... migration is **g** .... climate of **h** .... area where **i** .... birds breed, and **j** .... small number of birds remain in an area where there is **k** .... harsh winter. So in **l** .... Scandinavia **m** .... blackbird is **n** .... migratory bird, but it is not **o** .... migratory in **p** .... southern Europe where **q** .... winters are milder. Another factor is **r** .... type of **s** .... food involved. Some birds eat mainly **t** .... insects which are not available in winter, so these birds have to undertake **u** .... migration in order to find food. However, lack of **v** .... food is not **w** .... trigger for migration, and birds need to be well fed before they start **x** .... long-distance flight. The main reasons for **y** .... migrating seem to be partly genetic and partly as **z** .... result of **1** .... small changes in **2** .... weather or in **3** .... length of **4** .... day.

GLOSSARY

EXTENSION ACTIVITY

Choose a paragraph from a book and make a practice passage like the ones in Exercises 2 and 4. Remove all articles and leave a space, add spaces for zero article, and add some trick spaces. Ask someone else in the class to complete your practice passage, and show them the original passage so they can check their answers.

*Need more practice? Go to the **Review** on page 208.*

21 articles (2)

nationality

- We use *the* with nationality adjectives that end *-ese, -ch, -sh, -ss* and are used to refer to all the people of that nationality, eg *Chinese, Japanese, French, Spanish, British, Swiss, Dutch.*
  The French drink a lot of wine.
  The Swiss are famous for their banks.

- We use *the* with plural nationality nouns in same way, eg *Russians, Americans, Poles, Greeks, Turks, Germans, Belgians* etc.
  The Russians and the Poles are used to cold weather.

- We use *a / an* with singular examples.
  an Australian, a Greek, a Turk, a Russian, a Pole, a Romanian, a Bulgarian, an Egyptian, a Jordanian

  Some nationalities end in *-man / woman*, and others have unique names.
  an Englishman / an Irishman / a Scotsman / a Welshman / a Frenchman / a Dutchman
  a Spaniard / a Cypriot / a Pakistani / an Iraqi / a Saudi / a Filipino

  Some nationalities can only be used as an adjective with a noun, eg *Japanese person / man.*

geography

- We use *the* with the names of oceans, seas, rivers, geographical areas.
  *They crossed **the Pacific** / **the Atlantic** / **the Mediterranean** etc in a small boat.*
  *The sun sets in **the West**.   She travelled widely in **the Middle East**.*
  *We took a voyage down **the Danube**.*

- *The* is used with *north*, *south* etc. to indicate geographical areas, but zero article is used to describe general directions.
  *The sun sets in **the west**.   The road runs **from north to south**.*

- We use zero article with continents, countries, lakes.
  ***Lake Geneva** borders **France** and **Switzerland**.*
  *Morocco is in **Africa**.*

- We use *the* with plural or collective names.
  *From here you can see **the Alps**.*
  *She lives in **the Philippines** / **the Netherlands** / **the United Kingdom** / **the USA**.*

- Names of mountains vary.
  *He's climbed **Everest** and **Mont Blanc** but not **the Matterhorn**.*

- Names of islands normally use zero article unless they have post-modification with *of* ...
  *I've been to **Crete** / **Majorca** / **Cuba**.*
  *I haven't been to **the Isle of Wight**.*

- We use *the* with deserts.
  The Sahara is not as dry as most people think.

school subjects

- We use zero article when we talk about school subjects, such as *geography, history.*
  *I'd rather study **physics** than **biology**.*

- These can also be used as adjectives with article + noun.
  *I've started **a physics** course.*
  The biology teacher is really good.

calendar

- We use zero article when we refer to days, months or parts of the day.
  *I'll see you **on Monday at midday**.*   *School begins **in September**.*

- We can use *the* with a day of the week when we refer to a particular week, and *the* with a month when we refer to a particular year.
  *It started as an ordinary week but **on the Friday** I received a surprising message.*

- We use *a / an* with a day of the week when we refer to the day as a typical example.
  *It was **a Tuesday afternoon** in August and nothing much was happening.*

home, school, prison, hospital, work

- We use zero article with *at home, at school, in hospital, in prison, in bed* when we speak about the place in general, or with reference to its use.
  *Jack is **in hospital**.* (he's ill)
  *Sue is **at school**.* (she's a student)

- When we refer to something just as a building, place, etc we use *the*.
  *The bus stops **outside the school**.*   (the building)
  *Leave the towels **on the bed**.*   (the item of furniture)
  *I was walking **past the hospital**.*   (the building)
  *There was a riot **in the prison**.*   (the building)

- Compare: *Alan's **in bed**.*   (he's asleep)
  *There's something crawling **in the bed**!*   (the item of furniture)

other generalized locations and activities

- We use other phrases with zero article to describe what people are doing or where they are in general.
  on holiday   *on tour* (performers)   *on location* (place where a film is shot)
  on stage   *on duty*   *at work*

- Specific examples use *a / an* or *the*.
  *They decided to take **a holiday abroad**.*   *He ran **onto the stage**.*

changes of meaning

- Some nouns can be countable or uncountable and have different meanings according to the article they use.

a / an	*a coffee*	*a cup of coffee*	*Can I buy you **a coffee**?*
the	*the coffee*	*grains or beans etc.*	*Put **the coffee** in the jar.*
zero	*coffee*	*in general*	*Do you like **coffee**?*

- Many names of substances have a change of meaning when used as a single object.

glass	**a glass**	*for holding water etc*	**glasses**	*for helping the eyes*
iron	**an iron**	*for smoothing clothes*		
paper	**a paper**	*a newspaper or a piece of published research*		

- Some food nouns which usually have no plural can be used with *a / an* to talk about one particular type of that food.
  *I try to eat as much fresh **fruit** as I can.*
  *This is **a fruit** that only grows in the tropics.*

  Other foods used in this way are: *wine, beer, cheese, meat, oil.*

(See also **Unit 20**.)

articles (2)

Exercises in this unit also practise material from Unit 20.

1 Complete the sentence with *a / an* or *the*, or leave blank for zero article.

a The_____ victim was waiting for _____ bus outside _____ hospital when _____ offence took place.

b Maria forgot to turn off _____ iron when she went to answer _____ knock at _____ door, and she burnt _____ hole in _____ ironing board.

c We went to _____ Crete on _____ holiday and spent _____ week walking over _____ mountains admiring _____ scenery.

d After you put _____ coffee in _____ machine, fill it with _____ water, and make sure _____ water comes up to _____ level of _____ thick black line.

e When I'm at _____ work, I'm only allowed to take _____ personal calls in _____ emergency.

f Helen is in _____ bed with _____ temperature, so _____ trip to _____ country has been postponed until _____ next week.

g At _____ last minute, David decided to go away for _____ few days and stay in _____ hotel by _____ sea.

h _____ train to _____ Manchester was _____ half _____ hour late by _____ time it reached _____ Watford.

history

2 Complete the text with *a / an* or *the*, or leave blank for zero article.

The Great Wall of China

a The_____ Great Wall of b _____ China is one of c _____ wonders of d _____ modern world, and became e _____ UNESCO Heritage site in 1987. It is f _____ one of g _____ longest (6,700 km) structures in h _____ world, and has i _____ history of more than j _____ two thousand years. k _____ building of l _____ wall began between m _____ 7th and 8th centuries BC as n _____ means of defending most of o _____ China from p _____ invading people of q _____ north. r _____ rulers of different parts of s _____ country built sections of t _____ wall, and these were joined together in u _____ time of v _____ Qin dynasty. During w _____ Ming dynasty (1368–1644 AD) x _____ wall was repaired and extended and took on y _____ appearance it has today, with z _____ complex system of 1 _____ forts and towers. It has 2 _____ average height of ten metres and 3 _____ width of five metres, and it runs from 4 _____ east to 5 _____ west.

GLOSSARY

3 Complete the sentence with *a / an* or *the*, or leave blank for zero article.

a _The_ British are famous (or notorious) for _____ amount of _____ fast food they eat.

b We went on _____ field trip to _____ Lake District as part of _____ final year geography course.

c Jim is at _____ work at _____ moment. He's _____ personal trainer.

d _____ story begins on _____ quiet afternoon at _____ end of _____ July.

e Can I have _____ coffee in _____ glass with _____ milk, please.

f Helen works at _____ hospital at _____ end of _____ road.

g Peter was in _____ bed with _____ attack of _____ flu.

h _____ film was shot on _____ location in _____ Philippines.

i On my way to _____ work in _____ morning I usually buy _____ paper before I get on _____ bus.

j When he's on _____ duty at _____ prison, Jack has to wear _____ uniform.

geography

4 Complete the text with *a / an* or *the*, or leave blank for zero article.

The Dominican Republic

a _The_ Dominican Republic is b _____ country of approximately 8 million people, and is located on c _____ eastern two-thirds of d _____ Caribbean island of e _____ Hispaniola, which is f _____ second-largest of g _____ Greater Antilles islands. h _____ western part of i _____ island forms j _____ Republic of k _____ Haiti. l _____ capital of m _____ country is n _____ city of o _____ Santo Domingo and is located in p _____ southern part of q _____ island. r _____ second largest city is s _____ Santiago. t _____ country has three major mountain ranges, and u _____ highest peak is v _____ Pico Duarte (3,175m). w _____ geography of x _____ country is varied, and ranges from y _____ semi-desert plains to z _____ lush valleys of tropical rainforest. 1 _____ economy depends largely on 2 _____ agriculture, with 3 _____ sugar as 4 _____ main crop, though 5 _____ mining and 6 _____ tourism are also important.

GLOSSARY

EXTENSION ACTIVITY

Choose a paragraph from a book and make a practice passage like the ones in Exercises 2 and 4. Replace all articles with a space, add spaces for zero article, and add some trick spaces. Ask someone else in the class to complete your practice passage, and show them the original passage so they can check their answers.

*Need more practice? Go to the **Review** on page 208.*

22 | number and quantity

many, few, much, little

- With countable nouns we can use *too many, not many, (only) a few, (very) few*.
  There are **too many** mistakes here.   We've had **very few** complaints.

- *Few* is negative, *a few* is positive.
  I have **a few** friends in Germany.   (some)
  I have **few** friends in Germany.   (not many)

- With uncountable nouns we can use *too much, not much, (only) a little, (very) little*.
  We haven't got **much time**.   There is **too much smoke** in here.
  I need **a little help**.   There's only **a little milk** left.

a lot of / lots of, plenty, hardly any, not enough

- With countable and uncountable nouns we can use *a lot of / lots of, plenty of, hardly any, (not) enough, hardly enough*. (See **Unit 23** for the use of *much, a lot* as adverbs.)
  We've got **lots of** time.   We had **a lot of** complaints.
  There's **hardly any** milk.   There are **hardly any** seats.
  We haven't got **enough time**.   There aren't **enough chairs**.

- *A lot* and *lots* can stand alone as pronouns.
  How many complaints have you had?   **Lots / A lot**.

no, not any, none (of)

- *No* and *not any* can be used with countables and uncountables.
  There's **no time** to lose!   There **isn't any time** for that!

- *None* stands alone as a pronoun, often with *at all*. *None of* is used with nouns, with either a singular or a plural verb, though many users prefer a singular verb.
  There might be lots of customers, or there might be **none (at all)**.   **None of** the passengers was / were saved.

much / many with numbers and quantities

- *Many* can be used as an intensifier with *hundreds of / thousands of* etc.
  Many thousands of people took part in the demonstration.

- *A good many* is a colloquial way of describing a large number.
  A good many people were carrying banners.

- We use *as many as* or *up to* to indicate the highest number. We use *as much as* or *up to* to indicate the highest amount.
  As many as a hundred people were arrested.
  We spent **as much as** £300 yesterday.

- We use *more than* or *in excess of* to indicate the lowest number.
  More than £10 million has been spent already.

too much, too many, enough

- We use *too many* with countables and *too much* with uncountables to show that the number or amount is greater than necessary or more than is acceptable or possible.
  There are **too many cars** in the centre of the city.   There is **too much traffic**.

- We use *far* or *way* as intensifiers in everyday speech.
  There is **far too much** salt in this sauce.

- We use *enough* with countables and uncountables when we want to show that the number or amount is acceptable or sufficient.
  I'll give you **enough money** to buy tickets for all of us.

- *Hardly enough* means 'almost not enough'. *Just enough* means the right amount or number. *More than enough* means 'more than is needed' (*plenty of* has a similar meaning).
  There are **hardly enough chairs** for so many people.   There is **just enough food** for the three of us.
  Don't worry, we've got **more than enough chairs**.

quite a lot, rather a lot

- *Quite a lot* is a fairly large number, but not a very large one or more than we expected.
  There were **quite a lot of people** waiting outside.

- *Rather a lot* is generally a greater number or amount than *quite a lot*, almost too many.
  I can't come out. I've got **rather a lot of work** to do.

number and amount

- We use *a number* or *a large number / a small number* to describe how many. We use a singular or a plural verb, though many users prefer a singular verb.
  A number of houses have already been built.
  A large number of people was waiting outside.

- We use *a large / small amount* to describe how much.
  A large amount of money has been recovered by the police.

loads of, masses of

These are informal expressions meaning a large number or amount.
  Jim's a banker, and has got **loads of money**.

hundreds of, miles of etc

Measurement words can be used with *of*. Note that measurement words such as *litre, ton,* etc are also followed by *of*: *a litre of milk, a ton of earth.*
  Thousands of tons of earth had to be moved.
  Millions of litres of water are wasted every day.
  There were several **miles of** wiring in each machine.

twice as much as / as many as

- We use *twice as much, three times as much* etc to make comparisons between a larger and smaller quantity or number.
  Paula earns **twice as much money as** I do.
  There are **ten times as many students** here **as** in my last school.

- *(Just) as much / many* means an equal amount or number.
  Paula earns **as much as** I do.

every and each + noun

In some cases, the meaning of *every* and *each* is the same, though *each* is often used to mean *separately* or *one by one*, especially when we are thinking of a definite number.
  Every / Each time I have a holiday, I catch a cold.
  There is a café **in each corner** of the square.   (there are four cafés)

more, fewer, less

- *More* can be used with countables and uncountables to mean a larger number or amount.
  Bring **more** chairs.   We need **more** milk.

- We use *fewer* with countables to mean a smaller number, *less* with uncountables to mean a smaller amount.
  There have been **fewer storms** this year.   And **less rain**.

  In everyday speech, people often use *less* with countables, and this is becoming more common in print.

1 Underline the best option.

a There is <u>hardly any</u> / *too few* milk left, so we'll have to buy some more.

b I don't think there is *enough* / *plenty of* salt in the soup.

c You don't have to hurry. There's *lots of* / *much* time.

d There are *lots of* / *very few* books on this subject, so you might have difficulty finding one.

e There's *only a little* / *only a few* paint left. Do you think it will be enough?

f There's *not enough* / *too much* time to finish this exercise now, so we'll do it tomorrow.

g Can you wait a minute? There are *a few* / *few* things I have to do before I leave.

h It costs *a lot of* / *plenty of* money, and I don't think it's really worth it.

i We'll have to find a larger room for the lecture. *Not enough* / *Too many* people have turned up.

j I have to sleep with the window closed because there is *plenty of* / *too much* noise outside.

k When the money was counted, it was found that *as much as* / *as many as* £500,000 was missing.

l I'm sorry, but there aren't *too many* / *enough* books for everyone, so you'll have to share.

2 Choose the best option, A, B or C, to complete the sentence.

a Can you come and help me, because there's ___B___ of shopping to carry.

b Helen reads a lot, and has _____ books as I have.

c _____ of people gathered outside the town hall to hear the mayor speak.

d Many people write uninteresting diaries, and _____ of them are on the Internet.

e Have you got _____ paper to print twenty copies of this worksheet?

f An elephant drinks about a hundred and fifty _____ a day.

g If you're careful, there is _____ hot water for a bath.

h Only _____ people came to see the play on the first night.

i I tried _____ house in the street, but nobody had heard of Mrs Salkeld.

j It's a lovely house, but it cost them _____ money.

k There's no need to hurry. We've still got _____ time.

l _____ people nowadays are being taken in by fraudsters on the Internet.

a A *too many*	B *rather a lot*	C *thousands of*
b A *twice as many*	B *more*	C *a large number*
c A *Many thousands*	B *A large amount*	C *More than enough*
d A *just enough*	B *more*	C *a good many*
e A *much*	B *loads of*	C *enough*
f A *litres of water*	B *litres water*	C *water litres*
g A *hardly enough*	B *just enough*	C *too much*
h A *few*	B *quite a few*	C *a very small number of*
i A *each*	B *rather a lot of*	C *every*
j A *rather a lot of*	B *rather lots of*	C *a good many*
k A *much*	B *loads of*	C *quite a lot*
l A *Too many*	B *Enough*	C *A large number*

3 Put one suitable word in each space.

Salt consumption and health

Health experts believe that **a** _many_ people are consuming far too **b** .... salt, and that this is a health risk. There are plenty **c** .... studies which show that increased salt consumption raises blood pressure and can cause heart problems, and the recommendation is that we should all be consuming **d** .... salt. Even if we add **e** .... any salt to our food at the table, we may be consuming a **f** .... of salt without realizing. The daily recommended amount is 6 grams, but many people are consuming twice as much **g** .... this and the average daily consumption in the UK is over 9 g per day. Bread, biscuits, ketchup and ready made meals all contain **h** .... a lot of salt, so each time we eat a slice of bread, for example, we are adding to our daily intake. So what is the solution? We all need to be more aware of **i** .... much salt we are consuming, and try to limit our intake. Governments are encouraging food manufacturers to cut down on the **j** .... of salt they put into food, and every food product should state clearly on the wrapper how **k** .... salt it contains.

GLOSSARY

4 Write a new sentence with the same meaning containing the word in capitals.

a There's too little time to finish now.   NOT
   There's not enough time to finish now.

b All of my answers were right.   WRONG

c There isn't any money in your wallet.   IS

d There weren't many customers this morning.   VERY

e There were more crimes this year.   LAST

f The red one costs €50 and the green one costs €100.   MUCH

g Hundreds of people were queuing at the front entrance.   LARGE

h There is plenty of food for six people.   MORE

i The cupboard hasn't got any paper in it.   THERE

j There wasn't much snow last night.   ANY

number and quantity

5 Write a new sentence with the same meaning, beginning as shown.

a The traffic is heavy today.
There *is too much traffic today* .

b This coffee is too sweet.
There is ....

c This house is double the value of that one.
This house is worth ....

d A lot of money has been spent on this project.
A large ....

e I've got plenty of money to buy the tickets.
I've got more ....

f Nearly a thousand football fans were arrested.
As ....

g There are hardly any taxis at this time of night.
There are very ....

h This is a secret and not many people know about it.
This is a secret and only ....

i All of the paintings were undamaged.
None ....

j The tank hasn't got any water in it.
There ....

6 Complete the text with one word in each gap.

The 'flu pandemic of 1918–19

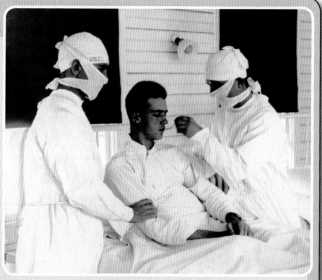

The influenza pandemic of 1918–19 killed millions
a ...*of*........... people at the end of World War One.
As **b** .... as 40 million people are believed
to have died and more or less **c** .... part
of the world was affected. As might be expected,
a **d** .... number of the victims were
soldiers. In fact, in some parts of the war zone,
e .... many soldiers died of influenza as
died in the fighting. In the US army at home and abroad,
ten **f** .... as many soldiers died of influenza.
Unusually, in the civilian population there were relatively
g .... victims among the young and elderly, the usual victims of influenza. Instead, most of the
h .... millions who died were the strongest members of the population, between the ages of
20 and 40. Doctors at the time had **i** .... little idea of how to treat the disease and it spread rapidly
as the war ended and **j** .... numbers of people returned home. At the time, **k** .... of
people believed that the epidemic was caused by biological warfare. However there is **l** ....
evidence to support this suspicion. Scientists now believe that a pandemic occurs **m** .... time the
influenza virus changes its genetic composition. This pandemic is sometimes known as the Spanish Flu because it
was believed to have caused as many **n** .... 8 million deaths in Spain in 1918. However the
outbreak is now believed to have originated in China.

GLOSSARY

7 Complete the text using one phrase from the list in each gap.

1 a few	5 hardly any	9 quite a lot of
2 ~~aren't enough~~	6 large numbers	10 too much
3 enough time	7 many	11 two or three times as much
4 lot of	8 more	12 very few

Women in power

More than a century after women started campaigning for the right to vote, it still seems that there **a** _2_ women in positions of power. In the world as a whole, there have been **b** _____ female heads of state, and in some countries women have **c** _____ political power. In industrialized countries where **d** _____ of women work, it still happens that men earn **e** _____ for doing the same job. Although there are **f** _____ successful female business leaders, there are clearly many **g** _____ men at the top. Many people believe that this situation reflects the fact that women haven't got **h** _____ to be successful in the work place, and in the home. There is much **i** _____ pressure on women, they say, to be good wives and mothers, and they are at a disadvantage in the job market. However, there is **j** _____ evidence to suggest that women can be more successful in the modern business environment than men. **k** _____ modern business operations now depend on co-operation and flexibility, and women are better at these skills than men. So it may well be that in the future, quite a **l** _____ important business will be run by women, and it will be the men who earn lower wages or stay at home.

GLOSSARY

EXTENSION ACTIVITY

A Write true sentences about yourself which include these words.

hardly any   too much   quite a lot   twice as much   every   fewer

B Write sentences about your town or country, beginning as shown.

*Many thousands of people ...   There are too many ...   There is far too much ...
We need more ...   We haven't got much ...*

23 nouns

nouns always ending in plural s

- Nouns ending -*ics* have no singular form, they use zero article and a singular verb, eg *mathematics, linguistics, physics, politics, athletics.*
  Mathematics is my favourite subject.

  When not used to mean 'subjects of study', nouns of this kind can use *the* + plural verb.
  Economics is a difficult subject.   *The economics* of this case *are* complex.

- Some nouns always ending in plural s are counted as singular, though they have no singular form, eg *the news, darts, billiards* (and other plural games), cities with plural forms *Naples, Athens* etc.
  The news is on at 10.00.   *Athens is* a beautiful city.

- Illness words always ending in plural s use a singular verb, eg *measles, mumps.*
  Measles is a highly infectious disease.

- Some nouns always ending in plural s can have a singular verb when singular, and a plural verb when plural, eg *crossroads, series, species, means.*
  This *species is* interesting.   Both *species are* now extinct.
  This *is a means* to an end.   *All means* have been exhausted.

- Some nouns always ending in plural s use a plural verb, eg *belongings, clothes, congratulations, earnings, goods, outskirts, remains, stairs, surroundings, thanks.*
  Are these your *belongings*?   These *are the remains* of my car!
  Some of these nouns have a singular form with a different meaning.
  looks   She was admiring Jack's good *looks*.
  look   Could I have *a look* at your answers?

nouns describing groups (collective nouns)

- Some nouns describing groups of people are singular only, but can be followed by a singular or plural verb, eg *the majority, the public.*

- Some singular nouns describing groups of people use singular or plural verb depending on how we think of them, eg *government, army, council, management,* etc.
  The government is planning to raise taxes.   (= one body)
  The government are undecided about this matter.   (= a group of individuals)

- Some nouns describing groups of people or animals have no plural s and use a plural verb, eg *people, the police, cattle.*
  The police are investigating the fire.

  People can be used with plural s to mean nationality or race.
  The peoples of the world are united in their desire for peace.

change of meaning

Some nouns have different meanings for singular and plural.
  damage   The insurance company paid for the *damage* to the house.
  damages   The court awarded *damages* of £50,000.
  custom   Giving eggs at Easter is a *custom* here.
  customs   When we passed through *customs*, we had to open our cases.

Others include, *expense / expenses* (money spent as part of a job), *manner / manners* (way of behaving), *work / a work, works* (of art, literature etc), *glass / glasses* (spectacles).

pairs

- Some nouns with plural form only can be used with a *pair of …/ two pairs of* etc, though this can be left out, eg *glasses, trousers, shorts, pyjamas.*
  Where are my glasses?   I've got two pairs of glasses.

- Other words which can be singular, and which can also be used with *pair* are *socks, shoes, sandals, gloves.*

collections

Some collections of nouns are described with *a + noun + of*, eg *a bunch of flowers, a circle of friends, a crowd of people, a gang of thieves, a herd of cattle, a flock of sheep, a pack of cards, a panel of experts, a team of lawyers / doctors.*

partitives

Some mass nouns eg *bread* have a countable item which describes a 'piece' of the whole, and which can be used when we want to specify 'one' of that item. eg *a loaf of bread, a bar of soap, a cloud of dust, a flash of lightning, a clap of thunder, a shower of rain, an item of news, a slice of cake etc.*

- container + of *a tube of toothpaste, a can of beer, a carton of milk etc*
- container: compound noun *a beer-can   a matchbox*

  The name of the container usually begins with the name of what is contained, with a singular noun if it is countable.

- small quantities *a speck of dust, a grain of rice, a scrap of paper*
- abstract nouns *a piece of advice / information, a spot of trouble*
- quantities *a litre of beer, a kilo of cheese etc*
- words describing types *a kind of, a type of, a variety of, a species of*
- game, round *a game of chess, a round of golf*

compound nouns

- Noun + noun The first noun is normally singular (but: *a clothes brush*). Check in a dictionary for the use of a hyphen, as this varies greatly.

  a bus ticket   a key ring

  Categories include:

type	*a seat belt a comedy film*
containers	*a milk jug a water bottle*
purpose (-er)	*a can opener* (a thing that opens cans)
(for)	*a book shelf* (a shelf for books)
place	*a bedroom chair a school playground*
part of a whole	*a car door a mouse button*

- *-ing* + noun *frying pan   writing desk*

- noun + *-ing* *sight-seeing   water skiing*

- from multi-word verb *a take-off   a hold-up*

of and possessive apostrophe

- Use *of* for things when there is no compound noun, for parts of things and for abstract ideas.
  *the **end of** the road   the **aim of** the project*

- Use possessive apostrophe for things belonging to people.

singular	apostrophe *s*	*Michael**'s** desk.*
plural with *s*	apostrophe only	*The boys**'** bedroom.*
plural without *s*	apostrophe *s*	*The children**'s** bedroom.*

- Names ending in *s* add apostrophe *s*, or apostrophe, but are pronounced as if they have apostrophe *s*.
  *the **Jones'** house / the **Jones's** house*   (both pronounced the same)

- We also use possessive apostrophe with references to time, and in some fixed expressions.
  time   *an **hour's** bus-ride, a **days'** work etc*
  expressions   *be at your **wits'** end*

Some exercises require the use of a dictionary.

1 Underline the best option.

a I'm afraid that the news *is* / *are* not very encouraging.

b It took Helen a while to get used to her new *surrounding* / *surroundings*.

c Athletics *is* / *are* a popular pastime in many countries.

d Do you fancy a game of *card* / *cards*?

e The cattle *has* / *have* got through the fence by the main road.

f Mumps *is* / *are* a serious illness for many older people.

g What do you think of my new *trouser* / *trousers*?

h The bathroom is on the left at the top of the *stair* / *stairs*.

i 'Extras' *is* / *are* the funniest comedy series I have ever seen.

j Local police *is* / *are* baffled by the disappearance of more than fifty pet dogs.

2 Complete the sentence with a singular or plural form of a word in the list.

custom   damage   expense   glass   manner   work

a You'll have to declare these items at _____customs_____ when you land in London.

b The newspapers were not impressed by the _____ of Mr Smith's election.

c The violent storm caused severe _____ throughout the west of the country.

d The school gave Tony the complete _____ of Shakespeare as a prize.

e You can put in a claim for your travel _____ when you come back from the trip.

f People here have the _____ of opening the front door at midnight on New Year's Eve.

g The waiter filled Maria's _____ with sparkling water.

h The injured passenger was awarded _____ of over £1 million.

i As far as I'm concerned, eating and drinking on buses and trains is simply bad _____.

j In this part of the country, factories have closed and many people have no _____.

k Have you seen my _____ anywhere? I can't see a thing!

l For most students, rent is their biggest _____.

3 Complete the sentence with a word from the list.

bunch   cloud   ~~crowd~~   flash   gang   item   pack   piece   shower   team

a The stars of the film were met outside the cinema by a _____crowd_____ of fans.

b A sudden _____ of lightening lit the night sky.

c The building crashed to the ground, leaving a _____ of dust.

d A _____ of doctors in south London is carrying out a new study into childhood illnesses.

e One of the soldiers produced a _____ of cards, and they started to play.

f After a heavy _____ of rain, the pitch was slippery.

g Let me give you a _____ of advice. Don't borrow any money from that bank.

h Harry bought a large _____ of grapes from the supermarket.

i The train crash was the first _____ on the late news.

j The bank was raided by a _____ of armed robbers.

4 Use the description to make a compound noun.

a A belt you wear when you sit in the seat of a car.　　a *seat belt*

b A shelf which you put books on.　　a ....

c A chemical which softens water.　　a ....

d A pot for making coffee.　　a ....

e A brush for cleaning teeth.　　a ....

f The window of a shop.　　a ....

g Climbing in the mountains.　　a ....

h Equipment used in the office.　　a ....

i Something used for sharpening pencils.　　a ....

j A network of computers.　　a ....

the arts

5 Add an apostrophe where necessary and <u>underline</u> the word.

Hamlet *by William Shakespeare*

<u>Hamlets</u> father the King of Denmark has died, and
his mother has married his fathers brother, Claudius.
Denmark is under threat of invasion by a foreign
princes army. Two soldiers on duty on the ramparts of
the castle see Hamlets fathers ghost. Later, the ghost
speaks to Hamlet and describes his brothers method
of murdering him. Hamlet promises to avenge his
murder, but pretends to be mad to escape his uncles
suspicions. Claudius asks Hamlets friends to find out
the reasons for his strange behaviour. Claudius adviser,
Polonius, the father of Hamlets girlfriend Ophelia,
suggests that his madness is caused by love. Hamlets
friends invite a troupe of actors to try to make Hamlet
less unhappy. Hamlet asks them to put on a play he
has written in which his fathers murder will be acted.
His uncles guilt becomes clear when he stops the play
and leaves with his courtiers. Hamlet kills Polonius in
error and is sent to England with his friends as part of
the kings attempt to kill Hamlet.

What happens next? You'll have to read the play!

GLOSSARY

EXTENSION ACTIVITY

A Choose a page in a magazine, newspaper or book and make a list of
any collective nouns, collections or partitives, and compound nouns.

B Choose twenty words from the explanation pages, and look them up
in a dictionary. How would you translate them into your language?

*Need more practice? Go to the **Review** on page 208.*

nouns

24 pronouns, *so*, *it*, *there*

each (of), both (of), either, neither

- *Each* as a pronoun (see **Unit 22**), refers to two or more things or people separately.
  If two players win, they **each** *get an extra card* / **each of them** *gets ...*
  The winners received £500 **each**.

- *Both* as a pronoun refers to two things or people together.
  They **both** *arrived at the same time.* **Both (of them)** *arrived at the same time.*
  I like them **both**. *I like* **both of them**.

- *Either (of)* means one or the other, when it doesn't matter which one. It uses a singular verb. *Not ... either* is also possible.
  These two colours are both fine. We can use **either**. **Either of them** *is suitable.*
  *No, we ca**n't use either** of them.*

- *Neither (of)* is the negative form, meaning not one nor the other.
  I don't like these two colours. We can't use either. **Neither of them** *is suitable.*

each other, one another, one ... the other

- *Each other* refers to two or more things or people each doing something to the other.
  The two men accused **each other** *of stealing the money.*

- *One another* has the same meaning. Some speakers prefer to use *each other* for two things or people, and *one another* for more than two.
  When they get into difficulties, all the children help **one another**.

reflexives

- Some verbs use a reflexive pronoun (eg *myself*) to refer back to the subject.
  I **blame myself** *for what happened.* *I hope* **you enjoy yourselves**.

  Other reflexive verbs include *cut, hurt, introduce.* These verbs can also have normal objects:
  We **enjoyed the play** *a lot.* *The police* **blamed hooligans** *for the problems.* (normal object)

- *Behave* is intransitive, and can have a reflexive but no other object, though the reflexive can be left out. *Make sure you* **behave yourself**. *Try to* **behave**!

- *Dress, wash, shave* often have a reflexive but it is not necessary.
  Hurry up and **dress (yourself)**.

- Reflexives are also used with verbs like *see, help, give* in some expressions.
  Then he **saw himself** *in the mirror.* *I couldn't* **help myself**. *She* **gave herself** *a pat on the back.*

someone, anyone, everyone, no-one, (somebody, something etc)

- These pronouns can be used:
  as a subject pronoun with a singular verb, or as an object pronoun. *Quiet!* **Someone's** *coming!*
  with an adjective.   *I've got* **something important** *to tell you.*
  with a comparative adjective.   *Have you got* **anything smaller**?
  with an infinitive.   *He says he's got* **nothing to do**.
  with *for* + pronoun + infinitive.   *Is there* **anything for us to drink**?

- The same uses also apply to adverbials *anywhere, somewhere, nowhere.*
  There's **nowhere** *nice to sit.* *Do you know* **anywhere** *cheaper?*
  I need **somewhere** *to stay.*

- *Else* can be added to all of these words to mean 'other'.
  I'm in love with **someone else**. *Do you want* **anything else**?
  There's **nothing else** *to say.* *There's* **nowhere else** *to sit.*

- There are problems with using personal pronouns or possessive adjectives to refer back to *somebody* etc, as the person could be male or female. Traditionally *he / his* was used.
  Someone / somebody has left **his** *wallet on the desk.*
  This is considered 'sexist' by many people, and an impersonal *they / their* is often used instead. In formal writing *he or she / his or her* is used.
  Does **everyone** *know what* **they** *are supposed to be doing?*
  Everyone should bring **his or her** *passport for inspection.*
- We use general *some / any* rules for negatives and questions.
  Is there **anyone** *there?   There's* **nobody** *here.   Do you want to see* **someone**? (specific person)

one / ones

- can be used to avoid repeating a countable noun.   *Are those* **the ones** *you meant?*
  One can also mean 'person'.   *She is* **the one** *I love!*
- can be used with an adjective.   *I like* **the red one**.
- can be used with *this / that* etc.   *Do you like* **these ones**?
- *One … the other* can be used to refer to two things.
  What's the difference between the M1 and a lawnmower?   **One** *is a motorway and* **the other** *is a way to mow.*

one, you

- We use *one* in formal speech or writing as an impersonal pronoun.
  One *grows to rely completely upon* **one's** *servants.*
- In everyday speech, we use *you*.
  I think **you** *soon get tired of commuting long distances.*

it

- *It* is used as an 'empty subject' for verbs that have no real subject.
  It's *6.30.*   **It's** *raining.*   **It** *was hot.*   **It's** *going to be 40°C.*   **It's** *200 miles to Scotland.*   **It's** *cold.*
- *It* is also used as a subject for *say*, to describe what is written; for *take*, to describe length of time; and in expressions *it doesn't matter* and *it's no use.*
  It says *here we have to be there an hour before.*   **It takes** *an hour to get there.*
  It doesn't really matter.   **It's no use**, *I can't make it work.*
- *It* is often used with *seem to* + action verb, and with *seem as if, seem that, look as if, appear that.*
  It seems to *snow a lot in this part of the country.*   **It seems as if** *everyone is having a good time.*
  It looks as if *we're going to be late.*   **It appears / seems** *that the meeting has been postponed.*
- *It* is used in phrases *it's a pity, it's a shame, it doesn't matter if.*
  It's a pity *you missed Jack.*   **It's a shame** *you didn't come to the party.*
  It doesn't matter if *I catch a later train.*

there

- *There* is used with *be, seem, appear* to introduce a statement about what exists or happens.
  There's *a shop at the end of the road.*
  There seems / appears *to be a problem.*
  There's been *a fire at the school.*
  There was *nobody in the building at the time.*
  There is *no point in doing the same thing over and over again.*
- After the statement of existence, other pronouns are used to refer back to the thing or person mentioned.
  There's *a shop at the end of the road.* **It's** *open until late.*
  There's *a girl outside.* **She** *says she knows you.*
- *There* is used in idiomatic phrases with *come, follow.*
  There comes *a time in everyone's life when …*
  There follows *a party political broadcast.*

1 Underline the best option.

a I'm really thirsty. Is there <u>*anything*</u> / *nothing* to drink?

b I've tried two phones so far but *each* / *neither* of them was out of order.

c I told you that knife was really sharp. Now I've cut *myself* / *yourself*.

d I read the two books you recommended, but I didn't like *either* / *both* of them.

e Do you know *anywhere* / *it* where I can get my bike repaired?

f You have to press both buttons at once. Nothing *either* / *else* seems to work.

g The lemon cakes are really good, but I don't really like *one another* / *the other ones*.

h Not those children again! Why can't they behave *theirselves* / *themselves*?

i We couldn't have finished the project so quickly if we hadn't helped *each other* / *ourselves*.

2 Choose the best option, A, B or C, to complete the sentence.

a The problem with this town, is that there is ....B.... to go in the evening.

b Someone seems to have left .... passport on the table.

c I'm looking for .... cheap to stay for a couple of nights.

d According to you, ... I do is wrong! I give up!

e Before you go, there was .... I wanted to talk to you about.

f Here's your chicken. I hope you enjoy it. Is there .... that you need?

g .... really understands me, except you!

h As far as I'm concerned, that is it! There is .... more to say!

a	A *nothing*	B *nowhere*	C *no-one*
b	A *its*	B *her*	C *their*
c	A *somewhere*	B *something*	C *everything*
d	A *something*	B *everything*	C *nothing*
e	A *nothing*	B *everywhere*	C *something else*
f	A *something else*	B *anything else*	C *nothing else*
g	A *someone*	B *no-one*	C *anyone*
h	A *nothing*	B *anything*	C *something*

3 Write a new sentence with the same meaning containing the word in capitals.

a Every person who picked the correct number won £500. EACH
  The people who picked the correct number won £500 each.

b Some children in the class were throwing pieces of paper at other children. ONE

c I've looked in all the other places. ELSE

d Are you hurt? HAVE

e What happened is my fault. MYSELF

f Don't worry if you can't get here by eight. IT

g Have a good time at the beach, children! ENJOY

h A lot of people were driving too fast, but they police stopped me. ONE

4 Complete each sentence with *it* or *there*.

a Look at the sky! ~~It~~ .... looks as if .... is going to be a storm.

b .... takes six hours to get there, and .... is only one train per day.

c .... is a slight problem with the air conditioning, but .... is not serious.

d .... says here that .... are volcanoes on Mars.

e .... is a bus strike tomorrow so .... is going to take me longer to get to work.

f .... is a shame that .... is raining, because .... means we can't play tennis.

g .... is no point in running. .... is no way we can get to school in time.

h .... comes a time when .... is a good idea to take more exercise.

i .... were some great goals in the match so .... is a pity you missed it.

j .... doesn't matter if .... isn't hot. I like cold pizza.

---

history

5 Choose the best option, A, B or C, to complete the text.

Robin Hood

Most of us are familiar with Robin Hood from Hollywood films. In the popular story, Robin has two main enemies, Prince John and the Sheriff of Nottingham. **a** *C* try to capture and kill him. Robin Hood's men and the local villagers, who are usually described as poor Saxons, help **b** ...... to defeat the Normans, who are the enemy. But did **c** ...... called Robin Hood really exist? As with most legendary figures, **d** ...... whether he really existed. **e** ...... from the early legends that he was an outlaw in Yorkshire, not Nottinghamshire, and in those times the name was given to **f** ...... who was an outlaw. In the earliest stories, he isn't **g** ...... who steals from the rich and gives to the poor. **h** ...... in his story to make him a hero: he is just a robber, and **i** ...... sense of heroism attached to him. **j** ...... we know from Hollywood films, Maid Marion, Friar Tuck, Little John and so on, has been added to the story over the centuries. **k** ...... a 'real' Robin Hood, just a story that has been changing for nearly a thousand years. But **l** ...... whether he was a real person or not. He is **m** ...... in the imagination of millions of people.

GLOSSARY

	A	B	C
a	*Either of them*	*All of them*	*Both of them*
b	*one another*	*themselves*	*both*
c	*anyone*	*no-one*	*someone*
d	*there is not clear*	*it is not clear*	*it seems clear*
e	*There is*	*Neither*	*It seems*
f	*anyone at all*	*nobody else*	*someone important*
g	*anyone*	*someone*	*either*
h	*There is nothing*	*There is something*	*There is*
i	*there is not*	*there is nothing*	*there is no*
j	*Somebody else*	*Everyone else*	*Nobody else*
k	*It seems*	*There isn't*	*It doesn't matter*
l	*it doesn't matter*	*there is no point*	*it's a pity*
m	*nobody who lives*	*anything that seems*	*someone who exists*

EXTENSION ACTIVITY

A Write ten more examples beginning 'It ...' and ten beginning 'There ...'

B Translate your examples into your language.

*Need more practice? Go to the **Review** on page 208.*

25 adjectives

adjective position

- attributive adjectives
  These come immediately before the noun.
  *an **old** building   a **heavy** suitcase*

- predicative adjectives
  These come after *be, become, seem, look, appear, feel*, and can be used without a noun.
  *This vase looks **old**.   It's **heavy** too.*

- The following adjectives are usually attributive (before a noun):
  classifying: *chief, entire, local, main, national, only, particular, sole, whole* etc.
  *This is the **main problem**.   I have **a particular reason** for asking.*

  emphatic: *mere, sheer, utter*
  *This is **utter nonsense!***
  *The **mere thought** of losing depresses me.*

  Other adjectives take on an emphatic meaning when attributive (before a noun):
  *complete, perfect, total, pure.   This is **pure** nonsense!*

- Some adjectives are only predicative:
  afloat, afraid, alight, alike, alive, alone, ashamed, asleep, awake, ill, well.
  *Are you **awake**?   Luckily they were both **alive**.*
  *I feel **ill**.   You look **well**.*

- Others are usually predicative: *glad, pleased, sorry, upset.*
  *You should be **pleased**.   I don't feel **sorry**.*

- *something, anyone* etc and adverbials *somewhere* etc can be followed by adjectives.
  *Do you want to know **something interesting**?   I need **somewhere quiet**.*

- When looking up adjectives in a dictionary, check whether the meaning you want is attributive or predicative.
  *Helen is **a responsible pupil**. (attributive – sensible, reliable)*
  *Who was **responsible** for the accident? (predicative – who caused it?)*

verbs of sensation

- *appear, feel, look, seem, smell, sound, taste* are followed by adjectives not adverbs.
  *This **smells bad**.   It **tastes awful** too.*

gradable and ungradable

- Gradable adjectives have degrees of meaning. They can be used with *very, too, enough* and have comparative and superlative forms.
  *It's **very heavy**.   This one is **heavier**.*

  Ungradable adjectives are absolute. They do not have comparative or superlative forms and cannot be used with *very* etc.
  *This tree is **dead**.   This vase is **unique**.*

nouns as adjectives

- Nouns that refer to substances, places, seasons and parts of a whole can be used as adjectives. Some substance words have adjectives ending *-en*: *wooden, woollen, golden*. Check with a dictionary for usage.
  *These are **cotton** trousers.   They are my **summer** clothes.*

participle adjectives

- We can use participles as adjectives.

  a **dripping** tap   (it's dripping now)
  a **broken** promise   (a promise that has been broken)
  an **accepted** idea   (an idea that is accepted)

- We can make compound adjectives by putting an adjective, adverb or noun before the participle.

  a **fast-flowing** river   a **freshly-made** footprint
  a **life-saving** operation   a **tree-lined** street
  a **French-speaking** area   a **self-employed** plumber
  a **tight-fitting** dress   a **mass-produced** product

- Some *-ing* adjectives and *-ed* adjectives which refer to feelings are easily confused.
  -ing adjectives describe the thing that is having the effect on others.
  *This news article is rather **worrying**.*   (It worries me)

  -ed adjectives describe the person and the way they feel because of the effect.
  *Helen looks **worried**.*   (Something has worried her)

  Other adjectives like this include *amazed / amazing, bored / boring, excited / exciting, exhausted / exhausting, interested / interesting, pleased / pleasing, tired / tiring.*

adjective + adjective

In the following three expressions, the first adjective functions as an adverb to say how wet etc something is.

  boiling hot, freezing cold, soaking wet

compound adjectives

Compound adjectives can be formed in the following ways:
- from adjective + noun.   de adj and noun

  a **cheap-rate** phone-call

- with numbers (plural *s* in never used).
  a **four-year-old** child   a **two-hour** meeting
  a **fifty euro** ticket   a **three-hour** journey

- with a noun + adjective.
  a **tax-free** car   an **air-tight** box

meaning

As many adjectives have a wide range of meaning, and may be used metaphorically, always check in a dictionary.

  *Janet is **a heavy smoker**.*   (= she smokes a lot)
  *I walked away with **heavy heart**.*   (= idiom: I felt sad or depressed)
  *This is a **heavy responsibility**.*   (= serious)
  ***Heavy fighting** continued all day.*   (= involving many people and weapons)
  *The lecture was a bit **heavy going**.*   (= hard to understand)

1 Underline the best word.

a Don't eat the fish. It smells _bad_ / badly.

b It's a *two-hours* / two-hour train journey from here to Manchester.

c I stumbled across *an asleep* / a sleeping man in the doorway.

d They ran home through the rain, and when they arrived were *sheer* / soaking wet.

e As far as Maria was concerned, it was a *losing* / lost opportunity.

f Tom opened the door and found a very *large* / enormous parcel on the doorstep.

g I read that article, but I thought it was *mere* / complete rubbish!

h The smell of *baking-fresh* / freshly baked bread made me feel hungry.

i That suitcase looks really *heavy* / heavily.

j What's the matter with you? You look *worrying* / worried.

2 Put *very* in front of the adjective where possible, or leave blank (–).

a I put my foot in the water, and it was __—__ freezing!

b Please don't make that silly noise! It's __VERY__ annoying!

c When we first saw the wave we were shocked, because it was __—__ enormous.

d You really should read this book. It's __VERY__ interesting.

e Jeff has been missing for two days, and we're __VERY__ worried.

f Unfortunately, the ring I found turned out to be __—__ worthless.

g At the end of the race, most of the runners felt __—__ exhausted.

h By the end of the second week, many of the villagers were __—__ starving.

i It's __VERY__ unusual for so much rain to fall here in July.

j I've checked the figures again, and I can assure you that they are __—__ correct.

k How do you do. I'm __VERY__ pleased to meet you.

l When I realized what she had said, I was __VERY__ upset.

3 Make an adjective + noun phrase which fits the explanation.

a Clothes you only wear in the winter. _winter clothes_

b Shirts made of silk. _silk – shirts_

c Batteries used for a torch. _torch -> Batteries_

d Sales held in the spring. _Spring sales._

e An overcoat made of leather. _leather – ouacoat_

f Equipment used in an office. _Office – equipment_

g Fans who are supporters of football clubs. _Football funs._

h A bowl made of glass. _Glass – bowl_

i Holidays we take in the summer. _Summer holidays._

j Software which is used on a computer. _Computer software_

k A bracelet made of silver. _Silver bracelet_

l Leaves that fall in autumn. _autumn leaves -> hojas de los árboles o matas_

4 Use the word in capitals to form an adjective + noun phrase which fits the explanation.

a A masterpiece which nobody cares about NEGLECT
  a neglected masterpiece

b The headlines at the end of a news broadcast. CLOSE
  a closing headlines

c Very low temperatures. FREEZE
  a freezing temperatures

d A door anyone can go through. UNLOCK
  an unlocked door

e Different feelings about something at the same time. MIX
  a mixed of feelings

f A marriage which the family of the couple organizes. ARRANGE
  an arranged marriage

g An author people think well of. RESPECT
  a respected author

h An attack that causes serious harm. DAMAGE
  a damaged attack

i A crime without a known culprit. UNSOLVE
  an unsolved crime

j A roof with a hole in it. LEAK
  a leaking roof

k The scene at the beginning of a play. OPEN
  the opening scene

l A taste for something that you develop after first disliking it. ACQUIRE
  an acquired taste

5 Complete the sentence with a compound adjective made from a form of the two words in brackets.

a Ticino is in the *Italian-speaking* area of Switzerland. (Italy, speak)

b I usually buy a *freshly baked* loaf from the local baker's. (bake, fresh)

c The dog fell into a *fast-flowing* river and was swept away. (flow, fast)

d We let our flat to a *newly-married* couple. (new, marry)

e The school believes it should educate children to be *open-minded* (mind, open)

f All we could see was a bare *windswept* landscape. (sweep, wind)

g The building fell to the ground with a / an *earth shattering* crash. (shatter, earth)

h I particularly like *chocolate coated* nuts. (coat, chocolate)

i It was a *heart breaking* decision, but we had to make it. (break, heart)

j The *tree covered* hills stretched into the distance. (cover, tree)

k The automatic ironing machine is described as a *time saving* device. (save, time)

l The *newly-discovered* tomb is being examined by archaeologists. (discover, new)

compound → se coloca todo antes del verbo

6 Choose the best option, A, B or C, to complete the sentence.

a Fortunately the surgeon was able to perform a __B__ operation.

b Two _____ children gave flowers to the president.

c The historic centre of the city is a _____ area.

d This kind of gambling machine is often called a _____ bandit.

e The narrow streets were lined with _____ shops.

f Julia's visit to India was a _____ experience.

g Brian looked out of the window at the _____ street.

h A spokesperson explained that there was a _____ situation.

i Please send me a _____ copy.

j It's a _____ journey from here to the other side of the island.

k There was an _____ explosion, followed by a thick cloud of smoke.

l Dogs used for hunting have a _____ sense of smell.

a A *life-saver*   B *life-saving*   C *life-saved*

b A *seven-year-old*   B *seven-years-old*   C *seven-year-olds*

c A *traffic-freed*   B *traffic-freely*   C *traffic-free*

d A *one-arm*   B *one-armed*   C *one-arm's*

e A *bright-lit*   B *bright-lighting*   C *brightly lit*

f A *life-changing*   B *life's-changing*   C *life-changer*

g A *rain-soaking*   B *rained-soak*   C *rain-soaked*

h A *rapid-changing*   B *rapidly changing* C *rapid-change*

i A *typewriting*   B *typewriter*   C *typewritten*

j A *three-hours*   B *three-hour*   C *three-hourly*

k A *ear-shattering*   B *ears-shattering*   C *ear-shattered*

l A *high-developed*   B *highly-developing* C *highly developed*

7 Complete each sentence with an adjective from the list. Use a dictionary to check the meaning.

> fine great heavy high light long low narrow open short small wide — *ancho grande*

a We didn't want to eat too much before the theatre, so we just had a __light__ meal.

b Jane is a very easy person to talk to, and is very friendly and __open__.

c There was a __heavy__ shower of rain, and we got soaked through.

d Bill was very thirsty and ordered a __long__ drink.

e They didn't have a lot to say to one another, but spent the time on __small__ talk.

f His name is Alexander, or Alex for __short__.

g If you're looking for gifts, try Bentley's which sells a __wide__ selection of local products.

h There's a very __fine__ line between being surprised and being amazed.

i Julia and I are __great__ friends, and we get on really well.

j I think it's __high__ time you stopped watching television and did some work!

k Ellis scored in the last minute, giving the team a __narrow__ 89–88 victory.

l The government has promised to do more to help people on __low__ incomes.

8 Complete the text with a compound adjective from the list in each gap.

> freshly prepared much-reduced home-cooked
> so-called time-saving far-reaching
> traffic-clogged hard-working ~~home-produced~~
> ready-made large-scale locally grown

Supermarket food

Few of us have the luxury of **a** _home-produced_ food fresh from our own garden, and increasingly we live in a world where such food is becoming rare. Although supermarkets can sell fresh fruit and vegetables at **b** _much reduce_ prices, not everyone buys them. Many people cook very little at home, and in some households few meals are **c** _freshly prepared_ Frozen and **d** _ready made_ meals are **e** _time-saving_ solutions for **f** _hard-working_ people, and **g** _so-called_ 'convenience foods' sold in supermarkets are beginning to replace more traditional **h** _home-cooked_ meals in many households. The consequences of such changes are **i** _far-reaching_ . Food which might have a long journey from the other end of the country has replaced **j** _locally grown_ food, which also means that huge supermarket lorries are added to **k** _traffic-clogged_ roads. Small farmers, who produce only small quantities of food, also find that supermarkets prefer **l** _large-scale_ production, and are often forced out of business.

GLOSSARY

EXTENSION ACTIVITY

A Choose ten participle adjectives from these pages and translate them into your language. Then write an example sentence for each one.

B Choose ten compound adjectives from these pages and translate them into your language. Then write an example sentence for each one.

26 adjectives with infinitive or -*ing*

adjective + *to*-infinitive

- *able / unable, careful, curious, due, foolish, free, inclined, prepared, ready, welcome, willing*
  *Sorry, but I'm **unable to lend** you the money.*
  *The train is **ready to leave**.*

- *it*-sentences
  advisable, best / better, difficult, easy, curious, impossible, nice, possible
  ***It's easy** (for people) **to make** mistakes.*
  ***It's curious to imagine** what people once used to think.*
  ***It's best to leave** before the rush hour.*

- *it's hard to please you / you are hard to please*
  Some adjectives (eg *easy, good, hard, impossible*) can follow this pattern.
  ***It's impossible** (for me) **to reach** the top shelf.   The top shelf **is impossible** (for me) **to reach**.*

  Adjectives describing feelings (eg *annoying, interesting, lovely, terrific, wonderful*)
  work in a similar way.
  *It was **interesting** to visit the castle.   The castle was **interesting** to visit.*

  However, not all alternatives work in the same context.
  *It was **wonderful** to see you.   ~~You were wonderful to see.~~*

- adjective + *of* + person + *to*-infinitive
  good, great, interesting, lovely, nice, wonderful
  *It was **good of you to see** me.   (= thanks for seeing me)*
  *It was **nice of you to think** of me.   (= thanks for thinking of me)*
  Compare: *It was **good to see** you.   (= I enjoyed it)*

adjective + *that*-clause or + *to*-infinitive

- *afraid, angry, annoyed, ashamed, astonished, certain, disappointed, glad, happy, pleased, shocked, sorry, sure, surprised, unhappy, upset, worried*

  In an infinitive construction the subjects of both clauses are the same.
  *We were **afraid to** go back to the house.*
  *I was **pleased to** see him again.*

- In a *that*-clause, the subjects of the clauses can be different.
  *I was **afraid that the bus** was going to crash.*
  *I'm **astonished that you** haven't won the prize.*

  Note that it is possible to leave out *that*.
  *I was **afraid the bus** was going to crash.*

- A past infinitive may be possible.
  *I was **disappointed not to have** won.*

adjective + *that*-clause

- *aware, it's clear, confident, hopeful, it's obvious, positive (very sure)*
  *I wasn't **aware that** the rules had been changed.*
  *It's **clear that** something has gone wrong.*

  Note that it is possible to leave out *that*.

- *feel + awful, bad, good, guilty, terrible*
  *I felt **guilty that** the others had been punished.*
  *I felt **good that** I had been proved right.*

adjective + *that*-clause with *should*

- Used in more formal speech and writing, and common in *it*-sentences.
  it's absurd, it's advisable, it's alarming, I'm angry, I'm anxious, I'm ashamed, it's awful, I'm content, I'm determined, I'm eager, it's essential, it's fortunate, it's funny, I'm keen, it's natural, it's unnecessary, it's odd, it's right, it's sad, it's silly, I'm sorry, it's strange, it's unusual, it's unfair, it's vital etc
  *It's **odd that you should say** that! I was just thinking the same thing.*
  *I'm **angry that they should take** that approach to this issue.*
  *We are **keen that he should take up** this post immediately.*

- Past simple is also possible.
  *It **was odd that** he should have forgotten.*

- These phrases can also be used informally without *should*.
  *I'm **angry that they are taking** that approach to this issue.*
  *It was **odd that he forgot**.*

adjective + *-ing*

- We can use *busy, no good, (not) worth + -ing*.
  We can use *feel + awful, bad, good, guilty, terrible + ing*.
  *Martin is **busy cooking** the dinner.   It's **not worth seeing** that film.*
  *I **feel terrible leaving** you alone like that.*

adjective + *to*-infinitive or *-ing*

- common in *it*-sentences
  *alarming, absurd, awful, cheap, dangerous, easy, *foolish, good, great, hard, hopeless, lovely, nice, pleasant, pointless, *rude, *sad, safe, *silly, strange, *stupid, *unwise, useful, useless, wise, *wrong*
  *It was pointless **to do that / doing that**.   It's **better** to go now.*
  *It was sad **to hear / hearing** your bad news.   It was lovely **to see / seeing you**.*

- Those marked * can also be used with a person, with a *to*-infinitive.
  *Jim was **foolish to give up** his job.   I'm **sad to say** I agree.*
  *You were **wrong to say** that.   She's **silly to spend** so much.*

- For *it's easy / hard* see above, adjective + *to*-infinitive

(it) makes me + adjective

- *(it +) make* + person + adjective + *to*-infinitive
  Use to describe how something makes us feel, with adjectives describing feelings: *angry, ashamed, aware, embarrassed, furious, glad, happy, miserable, nervous, sad, tired, uncomfortable, unhappy* etc.
  We can also use *it makes me feel* + adjective + *to*-infinitive.
  *This news **makes me feel embarrassed to be** a member of this company.*
  *Knowing that you love me **makes me glad to be** alive!*
  *It **makes me sad to know** that you feel you way you do.*

- We can turn the *it*-infinitive into an *ing*-form and use it as the subject.
  *Knowing that you feel you way you do **makes me sad**.*

- Informally we can also use *it makes me* + adjective + *-ing*, especially with *sad, happy, unhappy*.
  *It **makes me sad knowing** that you feel you way you do.*

be, seem, appear, look

- *Seem look, appear* can also be used instead of *be* in the constructions above.

1 Underline the correct form.

a Sorry, but I'm unable _to help_ / _helping_ you.

b It made me really angry _to find out_ / _finding out_ I'd been cheated.

c I think it's better _to leave_ / _leaving_ early.

d I'm sorry, but it wasn't clear _that you wanted_ / _to want_ the projects finished today.

e It's hard for some people _understanding_ / _to understand_ maths.

f It makes me angry _to see_ / _see_ so many people wasting their time.

g Helen is busy _getting_ / _to get_ things ready for her party.

h You are free _to go_ / _going_ whenever you want.

i This book about astrophysics is impossible _to understand_ / _understanding_.

j I was surprised _that I found out_ / _to find out_ what happened at the end of the film.

2 Write a new sentence with the same meaning, containing _should_.

a You are here at the same time! How odd!
  It's odd that you should be here at the same time.

b Why talk to me like that! It makes me angry!

c Maria has won first prize. And that's right.

d We have to work until 10.30! That's unfair!

e No repetition of today's unfortunate events! I'm determined about that.

f There's no security at all in the building! That's alarming!

g The employees feel badly treated. That's only natural.

h You have the same initials as me! That's strange!

3 Complete the sentences about sport training by writing one word in each gap. The first letter of the word is written for you.

a It's o obvious that if you have a serious sporting ambition, you should go about training in a serious manner.

b It's e_____ that you should follow a regular training programme.

c It's really p_____ to train a lot one week, and then miss training for two weeks.

d It's b_____ to work an another area of fitness (eg gym exercises, swimming etc) than do no training at all.

e You should also be a_____ that diet and rest are important.

f Too much training can m_____ you feel exhausted and unmotivated.

g It's also i_____ to get nutritional advice from an expert.

h Most athletes are c_____ not to train without proper warming-up.

i In some sports it is i_____ to improve your performance without visual recording and feedback from a coach.

j It's v_____ that you should refer any injuries to a sports clinic.

4 Write a new sentence with the same meaning containing the word in capitals.

a I'd put on plenty of sun-cream before you go out, if I were you. BEST
It's best to put on plenty of sun-cream before you go out.

b Your bad news upset me very much. SORRY

c I find this bad weather depressing. MISERABLE

d Something will have to be done, obviously. OBVIOUS

e Revising for exams takes up all my time at the moment. BUSY

f I really enjoyed meeting David Bowie. WONDERFUL

g I was unhappy that I had to lie to her. TERRIBLE

h I intend to make sure this doesn't happen again. DETERMINED

i Thanks for giving me a lift. GOOD

5 Complete the text with a word from the list in each gap.

aware   be able   clear   hopeful   impossible   possible   surprised   unusual   unwilling   unwise

Science news

Scientists carrying out research in swamps in Sumatra have discovered the world's smallest fish. The female is only 7.9 mm. It was thought to be **a** *impossible* that any living organism should survive in the swamps, as the water is extremely acidic. It is also very low in minerals and this is thought to explain why it is **b** .... for larger species to develop.

Researchers examining satellite data from the Antarctic have been **c** .... to find that there are large lakes and rivers beneath the ice sheets. 'It's **d** .... that Antarctic ice is moving much faster than we supposed,' said Professor Susan Graham from the Antarctic Survey. She was **e** .... to say whether this would mean a more rapid rise in sea levels due to melting ice. 'It's **f** .... to predict at this stage exactly what this discovery means, but it makes us **g** .... that Antarctic ice could be melting faster than we had thought.'

Scientists at NASA believe that they may **h** .... to detect earthquakes from space before they happen. It's **i** .... to monitor the build up of energy in the Earth's crust, and scientists are **j** .... that this information can be interpreted by computer programs which will give approximate predictions of future quakes.

GLOSSARY

EXTENSION ACTIVITY

Write five example sentences based on each of these patterns.

1 *I'm* + adjective + *that* clause   2 *It makes me* + adjective + *to* …

*Need more practice? Go to the **Review** on page 208.*

science

adjectives with infinitive or -*ing*

27 adverbs

adverbs and adjectives

- Some words ending *-ly* are not adverbs but adjectives: *friendly, lonely, silly, ugly* etc.
- Some adverbs and adjectives have the same form: *fast, dead, early* etc.
- *Hard* and *hardly* are both adverbs, but have different meanings.
  *I can **hardly** hear you.* (=almost not)   *You've worked **hard**.* (= with a lot of effort)

gradable and ungradable adjectives and intensifiers

- Adjectives that describe age, size, beauty etc can be measured or graded, and are called *gradable*. We can use intensifiers *very, extremely* with them.
  *This tree is **extremely old**.   It's a **very beautiful** painting.*
  *This problem is **extremely difficult**.   I feel **very unhappy**.*

- *Ungradable* adjectives cannot be graded because the qualities they describe are either present or absent.
  *This painting is **superb**.   This problem is **impossible**.*
  We cannot say   ~~This painting is **very superb**.~~

degree adverbs: *quite*

- With gradable adjectives (or adjective + noun) or adverbs, *quite* has a negative meaning: 'not very much' or 'less than expected'.
  *The film was **quite entertaining**, but I didn't really enjoy it.*
  *It's **quite a long way** to walk.*
  *They did the work **quite slowly**.*

- With ungradable adjectives and adjectives with an 'extreme' meaning, *quite* means *completely*. It can be used in the same way before a verb or adverb.
  *I'm sorry, but you are **quite wrong**.* (ungradable)
  *This puzzle is **quite impossible**!* (extreme meaning)
  *I **quite agree**.* (= I agree completely)
  *I can't **quite make** up my mind.* (not completely)

- *Quite* can be used with + *a* / *an* + noun to show that something is unusual or interesting.
  *That's **quite a car**!*

- *Quite* can be used with a superlative to mean 'very much'.
  *That's **quite the longest book** I've ever read!*

degree adverbs: *rather*

- With gradable adjectives (or adjective + noun) *rather* has a stronger meaning than *quite*. It can be used in the same way before a verb or adverb.
  *I think she's **rather clever**.   This is **rather a steep** hill.*
  *We all worked **rather hard**.   I **rather like** your friend Anna.*

- *Rather* is common with negative adjectives.
  *I thought the film was **rather uninteresting**.*
  *That was a **rather stupid thing** to do!*

- *Rather* is also often used with comparatives (see **Unit 28**).
  *This painting is **rather more** interesting.*

degree adverbs: *fairly*

● With gradable adjectives (or adjective + noun) *fairly* usually has a similar meaning to 'quite'.
  Fairly is less strong than *quite*. It can be used the same way before an adverb.
  *She's **a fairly good pianist**, I suppose.*   (= not <u>very</u> good)
  *They worked **fairly hard**, but that wasn't really good enough.*

Sophie is a fairly good pianist, but she needs to practise more.

intensifiers

● These are words that modify gradable adjectives and adverbs:
  very, extremely, really, terribly, particularly, awfully etc.
  *This is **really** tasty!   I thought the play was **terribly** boring.*

● *especially, particularly, really* are often used with verbs.
  *I **really admire** you!   I **particularly like** this one.*

● Some intensifiers tend to collocate with certain adjectives:
  absolutely ridiculous, completely useless, entirely unexpected, greatly admired, perfectly obvious etc.
  There are no rules to explain which intensifiers go with which adjectives.

● Some ungradable adjectives, usually with a negative meaning, can be modified by *utterly, completely, totally.*
  *The food was **completely awful**!*
  *The house was **totally destroyed** in the explosion.*

  These adverbs can also be used with verbs.
  *I **completely agree** with you.   We **utterly condemn** what has happened.*

comment and viewpoint adverbs

● Comment adverbs show the attitude of the speaker, eg *clearly, probably, luckily, surprisingly, foolishly.*
  *Sue **naturally** didn't agree.   We **obviously** liked it.*
  *Alan **kindly** gave us a lift.   **Stupidly**, I had left my wallet at home.*

● Other sentence adverbs indicate how we should understand what follows, eg *generally, apparently, supposedly.*

● Viewpoint adverbs tell us from what point of view the speaker is talking, eg *politically, financially, technically.*
  ***Environmentally**, this was a disaster.* (= From an environmental point of view …)
  ***Logically**, this can't be correct.*

  Sometimes phrases are used for emphasis, eg *politically speaking, from a political point of view, as far as politics is concerned.*

1 <u>Underline</u> all the forms which are correct.

a Bye for now. I'll see you *rather later* / <u>*soon*</u> / *obviously*.

b Everyone acted well, but I thought that Naomi did *absolutely* / *fairly* / *particularly* well.

c Tony can't *quite* / *really* / *surprisingly* decide what he wants to study at university.

d If you work *hard* / *extremely* / *hardly*, I'm sure you'll be a success.

e *Technically* / *Exactly* / *Apparently*, this is one of the best low-cost cameras currently available.

f Sorry, can you speak up – I can't *quite* / *rather* / *really* hear you.

g The thatched cottage was *completely* / *structurally* / *awfully* destroyed by a devastating fire.

h I'm leaving tomorrow *early* / *extremely* / *quite* in the morning, so I'll say goodbye now.

i See you again soon. Yours *truly* / *fairly* / *friendly*, Your friend Carl.

j *Luckily* / *Really* / *Fortunately*, we managed to catch the train at the last moment.

2 <u>Underline</u> all the words in brackets which can be used to complete the sentence.

a This French cheese you bought is _____ tasty. (absolutely, <u>really</u>, completely)

b The hotel turned out to be _____ expensive. (clearly, incredibly, luckily)

c Gina Evans is _____ expected to become deputy prime minister. (considerably, greatly, widely)

d The glue I bought was _____ useless so I had to buy some more. (completely, extremely, utterly)

e It was _____ obvious that Jack had made a mistake. (completely, perfectly, really)

f Sue was _____ disappointed to lose the match. (awfully, terribly, very)

g The police decided that Tom was _____ blameless. (entirely, extremely, greatly)

h We _____ appreciate all the help you gave us. (completely, greatly, widely)

i I _____ liked the first beach we went to. (absolutely, especially, particularly)

j Quite honestly, I think this is _____ ridiculous. (totally, utterly, very)

3 Write a new sentence with the same meaning containing the word in capitals.

a I really do understand how you feel. QUITE
 I quite understand how you feel.

b Nobody came to the party, which was unfortunate. UNFORTUNATELY

c I didn't find the match very exciting. RATHER

d The decision was disastrous from a financial point of view. FINANCIALLY

e We really didn't expect this result. ENTIRELY

f Mrs Burns has agreed to provide sandwiches, which is kind of her. KINDLY

g This printer is of no use at all! COMPLETELY

h I can't see the end of the road very well! HARDLY

i The answer is as obvious as it could be. PERFECTLY

j It's logical to suppose that the missing money must be in this room. LOGICALLY

4 Choose the best option, A, B, or C, to fill each gap.

Street design

People in some British towns are complaining about the **a** _B_ uninteresting streets and squares being designed by local council architects. It seems that one **b** _____ unexpected result of improved health and safety laws is a / an **c** _____ unimaginative approach to urban design. **d** _____ , street features such as fountains, steps and even cobbled roadways, are being excluded from our streets because of the risk of accidents. **e** _____ , many councils are paying out huge sums on claims for damages made against them by people who injure themselves in the street, and although it is **f** _____ possible to design a / an **g** _____ accident-proof urban environment, architects are taking the easy way out. Hence the **h** _____ dull designs we now see in some city centres. It seems **i** _____ obvious that streets should be safe, but it is also **j** _____ important that they should make us feel proud to be walking in them. **k** _____ , there are architects who have come up with **l** _____ more creative solutions, as a visit to many city centres will show. So in the end, it's up to local councils to try harder.

a	**A** *quite*	**B** *extremely*	**C** *hardly*
b	**A** *entirely*	**B** *very*	**C** *fairly*
c	**A** *rather*	**B** *fairly*	**C** *entirely*
d	**A** *Technically*	**B** *Financially*	**C** *Surprisingly*
e	**A** *Logically*	**B** *Apparently*	**C** *Naturally*
f	**A** *rather*	**B** *hardly*	**C** *fairly*
g	**A** *completely*	**B** *very*	**C** *extremely*
h	**A** *politically*	**B** *rather*	**C** *clearly*
i	**A** *extremely*	**B** *utterly*	**C** *perfectly*
j	**A** *surprisingly*	**B** *particularly*	**C** *hardly*
k	**A** *Fortunately*	**B** *Absolutely*	**C** *Really*
l	**A** *extremely*	**B** *fairly*	**C** *rather*

GLOSSARY

EXTENSION ACTIVITY

Give some opinions using *fairly, quite, rather* about the following:

  public transport in your town   TV in your country   learning a foreign language

*Need more practice? Go to the **Review** on page 208.*

adverbs

28 making comparisons

modifiers

- Comparisons can be modified to make them less extreme.
  *This is **probably the best** computer at the moment.*
  *Smiths is **one of the largest** companies in Britain.*
  *I've done **just about as much as** I can.*
  *This isn't **quite as easy as** I thought.*
  *The new one is **not nearly / half / nowhere near** as good as the old one.*
  *It is **nowhere near as good as** the old one.* **(informal)**

- Comparisons can be made stronger.
  *This is **easily the best** car in its class.*
  *Football is **far and away the most popular** sport in the world.*
  *It's **the most popular** sport in the world **by far**.*
  *Tennis is **far / a lot / much more** demanding.*
  *It's **much / miles / loads more** interesting.* (*miles* and *loads* are informal)
  *Golf is **every bit as interesting** as football.*
  *Golf is **rather more interesting** than I thought.*

comparative constructions

- *as* + adjective + *a* + noun + *as*
  *We asked for **as large a car as** possible.*
  *It's not **as long a journey as** I used to have.*

- *too* + adjective + *a* + noun
  *A nuclear war is **too terrible a thing** to contemplate.* **(formal)**

- *not as / so* + adjective + *to*-infinitive + *as*
  *It's not **as / so easy to explain** as I thought.*

- *sufficiently* + adverb + *to*-infinitive
  *Some students are unable to write **sufficiently well to pass** the test.* **(formal)**

- *more* + adjective + *than* + adjective, or *not so much* + adjective + *as* + adjective
  This construction can be used to make a distinction between two similar adjectives.
  *I was **more surprised than** angry.*
  *I was**n't so much angry as** surprised.*

be + comparative + to-infinitive

- *it* + *be* + comparative + *to*-infinitive
  *It's **cheaper to buy** a return ticket.*

- noun + *be* + comparative + *to*-infinitive
  *French is **easier to learn than** Chinese.*
  *Tennis is **more interesting to watch than** golf.* (= It's more interesting to watch tennis than golf.)

comparative + comparative

Two comparatives together are often used in descriptive writing, with verbs of becoming, changing, movement, etc.
  *The bike began to go **faster and faster**.*
  *The boat was getting **further and further away**.*
  *Jane was growing **more and more confused**.*

the + comparative or superlative + *of the* + number / quantity

- This structure can be used with a comparative to compare two things.
  *This is by far / easily **the more interesting of the** two.*

- *It* can be used with a superlative compare one thing with many things.
  *I think this one is **the best of the lot / them all / the bunch**.* (informal)

present perfect + superlative

We often use the present perfect with a superlative.
  *This is **the worst holiday I've ever had**.*   (I'm on holiday now)
  *That was by far / much **the best film I've seen** this year.*

the + comparative, *the* + comparative

- This structure is often used to give advice.
  ***The more** you put off going to the dentist, **the worse** you will feel.*
  ***The longer** you leave it, **the more painful** your tooth will become.*

- Adjectives and adverbs can be mixed.
  *The **more exercise** I take, the **more slowly** I run!*

- Fixed phrases include:
  The sooner, the better.**   **The more, the merrier.

like and *as*

- *as ... as*
  *Stay for **as long as** you want.   His hands were **as cold as** ice.*
  *You look **as white as** a ghost.*
  as ... as is often used in proverbial expressions.
  *He was **as good as** gold.   She's **as happy as** the day is long.*

- *like*
  *A caravan is **like** a house on wheels.* (it is similar)

- *look like, smell like*
  *The school **looks like** a prison.* (it resembles a prison)
  *You **smell like** a beautiful flower!* (the smells are the same)

- *look like, sound like*
  *It **looks like** rain.* (= it looks as if it's going to rain)
  *That **sounds like** the postman.* (= it sounds is if he has arrived)

- *feel like*
  *The pain **felt like** a burning needle in his arm.* (it is similar)
  *I **feel like** going out tonight.* (That's what I want to do)

- *work as / like*
  *Sue **works as a bar-maid** at weekends.* (She is a bar-maid)
  compare: *They **worked like slaves** to get the project finished.* (They are compared to slaves)

- *look as if* + present simple / unreal past simple
  *You **look as if you need / needed** a rest. You must be really tired.*

enough and *too*

- *not* + adjective + *enough* + *to*-infinitive
  *I wasn't **quite old enough to get** into the film* (= I was nearly old enough.)
  *He didn't **run fast enough to win.***

- *too* + adjective + *to*-infinitive
  *The rescue services arrived far / much **too late to save** him.*
  *It was **too great a temptation (for him) to resist**.*

making comparisons

133

1 Underline the best word.

a This camera is easily _the_ / _a_ best of its type.

b I wasn't so much surprised _as_ / _than_ shocked by the result.

c That was _probably_ / _not nearly_ the best football match I've ever seen!

d Politics is _too_ / _so_ important an activity to be left to politicians.

e It was _as_ / _too_ good an opportunity to miss, so I accepted the job.

f It's quicker to travel by bus _than_ / _like_ by car in the city centre.

g As the medicine took effect, Tina became _far and away_ / _more and more_ sleepy.

h You are _every bit_ / _miles_ as responsible for what happened as I am.

i Cats are _not nearly_ / _a lot_ harder to understand than dogs.

j This looks _like_ / _as_ the place. It fits the description, anyway.

k I think the Harry Potter films are _about as_ / _a lot more_ interesting than the books.

l This is definitely _the better_ / _the best_ beach we've been to so far.

2 Complete the sentence with one word in each gap.

a Budapest is one of the ___most___ beautiful cities in the world.

b You haven't really worked hard _____ to get a higher mark.

c The more exercise you take, the _____ you will feel!

d Quite honestly, I don't think this is as hard an examination _____ it used to be.

e This is _____ the most beautiful beach in the Mediterranean. Don't you think so?

f I've done just _____ as much shopping as anyone can do in one day!

g The film was every _____ as entertaining as I expected it to be.

h Most of Winterson's books are good, but I think this one is the best of _____ all.

i The boat drifted _____ and no-one noticed Sue had fallen into the sea.

j The hotel was a _____ more expensive than I expected, so I looked for a cheaper one.

k This crossword puzzle isn't quite as easy _____ I thought it was.

l Helen's paintings were far and _____ the best in the exhibition.

3 Complete the sentence with _like_, _as_, _too_ or _enough_.

a You can use the pool ___as___ many times as you like in a week.

b We called the fire brigade but they didn't get to the house soon _____ to save it.

c Wear some warm clothes. It looks _____ snow.

d Harry walked into the city centre, but it was _____ early to get any breakfast.

e A kilt is a bit _____ a skirt, but for men.

f At weekends Tony works _____ a cashier in a supermarket.

g They wouldn't let Dave into the club because he didn't look old _____ .

h You don't look as well _____ you did last week.

i Open a window! This room smells _____ a farmyard!

j The man next to me on the train was snoring _____ a pig.

k Quite honestly, I thought the news was _____ good to be true.

l The ladder wasn't quite long _____ to reach the upstairs window.

4 Choose the best option, A, B or C, to complete the sentence.

Memory

It's quite common to hear someone complain that their memory is a ___C___ as it used to be, or that the more things they try to remember, **b** _____ quickly they seem to forget. However, memory is **c** _____ complicated than we usually think. For example, remembering facts is not at all **d** _____ remembering how to perform an action, and it seems that we don't 'forget' how to ride a bicycle or drive a car. For some people, it may be **e** _____ to remember what they have just read **f** _____ recall where they left their car keys. Of course, **g** _____ interesting a topic is, the more we remember about it, and we are almost certainly **h** _____ to recall something we have read or seen recently, because it remains active in our memory. Where studying is concerned, there are certainly ways of making the memory **i** _____. It's **j** _____ to remember disorganized information, so note-making and summarizing are important, and the learner, not the teacher, has to do this. Regular reviewing of what has been learned is **k** _____ ways of strengthening memory. Some learners have **l** _____ visual than a verbal memory, and may remember more by associating ideas with visual images. There are plenty of books on the market which illustrate these techniques, always assuming that you can remember to buy one!

a	**A** less good	**B** worse	**C** not as good
b	**A** not nearly as	**B** the more	**C** it's just as
c	**A** by far	**B** easily	**C** a lot more
d	**A** the same as	**B** like	**C** as if
e	**A** probably	**B** much easier	**C** nowhere near as
f	**A** as	**B** than to	**C** the more
g	**A** just about as much	**B** more and more	**C** the more
h	**A** faster and faster	**B** far and away	**C** more likely
i	**A** more efficient	**B** as good as	**C** every bit as
j	**A** just as easy	**B** not so easy	**C** easier and easier
k	**A** as important	**B** more and more important	**C** one of the best
l	**A** just as good	**B** easily the best	**C** a better

GLOSSARY

EXTENSION ACTIVITY

A Make statements about these topics, including a comparative or superlative, and using some of the modifiers on the explanations page.

> a film, book etc   something you dislike   a sport   an activity

B Check these proverbial *as ... as* expressions. What is the equivalent in your language?

> as cool as a cucumber   as easy as pie   as free as a bird
> as hard as nails   as keen as mustard   as large as life

*Need more practice? Go to the **Review** on page 208.*

making comparisons

29 place and movement, prepositional phrases

prepositions and adverbs

- A preposition always has an object, but many prepositions of place can be used as adverbs (adverb particles) with no object.
  *What's **inside** the box?* (preposition)   *Shall we wait **inside**?* (adverb)

  Others include: *above, across, along, around, behind, below, beneath, by, in, inside, near, off, on, opposite, outside, round, through, under, underneath, up.*
  These adverbs often combine with verbs (see **Unit 31**).
  *Come **on**!   Please sit **down**.*

- Some adverbs cannot be used as prepositions and do not have objects.
  *Brian lives **abroad**.   The red car moved **ahead**.*

  These adverbs can often be used with a preposition and an object.
  *The red car moved **ahead of the** blue one.*

place

At, on and *in*, and their variations such as *within, upon* are used with *be* and verbs that describe position not movement, eg *sit, stand, live* etc.

- **at**   a place, an address, a house, a building, a point on a journey
  *She's **at the shops** / **at home** / **at 12 Green Street** / **at the cinema** / **at the Grand Hotel**.*
  *This train doesn't stop **at Acton**.* (point on a journey)

- **on**   *He was standing **on the chair** trying to reach the book on the top shelf.*
  *She was **on the bus** / **train** / **plane**.*

- **in**   a room, container etc, a city, country or area
  *It's **in the kitchen** / **in your pocket** / **in New York** / **in Greece** / **in the car**.*

movement

- With a verb of motion, eg *come, go* etc we use *to, into / onto, out of, towards* and other prepositions or adverbials that involve movement: *along, up / down, through, across* etc.
  *He ran **out of the house** and **down the street**.*

word list

- **round / around**
  These are used to talk about movement as in a circle.
  *Follow the road **round to** the left.   I've been walking **around** the centre.*

- **abroad, ahead, ashore**
  Ashore implies movement, while *abroad* and *ahead* can be place or movement.
  *Several boxes were washed **ashore** later that day.* (= to the shore)
  *Peter lives **abroad**.   I'm going **abroad** next week.*
  *Let's stop now we are **ahead**.   United have now moved **ahead** in the title race.*

- **across / over**
  With a verb of motion these often have the same meaning (from one side to the other).
  *She walked **across / over** the road.*

  Over can also mean 'covering an area' or 'above' with a verb of motion.
  *The police put a blanket **over his head**.   They flew **over the mountains**.*

- **along / on / alongside**
  Along means 'in the direction of a line'.   *He walked **along the top** of the wall.*
  On just describes place, not movement in a line.   *He sat **on the wall**.*
  Alongside means close to the side.   *The road runs **alongside the canal**.*

- *away (from), out (of), in, back (to)*
  Away (from) describes a movement, the opposite of *towards*.
  *Come **away from** the fire! It's dangerous.*

  To be away means you have left home for some time, perhaps to stay somewhere else.
  *Helen and Bill are **away** in France.   Anna is **away** from school today.*

  We often use *far* with *away*, or as an adjective to describe a place.
  *I wish I was **far away** from here.   It's at **the far end** of the room.*

  Out (of) can mean 'not at home', *in* can mean 'at home'. *Back (to)* describes a returning movement.
  *I'm afraid Maria **is out / isn't in** at the moment.   She's **out of town**.*
  *When will she be **back**?   Come **back**! I want to talk to you!*

- *backwards, forwards / forward*
  Both describe a direction of movement.
  *This bus is going **backwards**!   I reached **forward** and took her hand.*

  Backward and *forward* are also used as adjectives eg *a forward movement*.

- *by, past*
  Both describe something that passes, with verbs of motion.
  *We **walked past / by** the house twice before we recognized it.*
  *Someone **ran past / by** me and threw a bag to the ground.*

- *up / down*
  Often used with *road, street* etc to mean *along*.
  *I saw him as I was walking **up the road**.*

- *above, below, over, under*
  Above and *over* can be used to mean the same thing, especially when something is at a higher level exactly vertically.
  *We used to live in a flat **over / above** a restaurant.*

  In other contexts, *above* means at a higher level than something, and not touching it, while *over* means touching.
  *There is a forest **above the village**.   They put a blanket **over him**.*

  Under can mean 'covered by' while *below* has a more general meaning 'at a lower level'.
  *There's a cat **under the table**.   Terry lives in the flat **below us**.*

  Under can also mean 'less than' and *over* 'more than' with numbers and measurements.
  *The total cost of the project was **over £2 million**.*
  *There were **over 200 people** present.   Are you **over sixteen**?*

- *among, between*
  Among means 'in a number of things', *between* means 'in the middle of two things'.
  ***Among the guests** were several of Tom's old teachers.   We live half way **between** London and Oxford.*

- pairs
  Many adverbials are used in pairs to describe movement, usually in first one direction, then the other, and repeated.
  backwards and forwards   (back and forth)   to and fro   round and round   up and down   in and out
  *He's been pacing **backwards and forwards** for an hour.   The children were running **in and out** of the house.*

phrases

Many prepositions form phrases with nouns. Check meanings with a dictionary.

on	on trial	on average	on the way
in	in control	in charge	in the way
at	at war	at peace	at rest
above	above average	above the law	
below	below average		
under	under construction	under pressure	under suspicion

1   Underline the best word.

a   Jane isn't here at the moment. She's *in / <u>at</u> / to* the shops.

b   The children ran *at / down / on* the street shouting.

c   Does this bus go *at / to / in* Southampton?

d   Maria could see someone coming *at / towards / onto* her.

e   You'll find more coffee *in / on / at* the top shelf.

f   Are you coming *at / to / in* the cinema this evening?

g   Delivery on purchases is free *at / by / within* the London area.

h   With a shriek, Juliet fell senseless *at / upon / down* the floor.

i   Walk *along / on / through* Hillway Road until you come to the roundabout.

j   We spent an enjoyable evening *at / in / on* the theatre.

2   Write a new sentence with the same meaning containing the word in capitals.

a   Jim covered his head with a sheet and pretended to be a ghost.   OVER
    Jim put a sheet over his head and pretended to be a ghost.

b   Anna walked from one side of the street to the other.   ACROSS

c   I wish I were a long distance from here.   AWAY

d   When do you think Alan will return? I want to talk to him.   BACK

e   The dog was running in circles and barking furiously.   ROUND

f   I first visited Moscow more than forty years ago.   OVER

g   The temperature is lower than usual for this time of the year.   BELOW

h   The elephant was coming in Peter's direction at high speed.   TOWARDS

i   When he's not with his friends, David stops showing off.   AWAY

j   We paid less than €200,000 for this flat.   UNDER

3   Complete each sentence with a word from the list.

   abroad   among   ashore   away   by   backwards   ~~out~~   through

a   The Smiths aren't at home. They're ....*out*........ at the shops, I think.

b   The train went .... a long tunnel before it stopped in the station.

c   You have to stand the fridge at least 20 cm .... from the wall.

d   Helen has left the country and gone to live ....

e   Angela walked .... me without saying a word.

f   The boxes fell off the ship and were later washed .... 200 km away.

g   .... those present at the ceremony was the local MP, Claire Sims.

h   The car started slipping .... down the hill.

4 Complete the second sentence with one word so it means the same as the first. Use a dictionary if necessary.

a I really don't have any time to spare.

I'm ___in___ a hurry.

b Helen often travels abroad as part of her job.

Helen often travels abroad _____ business.

c As things are, we'll replace the faulty machine free of charge.

_____ the circumstances, we'll replace the faulty machine free of charge.

d Leave the building as quickly as you can. You are all at risk.

Leave the building as quickly as you can. You are all _____ danger.

e For ten long years, the two countries fought each other.

For ten long years, the two countries were _____ war.

f The company employees have stopped working in order to get what they want.

The company employees are _____ strike.

g After buying the remaining shares, Michael Wilson is now head of the company.

After buying the remaining shares, Michael Wilson is now _____ control of the company.

h I supposed that Jane would be bringing the keys with her.

I was _____ the impression that Jane would be bringing the keys with her.

i The police said that David was to blame for the accident.

The police said that David was _____ fault for the accident.

j Generally speaking, a child dies on the roads every day of the year.

_____ average, a child dies on the roads every day of the year.

5 Complete each sentence with one word.

a Please sit ___down___ over there.

b When the plane rose _____ the clouds, there was brilliant sunshine.

c The cat jumped _____ the wall and landed in next door's pond.

d I walked _____ the security check without noticing it was there.

e The policeman walked up and _____ the street checking the doorways.

f They're building a new house _____ our house and the primary school.

g We walked _____ the riverbank looking for a good place to fish.

h The teacher put Mark _____ charge of the class during her absence.

i Walking _____ is difficult if you don't look over your shoulder.

j After the murder, several people were _____ suspicion.

k The police officer stopped the fight and stood _____ the two men.

l You'd better turn round. The road is blocked further _____ .

6 Complete the text with one word in each gap.

How to find Fordwich House

Arriving by bicycle

Turn a *into* Fordwich Road from Malling Road.

Walk b _____ the visitors' car park until you come to the science building.

c _____ your right there is a footpath running d _____ the side of the building.

Take this footpath and follow it e _____ the left.

Directly f _____, there is a bicycle shed for visitors g _____ your left. Please leave your bicycle here. Fordwich House is h _____ the end of the footpath.

Arriving by car

Drive i _____ the town centre until you see a sign for Malling Road (A1202).

Once you have passed Downs Road take the second right, which is Fordwich Road.

Follow the blue signs for visitors' parking. Please park j _____ the visitors' car park. Walk k _____ the archway at the far end of the car park and take the footpath running l _____ the two large buildings. Fordwich House is at the m _____ end of the path.

7 Complete the sentence with one suitable word. Use a dictionary if necessary.

a The children kept running in and *out* of the room.

b The injured man was swaying to and _____ and looked as if he was about to collapse.

c That policeman has been walking _____ and down outside the house for an hour.

d I've been driving round and _____ this city all day!

e Next door's burglar alarm has been ringing _____ and off for two hours.

f People came from _____ and wide to see the Christmas lights in the main street.

g I've been going _____ and forwards to the hospital all this week.

h Our company offers cheap holidays both at home and _____ .

8 Complete the texts with a phrase from the list in each gap.

> along the western side   along the route   below average
> between   in danger   ~~in India~~   on the plains
> on the island   through the region   under construction

Global warming spells disaster for Ganges

Scientists **a** _in India_ have warned that an ancient glacier in the Himalayan region of Nepal is **b** of melting before the end of the century. Water from the glacier feeds the River Ganges which flows **c** , supplying water to millions of people. At present mountain rivers depend on glacial melt, and **d** , monsoon rains provide much of the water. However, these rains may well fall **e** levels in future as a result of climate change.

Hi-speed railway under construction

The high-speed rail project **f** in Taiwan promises to promote and balance economic growth **g** . The railway, which will run **h** of the country, involves the construction of a high-speed rail link **i** Taipei in the north and the port of Kaohsiung in the south. Six stations have been constructed **j** . (2005)

EXTENSION ACTIVITY

A   Translate the answers to Exercise 3 into your language.

B   Use a dictionary to find phrases beginning:

   above   below   under   above all else

   You can also use an Internet search engine.

30 time words

yet and already

- *Yet* comes at the end of questions and negatives, and in BrE is used with perfect tenses.
  *I haven't done it **yet**.   Have you seen that film **yet**?*

- *Already* is not normally used in negative sentences and it can take any position.
  *I've done it **already** / I've **already** done it.   He's **already** here.*

for, since, ago

- *For* is used with a period of time.
  *I haven't seen him **for weeks** / **for ages**.   I've been waiting **for an hour**.*

  For can be used with past simple as well as present perfect.
  *Maria lived in Rome **for a year**.*

- *Since* is used with a point of time, and comes before the time reference.
  *I haven't seen him **since last Thursday**.   I've been waiting **since 10.00**.*

- *Ago* refers to a period of time going back from now, and comes after the time reference.
  *I last saw him **a week ago**.   I started waiting **an hour ago**.*

by, until, so far

- *By* refers to an action which will happen at some point before a certain time, though we do not know exactly when.
  *I'll call you at six. I'll have finished my work **by then**.   (= at some point before)*
  ***By the time** I left, I was tired. (I became tired during the time before)*

- *Until / till* refers to a point of time at the end of a period of time.
  *I waited **until six**, and then I left.*
  *I'll be here **until Thursday**, but then I'm going to Paris.*

- For a situation that continues into the future, we use *so far*.
  *The police have been searching all day, but **so far** they haven't found anything. (and they are still looking)*

  Note that we cannot use *until now* in this context.

by, past

By or *past* with *go* can also describe time that passes.
  *A week went **by** / **past**, and no letters came for Helen.*

during, throughout

- *During* describes a point in a period of time, or a whole period of time.
  *The house was broken into **during the night**.   (point in a period)*
  ***During the day**, cats tend to sleep.   (whole period)*

- *Throughout* emphasizes 'from the beginning to the end'.
  *She had many successes **throughout her career**.   (all the time)*
  *There were several explosions **during the night**.   (at some points)*

after, afterwards, later

- *After* is a preposition and needs an object. *Afterwards* is an adverbial meaning 'after that', and can stand alone.
  *I'll see you **after the lesson**.*
  *I've got a lesson now. I'll see you **afterwards**.*

- *Later* or *later on* means 'at some time after this', and is more general. It can combine with a time word to make a more specific reference.
  *Bye for now. I'll see you **later**.   I'll see you **later this afternoon**.*

on time, in time

● *On time* means 'at the moment which was arranged'. The opposite is *late*.
*The train arrived exactly **on time**.*

● *In time* is the opposite of *too late*.
*The paramedics did not arrive **in time** to save the man's life.* (They were too late to save him.)

at last, finally, in the end, at the end

● *At last* is used when something you have been waiting for happens.
***At last** you are here! I've been waiting for so long to see you!*

● *Finally* introduces something that happened after a long time. It is usually positioned before the verb.
*We **finally** moved into the flat last Thursday.*

It also begins a sentence, to describe the last in a series of events or process, or introduce the last thing you want to say.
***Finally**, the products are packed in cardboard boxes and sent to the warehouse.*
***Finally**, I'd like to propose a toast to the bride and groom.*

nowadays, these days

Both are used to describe general present time.
***Nowadays** very few men wear hats.*
*Most people **these days** wear casual clothes.*

once, one day, at once

● *Once* refers to a past event, or something which used to exist but no longer does.
*I **once** ate nothing but apples for three days!*
*There was **once** a castle here, but it was destroyed many years ago.*

Once can also mean *as soon as*.
***Once** we got on the plane, we started to relax.*

● *One day* can have past or future reference.
***One day** I was waiting for the bus, when suddenly I saw …*
*I hope that **one day** everyone in the world will have enough to eat.*

● *At once* means *immediately*.
*Please make sure you complete the letter **at once**.*

● *All at once* means *suddenly*.
***All at once** there was a knock at the door.*

in, within

In and *within* can mean 'before the end of a period of time'. *Within* is more formal.
*Helen managed to finish the exam paper **in / within** fifteen minutes.*
*Please be sure to return the completed form **within fourteen days** of receipt.*

They can also have future reference.
*I'll see you **in four days / in four days' time**.*

next Tuesday etc

Although we use *on* with days and dates, we cannot use *on* if we use *next* or *last*.
*I'll see you **on Friday**.* *I'll see you **next Friday**.*

1 Underline the best word.

a Harry has *already* / *before* / *yet* decided which university he wants to go to.

b I've got to go now, but I'll see you *after* / *later*.

c If I haven't finished *past* / *by* / *until* six, I'll give you a call.

d Luckily, we landed exactly *in time* / *on time*, so we were able to catch our connecting flight.

e Apparently, Sam *at once* / *once* played football for Scotland.

f Kate waited for Pat *by* / *until* / *since* 6.30, but then gave up and went home.

g *Later* / *Once* / *One day* I got used to the water, it didn't feel so cold.

h Martin had a bad attack of hay-fever *within* / *during* / *on* the film and had to leave.

i *In the end* / *At the end* of the lesson Kate waited outside for her friend.

j I'll see you *on next Saturday* / *next Saturday* / *the next Saturday*, same place, same time.

2 Complete the sentence with one phrase from the list.

> at last   at once   by now   during the night   ever since
> for weeks   in half an hour   in the end   in time   until 5.30

a I'll be here _until 5.30_ , but I'll have to leave then.

b _____ , a tree next to the house was struck by lightning.

c The whole basketball team has been training hard _____ .

d Good news! The plumber has turned up to fix the shower, _____ .

e Wait for me here, and I'll be back _____ .

f That's very odd! Alan should have got here _____ .

g _____ , the whole trip turned out to be a disaster.

h I've been looking forward to meeting you _____ I heard you were coming.

i Tina arrived at the station just _____ to see the train draw away from the platform.

j I need to speak to you urgently. Please come to my office _____ .

3 Complete the text with one word in each gap.

Vesuvius

Vesuvius is a volcano which started forming about 25,000 years a _ago_ .
b _____ its best-known eruption in 79 AD, which destroyed the Roman cities of Pompeii and Herculaneum, the volcano had c _____ erupted many times, but its history had been forgotten. It seemed to have d _____ grown quiet, and was covered in gardens and vineyards. e _____ hundreds of years the Romans lived around the volcano without realizing the danger. f _____ the 79 AD eruption, which is thought to have lasted 19 hours, the volcano released about four cubic kilometres of ash and rock over a wide area. Down the sides of the mountain rushed a pyrocastic flow, a cloud of superheated gas and ash, which g _____ the time it reached the cities below had a temperature of about 350°C. This is probably what killed their populations. h _____ the eruption of 79 AD, Vesuvius has erupted around three dozen times, with four serious eruptions i _____ the past 100 years. It last erupted in 1944, and j _____ scientists learn to accurately predict the dates of serious eruptions, the risk of a sudden eruption remains a constant danger to the three million people living nearby.

GLOSSARY

4 Complete the sentence with one word.

a The convicted bank robber was sent to prison __for__ six years.

b I'm a bit busy now but I can see you _____ on.

c The contract should be ready for signing _____ a week.

d By the time we got to the theatre, the play had _____ started.

e It's ages _____ I last read a really good novel.

f There's no point in calling Chris, because he won't be awake _____ .

g I was _____ in your situation, so I know how you must feel.

h My project is due in on Friday, but I won't have finished it _____ then.

i The letter I had been waiting for _____ arrived on Saturday morning.

j Sam hasn't felt well _____ the beginning of the year.

5 Choose the best word, A, B or C, for each gap.

The Battle of Thermopylae

The Battle of Thermopylae took place nearly 2500 years **a** _C_ , when the Persian King Xerxes invaded Greece. A huge Persian army moved down the east coast of Greece **b** _____ it reached the narrow pass of Thermopylae, which was defended by Leonidas with 300 Spartans, 600 slaves and a small number of other Greeks. The Persian army halted, and soon **c** _____ a Persian scout reported to the king that the Greek defenders were combing their hair, their custom before battle. The Persians waited **d** _____ four days while they tried to persuade the Greeks to leave, but the Greeks held firm. **e** _____ on the fifth day the Persians launched an attack but the Greeks easily defeated them. **f** _____ the following two days, the Persians attacked again and again, but **g** _____ the end of the second day the pass had still not been taken, and thousands of Persians had been slaughtered. On the third day a traitor, Ephialtes, offered to show the Persians a secret path over the mountains to the rear of the Greek position. **h** _____ a large force set off and **i** _____ a brief battle with the Phocians who were defending the path, the main Greek army was surrounded. **j** _____ the small Greek force was completely destroyed, but their bravery and skill and the small size of their army shocked the Persians, and won them a place in history.

a **A** *since*	**B** *past*	**C** *ago*
b **A** *until*	**B** *after*	**C** *later*
c **A** *at once*	**B** *at last*	**C** *afterwards*
d **A** *since*	**B** *for*	**C** *within*
e **A** *Afterwards*	**B** *Finally*	**C** *Until*
f **A** *During*	**B** *By*	**C** *Already*
g **A** *by*	**B** *for*	**C** *later*
h **A** *On time*	**B** *Immediately*	**C** *Once*
i **A** *within*	**B** *until*	**C** *after*
j **A** *After*	**B** *In the end*	**C** *Already*

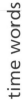

EXTENSION ACTIVITY

Write some examples which include these phrases.

since the beginning of the year   for three months   until the end of the week
by the time I leave today   later on   at the end   at once   one day

*Need more practice? Go to the **Review** on page 208.*

31 verb and preposition

This section lists verb + preposition followed by noun / verbal noun (-ing) patterns or a wh-clause. Some of these verbs also have verb + that-clause patterns, or can be followed by a wh-clause, or an infinitive, but these are not listed here.

Other meanings are also possible. Always check with a dictionary.

about

boast about / of	She is always **boasting about** her rich relatives.
dream about / of	I've been **dreaming about / of** you lately!
guess about	For centuries people have **guessed about** the nature of the universe.
protest about / against	The students are **protesting about / against** the war.

against

advise against	We **advise you against** travelling alone.
advise on / about	He **advises the government on / about** global warming.
argue for / against	The report **argued against** any change in the law.
argue with	Stop **arguing with** your sister!
decide against / in favour of	I've **decided against** buying a larger car.
decide on	We **decided on** Greece for our holiday.
insure against	You should **insure** all your belongings **against** theft.
vote against / for	More than a hundred MPs **voted against** the proposals.

at

glance at / through	I've only just **glanced at** the paper. I haven't read it in detail.
laugh at	We weren't **laughing at** you. (a person)
laugh about	Something silly happened, and we've been **laughing about** it all day.

between

choose between	You might have to **choose between** your work and your social life.

for

account for	Poor weather **cannot account for** the sheer number of accidents.
admire sne for	I **admire** you **for** your honesty.
allow for	In the financial plan, you have to **allow for** unforeseen future costs.
apologize for	I must **apologize for** being late. The traffic is a nightmare tonight.
blame sne for	I **blame myself for** everything that happened.
blame on	They **blamed the crash on** the bus driver.
charge for	We won't **charge you for** use of the gym. It's free for guests.
charge with	A man arrested nearby has now been **charged with** murder.
pay for	Let me **pay for** the coffee. You paid last time.

from

benefit from	Many people **have benefited from** the government's new policies.
deter from	The bad weather didn't **deter** people from travelling to the match.
differ from	How exactly does a toad **differ from** a frog?
distinguish sth from	It can be hard to **distinguish** fact **from** fiction.
distinguish between	Only experts can **distinguish between** genuine and fake paintings.
resign from	Tom was forced to **resign from** the company.
result from	The accident **resulted from** poor maintenance of the railway tracks.
result in	A three-hour delay **resulted in** the patient's death.
suffer from	After the accident, she **suffered from** double vision.

in

involve sne in sth	*The goal is **to involve workers in** the decision-making process.*
specialize in	*Anna **specializes in** Latin American dancing.*
succeed in	*Fortunately, we **succeeded in** rescuing all the passengers.*
trust in	*You should have **trusted in** me a little more.*

of

accuse sne of	*They **accused** Jim **of** stealing three cars.*
approve of	*I **don't approve of** children staying up too late.*
convict of	*After a long trial, he **was convicted of** theft and sentenced to four years.*
know of / about	*Do you **know of / about** any flats to rent in this area?*
remind sne of	*That old man **reminds** me **of** my grandfather.*
suspect of	*Police **suspect** the same man **of** breaking into four other houses nearby.*
taste of	*This is supposed to be chicken soup but it doesn't **taste of** chicken!*

on

base on	*The author **has based** the book **on** her experiences in China.*
concentrate on	*You need to **concentrate** more **on** your written work.*
congratulate sne on	*We must **congratulate** you **on** passing your driving test.*
depend on	*How much money you make **will depend on** how much you invest.*
elaborate on	*The prime minister refused to **elaborate on** his statement any further.*
impose on	*The council **has imposed** higher parking charges **on** 4x4 vehicles.*
insist on	*Jane **insisted on** seeing the doctor immediately.*

to

apply to	*The restrictions no longer **apply to** those over 75.*
attend to	*Please wait here. Someone will **attend to** you shortly.*
confess to	*Two men **have confessed to** stealing the lorry.*
devote sth to sne	*Louisa **devotes a lot of time to** her children.*
explain sth to sne	*Could you **explain** this **to** me please?*
object to	*Many local residents **have objected to** the redevelopment scheme.*
prefer sth to sth	*Personally I **prefer** tea **to** coffee.*
refer to	*Kate **referred to** the matter several times when I spoke to her.*
see to	*The central heating has broken down, but someone is coming to **see to** it.*

with

associate with	*Some people only **associate** sport **with** their school years.*
charge sne with	*They **charged** Bill **with** receiving stolen goods.*
collide with	*The speeding car **collided with** a tree.*
confuse with	*I'm sorry but you're **confusing** 'profit' **with** 'turnover'.*
deal with	*I've been **dealing with** this problem all morning.*
discuss sth with sne	*I need to **discuss** something **with** you.*
plead with	*She **pleaded with** her parents to let her go on the trip.*
provide with	*The school authorities **provides** all pupils **with** textbooks.*
tamper with	*Someone almost certainly **tampered with** the bus and caused the crash.*
trust with	*Can I **trust you with** a secret?*

(See also **Units 37, 38, 39**, phrasal verbs.)

verb and preposition

1 Underline the best word.

a The head teacher accused George *of* / *for* starting the fight.

b I haven't really read the report properly. I just glanced *for* / *at* it while I was on the train.

c I strongly object *to* / *for* the tone of the last paragraph of your letter.

d Sarah was involved *in* / *with* a traffic accident on her way to work.

e Harry pleaded *with* / *to* the judge not to send him back to prison.

f I always confuse Kate *with* / *on* her sister Maggie. It's hard to tell them apart.

g A diesel engine differs *from* / *to* a petrol engine in many important respects.

h Some business people find it hard to choose *with* / *between* their work and their family.

i I insisted *on* / *for* seeing the doctor at once, even though I did not have an appointment.

2 Complete the sentence with a preposition.

a The future of civilization depends __on__ our use of technology.

b I would advise you _____ taking any violent exercise before the leg has healed.

c The manager feels that nobody else can be trusted _____ the keys to the safe.

d Two boys have confessed _____ setting fire to the school.

e I'd like to congratulate you _____ passing the examination.

f We finally decided _____ a camping holiday in Greece.

g Jim has been suffering _____ severe headaches for some time.

h Helen voted _____ the proposal, but everyone else voted against.

i Harry says that his car accident has not deterred him _____ driving again.

3 Choose the best word, A, B or C, for each gap.

Goats in My Bathroom

Jane Howe's book *Goats in My Bathroom* is a __C__ her experiences on a Mediterranean island. Jane has always **b** _____ escaping from the rat race, but has never **c** _____ taking the plunge, and is trapped in a dull nine-to-five job in an insurance office. After a comic episode with an amorous boss, she **d** _____ the job and heads for the sun, and this is the story of her adventurous new life. And there is plenty to **e** _____ ! She has to **f** _____ short-sighted builders who can't understand a word she says, and then gets **g** _____ a dispute with her neighbours about the mysterious disappearance of twelve goats, which the whole village **h** _____ her. She is also the kind of person who seems to **i** _____ saying the wrong thing at the wrong time, but somehow, surprise, surprise, the local population ends up completely **j** _____ her. How does she do it? You'll just have to read the book.

a **A** *accounted for*   **B** *borrowed from*   **C** *based on*

b **A** *dreamed about*   **B** *benefited from*   **C** *advised against*

c **A** *concentrated on*   **B** *agreed on*   **C** *succeeded in*

d **A** *accounts for*   **B** *resigns from*   **C** *depends on*

e **A** *laugh about*   **B** *congratulate on*   **C** *confide in*

f **A** *choose between*   **B** *protest about*   **C** *deal with*

g **A** *provided with*   **B** *seen to*   **C** *involved in*

h **A** *accuses of*   **B** *blames on*   **C** *charges with*

i **A** *specialize in*   **B** *collide with*   **C** *involve in*

j **A** *marvelled at*   **B** *identified with*   **C** *devoted to*

4 Complete each sentence with a verb from the list.

> advise   apply   benefit   blame   boast   concentrate   provide   refer   specialize   tamper

a   If I were you, I'd __concentrate__ more on studying, and forget sport for a while.
b   We will _____ you with all the necessary equipment.
c   Richard likes to _____ about his success as a footballer.
d   Some people always try to _____ their poor performance on others.
e   A security guard caught someone trying to _____ with the CCTV camera.
f   I think you should _____ this problem to an expert.
g   Helen would like to _____ in psychiatric medicine.
h   Everyone in the area will _____ from the new social centre and sports club.
i   The new regulations _____ to anyone parking in the area between 8.00 and 20.00.
j   I _____ you against taking this case to court, as it will not succeed.

5   Complete the text with one word in each space.

Women and the First World War

After the outbreak of war in August 1914, as more and more men became a __involved__ in the war effort, many women replaced them at work. However, most employers **b** _____ between jobs they thought were suitable for women, such as office work and work in the clothing industry, and others, such as in heavy industry, where they believed women's skills **c** _____ greatly from those of men. There were other reasons why they did not **d** _____ of women working in heavy industry. They felt that women would not be able to **e** _____ in skilled engineering work, and they also feared that the unions would **f** _____ on restricting such jobs to men only. By 1916 the war effort had **g** _____ in a severe labour shortage, and the employment of women was to some extent **h** _____ on an unwilling nation by circumstances. Soon government industries such as munitions manufacturing **i** _____ on women to a great extent, and those who had **j** _____ to women in men's jobs were proved quite wrong, as women took on a range of jobs – engineering, welding, steel working, bus driving – which had previously been **k** _____ exclusively with men.

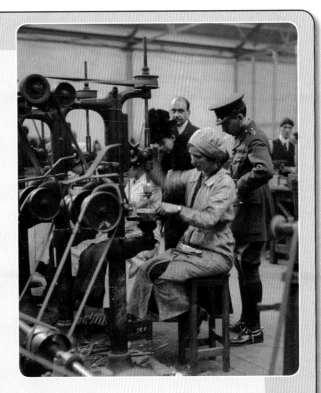

GLOSSARY

EXTENSION ACTIVITY

Write some examples describing things you:

> argue about   dream about   admire someone for   approve / don't approve of

*Need more practice? Go to the **Review** on page 208.*

verb and preposition

prepositions with adjectives and nouns

A selection of phrases is given here. Always use a dictionary to check meaning and context. Note that other prepositions may be possible, with different meanings. The most common are given here.

adjective and preposition

- *about*
  angry / annoyed about something
  anxious about the test results
  upset about / over / by something
  not sure about the answer

  curious about the subject
  pleased about / with your performance
  right / wrong about something
  sorry about / for being late

- *at*
  amazed at the difference / **by** the difference
  (+ similar words *shocked, surprised*)

  angry / annoyed at / with someone
  good / bad / awful / terrible etc **at** tennis

- *for*
  eager / desperate / impatient for news
  famous for its cheeses
  feel **sorry for** a person

  ready for something different
  responsible for the damage

- *from*
  absent from school
  different from / to the others

  free from additives
  safe from harm

- *in*
  interested in ballet

- *of*
  afraid of the dark
  ashamed of myself
  (un)aware of the problem
  (in)capable of doing better

  fond of children
  free of charge
  jealous of his brother

- *on*
  keen on gardening

- *with*
  satisfied with the work

  good with his hands

be + participle -ed + preposition

Note that many participles are used as adjectives, see also the list above.

- *about*
  I'm **concerned / worried about** Tom.

- *in*
  She was **absorbed in** her work.

  I'm not **interested in** buying the house.

- *to*
  I'm now **resigned to** the fact that I was wrong.
  Peter wasn't **used to** the hot climate.

  Maria is **addicted to** Internet chatrooms.

- *with*
  We are **faced with** serious social problems.
  Are you **acquainted with** this article?
  This meeting is **concerned with** the details of the scheme. (formal: *is dealing with, is about*)
  I was bored **by/with** this film.

  He was **confronted with** a difficult situation.
  The train was **packed with** people.

noun + preposition

- **for**
  *I have no **sympathy for** you.*
  *I have a lot of **respect for** your view.*
  *Is there **room for** one more?*
  *You must **take responsibility for** your actions.*

- **on**
  *Kate is an **authority on** Picasso.*
  *Coffee can have an **effect on** appetite.*

- **over**
  *You have no **control over** this dog!*

- **to**
  *This is an **exception to** the rule.*
  *We need a **solution to** this problem.*

- **with**
  *Sue has a good **relationship with** her parents.*

preposition + noun phrases

- **at**
  *More than a hundred homes are **at risk**.*
  *The company was **at fault** for the power cut.*
  ***At any rate**, nobody was injured.* (= anyway)

- **by**
  *I went to the wrong house **by mistake**.*
  *The antique vase was broken **by accident**.*
  *The army took over the country **by force**.*
  *We met completely **by chance**.*
  *Can I pay **by cheque / by credit card**?*
  *I know this poem **by heart**.*

- **for**
  *I'll be staying here **for the time being**.*
  *Our team won yesterday **for a change**.*
  *Sorry, but the car is not **for sale**.*

- **in**
  *Please describe what happened **in detail**.*
  *Jim was **in danger** and had to be rescued.*
  *You need to come to the office **in person**.*
  *The doctor asked if I was **in pain**.*
  *Vicky is **in trouble** with the police.*
  ***In theory** this works, but not **in practice**!*
  ***In business**, mistakes can be costly.*
  *Sam was **in tears** at the end of the film.*

- **on**
  *Storms occur once a month **on average**.*
  *Run! The house is **on fire**!*
  *I think Helen broke the cup **on purpose**.*
  *The railway workers are **on strike** again.*

- **out of**
  *I think that attitude is rather **out of date**.*
  *It's **out of stock** but we can order it for you.*
  *The books were **out of reach** on the top shelf.*
  *What a terrible shot! I'm **out of practice**!*
  *I'm afraid the lift is **out of order**.*
  *You're singing **out of tune**!*
  *I've been running and I'm **out of breath**.*
  *Good news. Jan is now **out of danger**.*

- **under**
  ***Under the circumstances**, we accept your excuse.* (= considering the special difficulties)
  *I was **under the impression** that you had finished the work.* (that's what I thought)
  *The fire was brought **under control** after an hour.*

- **without**
  *Please send my order **without delay**.*
  *This is **without (a) doubt** an important day.*
  *You must be here at 8.00 **without fail**.*
  *Everyone must be here, **without exception**.*

1 Underline the best word.

a Jane has been absent _from_ / at school for several days this month.

b Charles is very fond *for* / *of* the sound of his own voice.

c Sorry, but I'm not acquainted *with* / *in* the details of the plan.

d Kate is still anxious *for* / *about* her exam results.

e You know that stealing is wrong! You should feel ashamed *with* / *of* yourself!

f Because we are students, we get into all the museums free *from* / *of* charge.

g Our town is famous *for* / *from* its medieval churches.

h Is anyone interested *in* / *with* starting a tai-chi club?

i The transport system is incapable *from* / *of* dealing with the increasing number of commuters.

j The minister said she was sure the stadium would be ready *for* / *with* the opening of the Games.

2 Complete each sentence with a noun from the list.

> chance   date   detail   effect   fault   person   practice   purpose   room   time

a The teacher accused Tim of breaking the window on ....purpose........ .

b What .... did the closing of the factory have on you?

c My French is terrible! I'm really out of ....

d I found the address I was looking for completely by ....

e Before my parachute jump, the instructor explained in .... what would happen.

f The computer software I've been using is now out of ....

g Alan was unable to receive the award in .... but his manager received it on his behalf.

h There's .... for at least three more people at the back.

i I've decided to stay here for the .... being, and think about moving next year.

j The inquiry found that the builders were not at .... for the collapse of the building.

3 Complete the text using a phrase from the list in each gap.

> an effect on   annoyed by   at fault   aware of   better at   by mistake
> different from   ~~in business~~   without exception   wrong about

EFFECTIVE COMMUNICATION

a ...In business..... how staff communicate with each other and with customers is vitally important. Not everyone is b .... the importance of using both the right language and the appropriate tone of voice. You can give someone the right information, but be c .... the way you have chosen to express yourself when you do this. In this case, you could be sending the wrong message d .... , by putting it in an inappropriate way. The same issues apply to writing. The way you come across in an email may be very e .... the way you speak on the phone, or talk to someone face to face. Some people may even be f .... what you say if you appear too friendly or too distant. In writing, the organization of a letter or email, its typeface and general appearance can also have g .... how the message is understood. In this case your style of writing may be h .... , and you may need more practice. It may be true that some people are naturally i .... communicating than others, but all staff, j .... , need training in this area, and their performance should be monitored.

4 Write a new sentence with the same meaning, containing the word in capitals.

a I didn't know about the problem.   UNAWARE
   I was unaware of the problem.

b The drinks machine isn't working.   ORDER

c You didn't damage this chair by accident!   PURPOSE

d David was concentrating totally on his work.   ABSORBED

e Mr Gordon gets on well with his employees.   RELATIONSHIP

f Many people in the crowd were crying.   TEARS

g Send in your application at once.   DELAY

h Harry can't stop playing computer games.   ADDICTED

i We don't have this book in the shop, but we can order one.   STOCK

j Robert knows a lot about genetic engineering.   AUTHORITY

5 Complete the text with one word in each space.

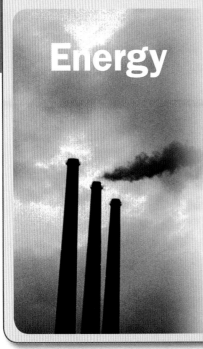

Energy

Nowadays we are all well **a** _aware_ of the problem of global warming, and it is generally agreed that we are all at **b** _____ from rising temperatures, climate change, and changes in sea levels. Massive consumption of fossil fuels, such as oil, coal and wood, is **c** _____ for greatly increasing the amount of CO_2 in the atmosphere, and many people believe that we are **d** _____ with possible catastrophe if we cannot bring this situation under **e** _____. However, there is another side to the fact that we are a world **f** _____ to the use of petrol, oil, coal and wood. In **g** _____, there is enough oil and gas to keep industrial societies going for several centuries, but in practical terms, we might have to get **h** _____ to looking for energy elsewhere, as resources dwindle and become more expensive. There is no **i** _____ for complacency when, on **j** _____, an American home uses more than 30 times as much electric light as an Indian one, and 1.6 billion people in the world have no electricity at all.

GLOSSARY

EXTENSION ACTIVITY

A Choose ten example sentences from the explanation pages, and translate them into your language.

B Choose twenty phrases from the explanations pages, and look them up in a dictionary. Note any other uses.

*Need more practice? Go to the **Review** on page 208.*

science

prepositions with adjectives and nouns

33 verbs followed by -ing or infinitive

followed by -ing

- *admit, avoid, *consider, delay, *deny, dislike, enjoy, escape, face, fancy, feel like, finish, can't help, involve, keep, *mention, mind, miss, practise, risk, spend / waste time*
  *If you do that, **you risk losing** the contract.*

- Verbs marked * can also be followed by a *that*-clause.
  *He **admitted that** he was wrong / **being** wrong.*

- Note that the *-ing* form can be preceded by a possessive.
  *I **dislike your being** on your own so much.*

followed by -ing or to-infinitive

- *mean doing, mean to do*
  *If you accept the job, **it means moving** to Scotland.* (= involve)
  *I **meant to post** these letters, but I forgot.* (= intend)

- *suggest someone does, suggest doing, suggest that someone should*
  *I **suggest we take** the bus as far as the square and then walk.*
  *In that case, I **suggest going** to see a physiotherapist.*
  *I **suggest that** you should re-apply next year.* (formal)

- *can't bear, love, like, hate, prefer*
  Normally followed by *-ing*, though *to*-infinitive is common in US English. In GB English, using *-ing* means that the activity is enjoyed (or not).
  *I **love going** to the cinema.   I **can't stand working** on a Saturday.*

  To-infinitive with these verbs describes a habit, what you choose to do, or think is a good idea.
  *I **like to get up** early on Saturday.   I **prefer to buy** organic vegetables*

  They can be used with a person + *to*-infinitive, to talk about another person's wishes.
  *My boss **prefers me to dress** formally at the office.*

- *forget, remember*
  Forget / remember to do are used for things we intended to do (often used when we didn't do them).
  *Did you **remember to** phone Jack?   I **forgot to** post my letter.*

  Forget / remember doing are used for thinking about a past event.
  *I **don't remember leaving** the party. I have no memory of it at all.*

- *try*
  Try to do describes an attempt.
  *I **tried to stop** him, but I failed.*

  Try doing describes an experience, or an experiment.
  ***Have you tried changing** the batteries? That might work.*
  *If you feel faint, **try putting** your head between your knees.*

- *go on, continue*
  Go on / continue doing and *continue to do* are used to talk about a continuing action.
  *The guests **went on eating and drinking** for three hours.*

  Go on to do is used to talk about the next in a series of events or actions.
  *Hillary Clinton **went on to become** president three years later.*
  *The prime minister began by describing what measures had already been taken, and **went on to outline** new proposals.*

- *regret*
  Regret doing describes being sorry for a past action.
  *I **regret not learning** to play the piano when I was younger.*

  Regret to do describes a person's feelings when something happens.
  *We **regret to announce** the death of Professor Angela Jackson.*

- *stop*
  Stop doing describes stopping an action.
  Please **stop shouting** at me like that.

  Stop to do is used when we stop one action in order to do another.
  The lecturer **stopped to have** a drink of water.

- *consider doing*, and *be considered to be*
  I'm **considering getting** a new job.
  She **is considered to be** the greatest tennis player in the world.

- *imagine doing*, and *imagine something to be*, *imagine that*
  I can't **imagine living** in a really hot country.
  I **imagined skiing to be** a lot easier.
  I **imagined that** skiing was a lot easier.

- *need / require doing, need / require to be done, need / require someone to do something*
  The windows **need cleaning**.
  These books **need to be put** back on the shelf.
  I **need you to help** me.

followed by *to*-infinitive or *that*-clause

- *agree, arrange, decide, demand, expect, hope, hurry, learn, plan, pretend, promise, swear, threaten, wish*
  We **agreed to meet** again the next day.
  We **agreed that** we would meet again the next day.

- *appear, happen, seem*
  followed by a *to*-infinitive, or with *it* + verb + *that*-clause.
  We **appear to** be lost.
  It appears that we are lost.

followed by bare infinitive or *to*-infinitive

- *help*
  We **helped** them **(to) find** a hotel.

- *make, force*
  make + object + bare infinitive, but with a passive *be made* + *to*-infinitive
  They **made him give** them the money.
  He **was made to give** them the money.

followed by bare infinitive

- *let*
  My parents **didn't let me go** to the club.

followed by an object and *to*-infinitive

- *assist, beg, command, dare, employ, enable, encourage, invite, select, send, *teach, *tell, train, *warn*
  Sarah **dared me to write** my name on the desk.

- verbs marked * can also be followed by a *that*-clause.
  They **warned him that** he was in danger.
  They **warned him not to** interfere.

- With *to*-infinitive: *advise, instruct, order, persuade, recommend, urge*

  (See also **Unit 18** report verbs.)

verbs followed by *-ing* or infinitive

155

1 <u>Underline</u> the correct form.

a Joe dared his brother *to kick* / *kicking* the ball out of the window.

b I used to spend a lot of time *to worry* / *worrying* about the future.

c Gina tried *to open* / *opening* the door, but it seemed to be stuck.

d The police made the two boys *to pick up* / *pick up* the litter they had dropped.

e All night people kept *to bang* / *banging* car doors outside in the street.

f I remember *to appear* / *appearing* in the Christmas play when I was at primary school.

g Our teacher likes us *to stand up* / *standing up* when she enters the room.

h Your car really needs *to clean* / *cleaning*! It's filthy!

I I can't help *to wonder* / *wondering* whether we are going in the right direction.

j My parents always encouraged me *to think* / *thinking* for myself.

2 Complete each sentence with a verb from the list.

avoid   bear   consider   deny   ~~involve~~   imagine   mind   regret   risk   stop

a This construction project will ____involve____ demolishing part of a run-down industrial area.

b Helen says she doesn't _____ coming in early tomorrow and dealing with that problem.

c Both teenagers _____ taking part in the robbery, and claim they were not in the area.

d I think we should _____ causing unnecessary damage to the woodland area.

e If you exercise without warming up, you _____ pulling a muscle.

f I can't _____ wearing the sort of clothes they wore in the 19th century!

g Please _____ staring at me like that! It makes me nervous!

h People often _____ not studying seriously during their schooldays.

i Would you _____ selling this painting if you received a suitable offer?

j Sheila can't _____ being pestered by fans who want her autograph.

the arts

3 Complete the text using one word in each gap.

Vincent Van Gogh

Vincent Van Gogh a ____spent____ the 37 years of his life as a more or less unknown artist. He did not b _____ painting seriously until his late twenties, and at one time c _____ becoming a priest because of his beliefs. His beliefs also d _____ him living in extreme poverty among the outcasts of society. His brother Theo, who was an art dealer, e _____ him to take up painting, and f _____ to support him financially throughout his life. Vincent's precarious mental state g _____ to have been made worse by alcohol and ill health. A stay in Paris from 1886 to 1888 h _____ Vincent to study Impressionists such as Manet and Degas, and i _____ getting to know many artists, including Paul Gauguin. Van Gogh and Gauguin painted together at Arles in the south of France, where Vincent's mental state worsened and he j _____ to murder Gauguin, before famously cutting off part of his ear. Two years later Vincent committed suicide. Since his death, his paintings have k _____ on to become among the most famous of the 19th century.

GLOSSARY

4 Write a new sentence with the same meaning, containing the word in capitals.

a Apparently, the match will be cancelled.   APPEARS
   It appears that the match will be cancelled.

b The burglars jumped out of the window so they weren't caught.   AVOID

c People think *Ulysses* is Joyce's greatest work.   CONSIDERED

d They intend reaching the mountains by the end of the week.   PLANNING

e I don't like wasting time watching television.   PREFER

f Would you like to go skating on Friday?   FANCY

g We can't continue to ignore this problem.   GO ON

h My parents didn't allow me to stay out late.   LET

5 Complete the text using one word or phrase from the list in each gap.

continued to   decided to   demand   expected   forced   involved
persuade   regretted   seemed to   stopped   urged   warned

The decision to drop atomic bombs on Japan

Since the US dropped the first atomic bombs on Japan in 1945, historians
have a **continued to** argue about whether or not this was justified. By
1945 Japanese forces had been severely damaged, but they had not
b .... fighting. American forces had c .... invade
Japan, but an invasion would have d .... landing in several
places, and military planners e .... that there would be at least a
million US casualties, and far more Japanese ones. Dropping the newly-tested
atomic bomb f .... be a better alternative, which might
g .... the Japanese government that surrender was the best
option. After the first bomb was dropped on Hiroshima on 6 August, killing
and wounding over 150,000 people, the American government
h .... the Japanese that further bombs would follow, and i .... them to surrender.
A second bomb dropped on Nagasaki three days later, which j .... the Japanese to accept that
they were in an impossible situation, and the government surrendered on 14 August. Only when US scientists
and medical experts finally examined the devastated cities and their suffering populations did the terrible
effects of atomic weapons become clear. Many Americans k .... that such weapons had
been used, and began to l .... they would never be used again.

GLOSSARY

EXTENSION ACTIVITY

Write examples of things you like / can't bear / regret / want to stop doing.

*Need more practice? Go to the **Review** on page 208.*

verbs followed by *-ing* or infinitive

157

34 relative and non-finite clauses

defining relative clause

A defining relative clause gives information about a person or thing etc. It comes immediately after the thing it defines, and is not separated from it by a comma. It is central to the meaning of the sentence and cannot be removed without changing this meaning.

*There are only one or two Greek Islands **that I haven't visited**.*

non-defining relative clause

A non-defining relative clause gives extra information which does not define the person or thing etc it follows. It is separated from the main clause by commas.

*Naxos, **which I've visited several times**, is my favourite island.*

which and *that*

- We can use *which* or *that* in defining clauses. *Which* is more formal.
  *There are only one or two Greek Islands **which / that I haven't visited**.*

- *Which* is used in a non-defining clause.

- *That* cannot follow a preposition.
  *It is an island **on which / where** important excavations have taken place.*

who and *whom*

- *Who* is often replaced by *that* in everyday use in defining clauses.
  *The people **who / that** own that house are away on holiday.*

- *Whom* is the object form of *who*, and is used formally in object clauses.
  *He was exactly the person **whom** I wanted to see.*

  However, *who* or *that* are used in everyday speech instead of *whom*, or *whom* can be left out. (see below)
  *He was exactly the person (**who / that**) I wanted to see.*

- *Whom* is used after a preposition, but this is often avoided in everyday use by putting the preposition at the end of the clause.
  *A hundred adults were asked to detail the individuals **with whom** they had conversed over the period of one day.* (formal)
  *They were asked to list **all the people they had spoken to**.* (less formal)

whose

- *Whose* is the possessive form of *who*, and is used in both defining and non-defining clauses. It can apply to both people and to things.
  *Make a list of everyone **whose** last name ends in '-son'.*
  *Make a list of countries **whose** population is greater than 20 million.*

prepositions and relative pronouns

- In everyday use we often put the preposition at the end of the clause to avoid over-formality.
  *The hotel room, **for which we had already paid**, turned out to be very noisy.*
  *The hotel room, **which we had already paid for**, turned out to be very noisy.*
  *The minister, **from whose office the e-mail originated**, denied being involved.*
  *The minister, **whose office the e-mail originated from**, denied being involved.*

- We do not split phrasal verbs in this way.
  *The story, **which** she had **made up**, was accepted as the truth.*
  **The story, ~~up which she had made~~, was accepted as the truth.* (not possible)

when, where, why, how

- in defining clauses
  *That's **the office where my brother works**.   I can't think of **a time when I wasn't** mad about football.*

- in non-defining clauses
  *Kate loved being in London, **where there was** so much to do.   I left at 5.00, **when it started to get dark**.*

- We often use *why* after reason.
  *I can't think of a **reason why I should help** you.*
  ***The way that** can be used instead of* how.
  *Tom didn't understand **the way that** the photocopier worked.*

leaving out the relative pronoun

- In defining object clauses it is possible to leave out the relative pronoun.
  *This isn't the book (**that / which**) I ordered.*

- In a non-defining clause it is not possible to leave out the relative pronoun.
  *This book, **which** I bought secondhand, was really cheap.*

reduced relative clauses

- In defining clauses we can leave out the relative pronoun and part of the verb phrase to leave
  a participle acting as an adjective defining the noun.
  *Peter was the only one of the group (who was) **not arrested** after the match.*
  *Tell the people (who are) **waiting** outside to come in.*

- We also use reduced relative clauses in non-defining clauses, usually in descriptive writing.
  *The two friends, (who were) **soaked to the skin**, eventually arrived home.*

anyone who etc, those who etc

- We can use relative clauses after *anyone*, *something* etc, and after *this / that / these / those*.
  *Have you seen **anyone who** looks like this?   I think there is something **(that) we need** to discuss.*
  ***Those who stayed** to the end saw an exciting finish to the match.*

- Reduced clauses are also possible with a participle acting as an adjective.
  *We went back and picked up all **those** (who had been) **left** behind.*

sentence relative: which

- We can use *which* to relate a non-defining clause to the main clause, and act as a comment upon it.
  *Several people turned up late, **which wasn't surprising**.*

- We can use other phrases in the same way: *at which time / point, by which time, in which case*.
  *You may experience swelling or discomfort, **in which case** contact your doctor.*

what, whatever, whoever, whichever

- *What* can be used as a relative pronoun meaning *the thing* or *things which*.
  *I don't know **what to do**.*

- We can use a *what*-clause as a subject for emphasis.
  ***What I really want** is a new bike.*

- *Whatever* and *whoever* meaning 'anything / anyone at all' can be used in the same way.
  ***Whatever** you do, do it now!   You can bring **whoever you like** to the party.*

- *Whichever* can be used instead of *whatever* when there are more than two items to choose from.
  *There are three rooms, You can sleep in **whichever you prefer**.*

all of, most of, some of, none of etc

- These can combine with *which* and *whom*.
  *He owns three cars, **one of which** is over fifty years old.*

1 <u>Underline</u> the best word or words.

a The historic castle, <u>*which*</u> / *what* was rebuilt after the war, contains the city museum.

b *What* / *Whatever* I would like to do next is go and visit the Modern Art Gallery.

c I didn't know exactly *whom* / *who* I was working with on the project.

d You may tick the 'No Publicity' box, in *that* / *which* case no details of your win will be given to the press.

e I've never seen anyone *who* / *which* can kick a ball as hard as David can!

f I'm afraid this isn't the meal *whom I asked for* / *I asked for*.

g Can someone tell me *that* / *what* I am supposed to be doing?

h Brussels, *that* / *which* I've visited several times recently, is a good place to spend a weekend.

i After eating so much I felt sick, *that* / *which* wasn't so surprising!

j The police asked me if I had seen anyone *who* / *which* fitted the description.

2 Complete the sentence with the correct word.

a Many Asians live in mega-cities, that is, cities ___*whose*___ population is greater than 10 million.

b Tony, _____ brother Dave also played for Scotland, eventually became team captain.

c I'm the sort of person _____ likes being busy all the time.

d We looked at three flats to let, one of _____ seemed suitable, though it was expensive.

e Elsa seemed like the kind of person to _____ happiness came almost naturally.

f This e-mail is intended solely for the use of the person to _____ it is addressed.

g It was a mistake _____ both generals were to regret before the day was over.

h The buildings _____ were damaged in the earthquake were marked with a red cross.

i Sophia lived alone in a house owned by her father, for _____ she paid no rent.

j That's the building _____ I used to work.

3 <u>Underline</u> the best word or blank (–) for no word.

Are men better at maths than women?

One of the stereotypes about the differences between men and women, **a** *who* / <u>*which*</u> / *–* seems to be supported by some research, **b** *what* / *–* / *where* is that men are better at maths. According to brain research, levels of grey matter, **c** *it* / *who* / *which* creates processing centres in the brain, are higher in men than they are in women. On the other hand, it is women **d** *who* / *-* / *they* have more white matter, **e** *–* / *it* / *which* creates the links between processing centres in the brain. **f** *Does* / *Which* / *What* this seems to suggest is that while the male brain **g** *–* / *that* / *it* contains more areas for processing information, **h** *which* / *what* / *who* means that the male brain has more capacity to solve maths problems, it is the female brain **i** *it* / *that* / *and* has the greater ability to perceive patterns. In other words, it is brain structure **j** *what* / *it* / *that* makes men better at maths, but **k** *whose* / *which* / *where* also makes women better at communicating. However, other researchers argue that it is the stereotyping itself **l** *it* / *–* / *that* causes the difference in performance in maths, rather than any innate ability. Women **m** *–* / *who* / *which* believe they are inferior at maths, especially when they take maths tests in rooms **n** *where* / *whose* / *which* men are present, tend to produce the kind of results **o** *–* / *and* / *they* expect to produce. Research **p** *–* / *which* / *what* analyses maths test results on a large scale suggests that the results attained by women are just as good as those attained by men.

GLOSSARY

4 Write a new sentence with the same meaning, containing the word in capitals.

a This man jumped over the counter and took the money. WHO
This is *the man who jumped over the counter and took the money* .

b It wasn't unusual for George to turn up late. WHICH
George turned ....

c Some of the many people we questioned gave us good descriptions of the robber. WHOM
We questioned ....

d My aunt and uncle live in that house. WHERE
That's ....

e Everyone likes Angela when they meet her. WHO
Everyone ....

f Many people came to the meeting but some were half an hour late. WHOM
Many people came to the meeting, some ....

g We sheltered from the rain in a shepherd's hut that we found eventually. WHERE
We eventually ....

h The train was extremely crowded and stopped at every station. WHICH
The train, ...

i I thought the bus stopped outside a different building. ISN'T
This ....

---

5 Complete the text with one word in each gap, or leave blank where possible.

Jane Austen

Jane Austen, **a** *whose* novels feature many clergymen, had two brothers
b .... joined the church, and two others **c** .... careers in the navy
are also reflected in her novels, in **d** .... several naval officers appear.
She also had a sister, Cassandra, with **e** .... she had a close relationship.
They exchanged frequent letters, from **f** .... historians have learnt much
about **g** .... Jane was doing and thinking during a life **h** .... was
fairly uneventful. All **i** .... we know of Jane Austen's appearance is based
on Cassandra's coloured sketch **j** .... hanging in the National Portrait
Gallery in London. We know Jane was encouraged to write by her brother Henry, **k** .... also wrote
himself, and that the family borrowed novels from the local library, **l** .... influenced Jane's writing.
Although Jane Austen wrote during the period of the French Revolution and the Napoleonic Wars,
m .... she wrote about was largely confined to **n** .... she knew: the manners of mainly well-
off people **o** .... living in small-town society near London, and the problems **p** .... faced by
women in choosing a marriage partner. Her novels also show women **q** .... have chosen the
wrong partner, or those **r** .... difficult financial situation influences their behaviour.

GLOSSARY

the arts (sidebar)

EXTENSION ACTIVITY

Complete these sentence examples.

... is a place where ...   ... is someone who...   What I really want is ...

*Need more practice? Go to the **Review** on page 208.*

relative and non-finite clauses (sidebar)

35 adverbial clauses

time

- Adverbial time clauses are introduced by time conjunctions: *when, after, as, as soon as, before, by the time, during the time, immediately, the moment, now, once, since, till / until, whenever, while.*
  Anna started to play the piano **when she was five**.
  Keep the book for **as long as** *you like*.

- If the clause comes first, we usually put a comma after it.
  The moment he came into the room, *I recognized him*.
  As I was going upstairs, *I heard a strange noise*.

- In adverbial time clauses referring to the future we do not use *will*; we use present simple, or present perfect to emphasize completion.
  As soon as I hear *any news, I'll let you know*.
  Let me know **as soon as you've** *finished*.

  Note that we can use *will* future in relative clauses beginning with *when*.
  Can you let me know **when you'll be** *coming back*.

- Note that *as long as* has a similar conditional meaning to *provided*.
  You can borrow my bike, **as long as** *you bring it back tomorrow*.

  As long as can also mean 'for the length of time'.
  You can keep that book for **as long as** *you like*.

place

- Introduced by *where, wherever, anywhere, everywhere*. Clauses beginning *where* normally come after the main clause.
  There is an impressive monument **where the battle was fought**.
  You can sit **wherever you like**.
  Everywhere David goes, *people ask him for his autograph*.

manner

- Introduced by *as*, and normally coming after the main clause.
  I took the train, **as you recommended**.

- Introduced by *the way* in colloquial English.
  You didn't write this **the way I told you to**.

- Often used in comparisons with *(in) the way (that), (in) the same way (as)*.
  You're not doing it **in the same way that** *you did it before*.

- *As if* and *as though* can be used after *be, act, appear, behave, feel, look, seem, smell, sound, taste*.
  He acted **as if he had seen** *a ghost*.
  It sounds **as though they are having** *a good time*.

reason

- Introduced by *as, because, since, seeing (that)*.
  Because I'm late, *I won't be able to meet you after all*.
  Since you refuse to answer my letters, *I am referring this matter to my lawyers*.
  Seeing that I am paying for the tickets, *I think I should decide what we see*.

- Introduced by *for*, but coming after the main clause. This is often formal or literary.
  They said nothing to anyone, **for they were afraid**.

contrast

- Introduced by *although, though, even though, considering (that)*.
  Even though Tim goes to fitness classes, he is a very poor runner.
  *Helen plays extremely well, **considering how young she is**.*

- Introduced by *while, whereas*, in formal speech and writing, and by *much as*, usually followed by verbs of liking etc.
  Much as / While we appreciate your work, I'm afraid we have to let you go.
  *The research found that **whereas** women under stress talk about it with other women, men under stress tend to keep their problems to themselves.*

- *however* + adjective
  *We are determined to complete the project, **however difficult it is**.*

- *no matter* + question word
  ***No matter where you live**, the weather will have some effect on you.*

- *wh*-question word + -*ever*
  ***Wherever you live**, the weather will have some effect on you.*
  *I'm going to do it anyway, **whatever you think**.*

purpose

- Introduced by *so (that)* usually followed by a modal auxiliary.
  *I asked you to come early **so (that) we could** discuss last night's meeting.*

- Introduced by *in order that* in formal speech and writing.
  *Legislation is needed **in order that this problem** may be dealt with effectively.*

- *So as (not) to* is used with infinitive constructions.
  *I closed the door quietly **so as not to disturb** anyone.*

- Introduced by *in case*, meaning 'to be prepared for a possible event'.
  *We turned down the music **in case it disturbed** the neighbours.*

result

- Introduced by *so* + adjective / adverb + *that*, or *such (a)* + (adjective) + noun + *that*.
  *He's **so tall that** he can easily touch the ceiling.*
  *They ran away **so fast that** nobody could catch them.*
  *He's **such a tall boy that** …   They were **such fast runners that** …*

- Introduced by *so much / many / few / little + that*
  *There were **so many people in the room that** some had to sit on the floor.*

- In reduced clauses.
  *He's **so tall!**   He's **such a tall boy!***
  *There were **so many people** in the room!*

1 Underline the best words.

a Tina was given the job, _even though_ / _seeing that_ she did not have the required experience.

b _Seeing that_ / _Considering that_ it's his birthday today, Tom has decided to take a day off.

c This is _the way_ / _as if_ we deal with hooligans in this country.

d We'd better take some money with us, _seeing that_ / _in case_ we can't find a cash machine.

e _However_ / _Much as_ I admire his earlier work, I think that his recent novels are rather poor.

f _The moment_ / _until_ you see anything move, press this alarm bell.

g _No matter what_ / _However_ you say, I still can't really forgive you for what you have done.

h Unfortunately Carol didn't pass the exam, _although_ / _however_ she studied really hard.

i _As soon as_ / _Everywhere_ I look these days, I seem to see people dressed the same.

j _In case_ / _Considering that_ she's only been learning the piano for six months, Jan plays really well.

2 Rewrite each sentence without the word or words <u>underlined</u>, and using a word or words from the list.

> anywhere   as soon as   now   once   until   when   whenever   where

a <u>Any time</u> you're in the area, drop in and see us.
  Whenever you're in the area, drop in and see us.

b <u>The moment</u> I saw you, I knew I liked you!

c Fiona started training as a ballet dancer <u>at the age of</u> six.

d I won't leave <u>before</u> you come back.

e You can park your car <u>wherever</u> you like outside.

f You're <u>finally</u> here, so you'd better sit down.

g <u>When</u> the exams are out of the way we can start learning something new.

h The memorial shows <u>the site</u> of the plane crash.

3 Complete the text with one word in each gap.

The Earth and the Sun

a _Although_ most ancient Greek philosophers considered the Earth to be flat, Eratosthenes calculated that it was a sphere and worked out its circumference around 240 BC. b _____ that he used only rough estimates, his calculation is surprisingly accurate. c _____ it seemed obvious that the Sun moved in the sky and the Earth stood still, this was the basis of astronomy d _____ the work of Copernicus in the 16th century.
e _____ Copernicus's work was published in 1543, it became increasingly difficult for scientists to see the universe in the f _____ they had done before, with the Earth at the centre of the universe. However, the theory was g _____ controversial for religious reasons that it did not become widely known.
h _____ Galileo came to the same conclusions as Copernicus in 1610, he was accused of heresy by the Church and imprisoned, in i _____ his view of the universe encouraged people to doubt the existence of God.

4 Write a new sentence with the same meaning, containing the word in capitals.

a They seem to be having a good time. SOUNDS
 It sounds as if they are having a good time.

b You are supposed to be doing this differently. THE WAY

c He seemed to be carrying something. LOOKED

d You suggested I took up jogging, and I did. AS

e By the way he behaved, I thought he owned the place. AS THOUGH

f By the taste, the meat hadn't been cooked properly. TASTED

g Peter didn't conduct the experiment according to instructions. THE WAY

5 Choose the best word, A, B or C, for each gap.

Will human beings ever live on other planets?

a **B** we have become accustomed to the idea of space travel, and in films and fiction it seems b .... space travel is inevitable, it appears unlikely that human beings will ever get any further than Mars, our nearest neighbour. c .... films we make about space travel, the fact is that it remains technologically challenging, and extremely expensive. d .... the distances involved are immense, any voyage outside our solar system would take hundreds of years using current technology. e .... human beings went into space, they would have problems of how to eat and breathe, and their spaceship would have to carry vast amounts of fuel f .... cover the distance. Even Mars is g .... far away that it would take about six months to get there. h .... the distance between Earth and Mars varies, astronauts would have to wait for nearly two years i .... they could return using the shortest journey time. j .... it could cost as much as $100 billion, a manned mission to Mars is planned for sometime between 2010 and 2020.

	A	B	C
a	A *Since*	B *Although*	C *So*
b	A *the moment*	B *since*	C *as though*
c	A *Although*	B *Considering*	C *No matter how many*
d	A *Since*	B *In order that*	C *So*
e	A *Wherever*	B *Although*	C *Before*
f	A *even though*	B *in order to*	C *as if*
g	A *so*	B *as*	C *after*
h	A *So*	B *Wherever*	C *As*
i	A *when*	B *since*	C *before*
j	A *As if*	B *Even though*	C *So that*

Surface of Mars

GLOSSARY

EXTENSION ACTIVITY

Write some examples beginning or ending as shown.

 The moment I ...   Everywhere I go ...   You look as if ...   Even though I'm ...

*Need more practice? Go to the **Review** on page 208.*

science

adverbial clauses

36 adverbial participle clauses

participle phrases

- A participle phrase (eg *noticing the door was open*) can be added to a clause to give more information, or describe the time, the manner or the result of the event in the main clause.
  Noticing the door was open, I walked in.
  This means the same as *'I noticed the door was open, and I walked in.'*

- If the participle phrase comes before the main clause, it must refer to the subject of the main clause. It is usually followed by a comma.
  Walking up the street, I heard a bell ring.
  (= I was walking up the street and I heard a bell)
  Walking up the street, a bell rang.
  (= The bell was walking up the street when it rang)

- If the participle phrase follows the main clause then either the subject or the object (if there is one) of the main clause can be the subject of the participle phrase. This will depend on the meaning of the sentence.
  We saw Jim **walking up the street**. (= We saw Jim while he was walking up the street)
  The boat struck a rock, **throwing the crew into the sea**.

one action before another performed by the same subject.

- Both present and past forms are possible.
  Leaving the parcel on the doorstep, he drove away.
  Having left the parcel on the doorstep, he drove away.

- When a phrase is negative, *not* normally goes before the participle.
  Not having an umbrella, I got really wet.

- *Not* may occur elsewhere in the clause, if another part of it is negative.
  Having decided **not** to stay longer, I went home.

- Using a past form can show that one action is the consequence of the other.
  Having forgotten my keys, I had to climb in the window.

- This kind of clause often explains the reason for something happening. We can put *on* or *upon* before the participle.
  On / upon noticing a policeman coming down the street, he ran off.

- A passive participle can sometimes also be shortened.
  Having been introduced to the president, he could think of nothing to say.
  Introduced to the president, he could think of nothing to say.

time phrase with *after, before, since, when, while*

- The participle follows the time word.
  After reading the letter, she burst into tears.
  Clean it thoroughly with warm soapy water **before using it for the first time**.
  Since talking to Mr Ashton, I've changed my mind about my career.
  When taking this medication, avoid drinking alcohol.
  While waiting for the train, we had a meal in the station restaurant.

time phrase with *on, in*

- *On* + participle describes an event immediately followed by another event.
  On hearing a noise at the window, I looked out.

- *In* + participle describes how one action causes something else to happen.
  In trying to adjust the heating system, I managed to break it completely.

manner phrase with *by, as if*

- *By* + participle describes the method you can use to do something.
  By using the Internet, it's possible to save money.

reason phrase

- To explain the reason for something we can use *being* to replace *because / as + be*.
  Because I was afraid to go on my own, I asked Sam to go with me.
  Being afraid to go on my own, I asked Sam to go with me.

past passive participle

- We can replace a passive verb with a past passive participle.
  I *was offered* a higher salary, so I took the job.
  Having been offered a higher salary, I took the job.

subject and participle phrase

- A noun and participle can be used to give extra information about the subject of the main clause.
  His ears bursting from the water pressure, he rose to the surface.
  All three goals were excellent, *the first one being the best*, I think.

- *It* or *there* can also be used as a subject in formal speech or writing.
  There being no further time today, the meeting will continue in the morning.
  It being a Sunday, there were fewer trains than usual.

with and *without*

- These are often followed by participle constructions in descriptive writing.
  With blood pouring from his wounds, he staggered into the room.
  Without making a sound, she opened the door.

reduced adverbial clauses (see Unit 35)

- Clauses of time, place, manner and contrast and conditional clauses often have the verb reduced to the present or past participle, or omitted in the case of *be*. This is more common in formal writing.
  While (she was) *at the shops*, Helen lost her wallet.
  Where (it is) *indicated*, use one of the screws labelled A.
  She waved her arms about, *as if* (she was) *swatting* a fly.
  Though (he was) *feeling ill*, he was determined to play in the match.
  Although feeling ill, I went to the meeting.
  If studying full-time, expect to spend 20 hours a week outside of set lectures.
  Unless travelling in an organized tour group, you will require a visa.

1 Tick the correct sentences and <u>underline</u> and correct any mistakes.

a Not knowing the way, I got lost several times.   ✓

b <u>After leaving</u> the room, the telephone rang.   *After I had left ...*

c Having lost my money, the conductor wouldn't give me a ticket.

d While falling asleep, there was a loud knock at the front door.

e By forcing open the window, I was able to get into the house.

f Not wishing to be a nuisance, I left as early as I could.

g Having opened the box, it turned out to be empty.

h Though feeling tired, Helen went out clubbing with her friends.

i Having asked my name, I was taken to meet the prime minister.

j On arriving at the station, the train had already left.

2 Complete the sentence with a word from the list.

> abandoned   although   being   by   if   it   there   though   while   without

a *Although* feeling dizzy, Sarah managed to play on until the end of the match.

b _____ a powerful swimmer, George reached the island in less than an hour.

c _____ waiting for a reply, the mysterious stranger vanished into the night.

d _____ being a Friday, everyone in the office was in a good mood.

e _____ walking across the field, Rita noticed something glittering by the path.

f _____ by its owner, the old dog sat by the side of the road and howled.

g _____ shocked by what he had seen, Martin tried to keep calm.

h _____ being no chance of escape, the two men gave themselves up to the police.

i _____ using a fan-assisted oven, reduce cooking time by half an hour.

j _____ signing your name here, you agree to the conditions listed below.

geography

3 Complete the text using one word in each gap.

The Galapagos Islands

a *Located* near the equator, the Galapagos islands are a group of volcanic islands off the coast of Ecuador. **b** _____ by Spanish colonists in 1535, and first **c** _____ on maps in about 1570, the islands were rarely visited, **d** _____ a haven for pirates. **e** _____ developed their own specializations and escaped the attentions of predators common elsewhere, the Galapagos species had became unique and unafraid of people. Passing ships hunted seals and giant tortoises. Once **f** _____ the tortoises were kept alive on ships for long periods and later eaten. After **g** _____ near extinction, few of these creatures remain today. **h** _____ by the naturalist Charles Darwin in 1835, the islands still have a close association with Darwinian theory, **i** _____ the home to many species isolated from the mainland. **j** _____ later that birds which differed from island to island were in fact the same species, Darwin used evidence from the Galapagos in the development of his theory of natural selection. Now **k** _____ as part of a national park, the islands are popular with 'eco-tourists'. Efforts are continuing to save their wildlife.

GLOSSARY

4 Write a new sentence with the same meaning, containing the word in capitals and a participle clause.

a As it was a public holiday, there was a lot of traffic on the roads. BEING

It being a public holiday, there was a lot of traffic on the roads.

b When I opened the letter, I realized it was from Professor Alton. ON

c The palace was destroyed by fire during the war but later reconstructed. THOUGH

d As Carol walked from the room, tears streamed from her eyes. STREAMING

e I broke the camera as I tried to remove the memory card. IN

f My hair has become soft and shining since I've used Glosso shampoo. USING

g Jan was taken to hospital after she was knocked down by a car. BEING

h After he had been shown to his room, George lay down on the bed and slept. HAVING

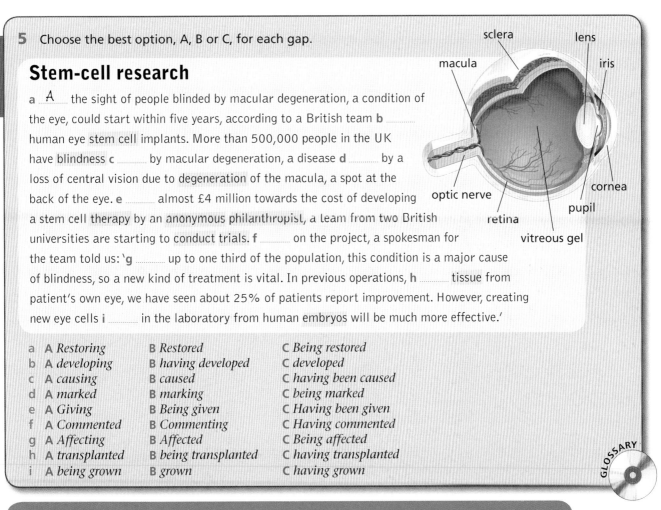

5 Choose the best option, A, B or C, for each gap.

Stem-cell research

a __A__ the sight of people blinded by macular degeneration, a condition of the eye, could start within five years, according to a British team **b** .... human eye stem cell implants. More than 500,000 people in the UK have blindness **c** .... by macular degeneration, a disease **d** .... by a loss of central vision due to degeneration of the macula, a spot at the back of the eye. **e** .... almost £4 million towards the cost of developing a stem cell therapy by an anonymous philanthropist, a team from two British universities are starting to conduct trials. **f** .... on the project, a spokesman for the team told us: 'g .... up to one third of the population, this condition is a major cause of blindness, so a new kind of treatment is vital. In previous operations, **h** .... tissue from patient's own eye, we have seen about 25% of patients report improvement. However, creating new eye cells **i** .... in the laboratory from human embryos will be much more effective.'

sclera lens macula iris optic nerve cornea pupil retina vitreous gel

a **A** *Restoring*   **B** *Restored*   **C** *Being restored*
b **A** *developing*   **B** *having developed*   **C** *developed*
c **A** *causing*   **B** *caused*   **C** *having been caused*
d **A** *marked*   **B** *marking*   **C** *being marked*
e **A** *Giving*   **B** *Being given*   **C** *Having been given*
f **A** *Commented*   **B** *Commenting*   **C** *Having commented*
g **A** *Affecting*   **B** *Affected*   **C** *Being affected*
h **A** *transplanted*   **B** *being transplanted* **C** *having transplanted*
i **A** *being grown*   **B** *grown*   **C** *having grown*

EXTENSION ACTIVITY

Write sentences beginning *Having …   On realizing …   While waiting …   If using …*

*Need more practice? Go to the **Review** on page 208.*

adverbial participle clauses

37 | phrasal verbs (1)

This unit and **Units 38** and **39** list both two-part and three-part phrasal verbs. Some phrasal verbs are colloquial, and most have a more formal equivalent. Many phrasal verbs have multiple meanings, not all of which are included here.

key points

- An *intransitive verb* is one which does not take an object.
  His story just doesn't **add up**.

- object positions
  bear (someone / something) out (someone / something)
  This indicates that *bear out* can have an object either after *out* or between *bear* and *out*.
  Jackson's new research **bears out his earlier claim** *that sea-levels are falling.*
  The research **bears him out**.   *The research bears* **this claim out**.

  If the object is a pronoun, it always comes between the verb and particle.
  This bears **it** *out.*   *It bears* **this** *out.*

- Avoid putting a long phrase between verb and preposition / particle.
  Tom explained that bad weather always **brought his illness on**.
  Tom claimed that the dusty room had **brought on a severe attack of asthma**.

add up (not) (intransitive)
make sense
I'm afraid your story **just doesn't add up**.

allow for (something)
consider when making a plan
You **haven't allowed for** *the cost of all the materials.*

bear (someone / something) out (someone / something)
confirm the truth
The police investigations **didn't bear out** *the victim's claims.*

break down (intransitive)
lose control of one's emotions
A friend of the dead man **broke down** *and wept when he told how he found the body.*

break off (something)
stop doing something
She **broke off** *their conversation to answer her mobile phone.*

break up (intransitive)
come to an end
The meeting **broke up** *in confusion.*

break out (intransitive)
when a war or disease begins
Fighting **has broken out** *on the southern border of the country.*

bring (something) about (something)
cause to happen
The digital revolution **has brought about** *profound changes in our society.*

bring (something) on (something)
cause an illness to start
Tom claimed that the dusty room **had brought on** *a severe attack of asthma.*

bring (something) on / upon (oneself)
cause a problem for (yourself)
I sympathize with your problem, but really, you **brought it on yourself**.

bring (something) out (something)
publish, release
David is **bringing out** *a new DVD next summer.*

bring (someone) round (to your point of view)
persuade someone to agree
I argued with her all day, but couldn't **bring her round** *to my point of view.*

bring (something) up (something)
mention
I'd like to **bring up** *another matter, if I may.*

build up (intransitive)
increase in size (negative)
Tension between the rival groups **has built up** *over the past few weeks.*

call (someone) up (someone)
order into military service
A week after the war started, Jim **was called up**.

carry (something) out (something)
complete a plan
Please make sure you **carry out** *these instructions.*

catch on (intransitive)
become popular (informal)
Camera phones **have really caught on** *lately.*

come about (intransitive)
happen
Many positive changes **have come about** *as a result of his efforts.*

come down to (something)
in the end be a matter of
In the end, this problem **comes down to** *overpopulation.*

come in for (something)
receive blame, criticism etc
*The Government's proposals **have come in for** a great deal of criticism.*

come into (something)
inherit
*Sarah **came into** €20 million when her grandfather died.*

come off (intransitive)
take place successfully
*Everyone is hoping that the new plan **will come off**.*

come out (intransitive)
appear, be published
*Her new book **comes out** next month.*

come up (intransitive)
when a problem happens
*I'm going to be home late. Something **has come up**.*

come up to (something)
be as good as (one's expectations)
*The restaurant **didn't come up to** our expectations.*

come up with (something)
think of an idea, plan etc
*Sue **has come up with** a really good idea.*

count on (someone)
rely on
*You **can count on me** for support at the meeting.*

crop up (intransitive)
happen, appear unexpectedly (informal)
*The same names kept **cropping up** during the investigation.*

do away with (something)
abolish
*The school decided **to do away with** uniform, and let pupils wear whatever they liked.*

do without (something)
manage without
*I **can't do without** a cup of coffee when I get up. It's essential.*

draw (something) up (something)
prepare a plan or document
*The lawyers **are drawing up** the contract.*

draw up (intransitive)
come to a stop
*Two police cars **drew up** outside the door.*

drop in (intransitive), **drop in on someone**
visit (informal)
*Do **drop in** if you're in the area.*

drop off (intransitive)
fall asleep
*Several people at the back of the hall **had dropped off** and were snoring.*

end up (intransitive)
finish in a certain way or place
*We missed the bus and had to walk, and **ended up** getting home at 4.00 am.*

fall back on (something)
use after all else has failed
*His father persuaded him to finish college so he would have something **to fall back on**.*

fall for (someone)
fall in love with (informal)
*Kate **has fallen for** George's brother.*

fall for (something)
be deceived by
*Harry **fell for** the oldest trick in the world.*

fall out (with) (someone)
quarrel (with)
*Paul and Jim **have fallen out** again.*

fall through (intransitive)
when a plan or arrangement fails
*We thought we had agreed to buy the house, but the deal **fell through**.*

fit in with (something)
be included in a plan
*I'm afraid your suggestion **doesn't fit in with** my plans.*

get (something) across (or intransitive)
make others understand
*Chris has some great ideas, but can't always **get them across**.*

get at (something)
suggest meaning
*What exactly **are you getting at**? I don't understand.*

get down to (something)
start to deal seriously with
*It's time you **got down** to some serious work.*

get (someone) off or **get off** (intransitive)
avoid punishment (informal)
*Terry was charged with murder, but her lawyers managed **to get her off**.*

get on for (something)
approach a time, age or number
*It's **getting on for** six, so it's time we were going.*

get on (intransitive)
make progress
*How are you **getting on** in your new job?*

get (something) over with
finish something unpleasant
*I always try to **get my homework over with** as quickly as possible.*

get round / around to (something)
find time to do
*I'll try and **get round to** writing some letters later.*

get up to (something)
do something you shouldn't do
*What are the children **getting up to** in the garden?*

phrasal verbs (1)

1 Choose the best phrasal verb, A, B or C, to complete the sentence.

a I'm sure we'll be able to ...C... to our way of seeing things by the end of the meeting.

b We haven't really .... a solution to the problem yet.

c Don't forget that you have to .... the expansion of the metal in your calculation.

d Wrist watch television was an interesting idea but didn't really ....

e Helen .... the issue at the next meeting.

f To be honest, the hotel didn't .... to our expectations.

g I hate going to the dentist's, so I try to .... as soon as I can.

h David .... his business partner over the plans to reduce the workforce.

i Kate says she can't .... a cup of coffee in the morning.

j Sorry, but something important has .... and I'll have to ring you back.

a	A *draw him up*	B *bear him out*	C *bring him round*
b	A *come up with*	B *fallen back on*	C *brought on*
c	A *get over with*	B *build up*	C *allow for*
d	A *carry out*	B *get round*	C *catch on*
e	A *brought up*	B *fell for*	C *came up with*
f	A *get up*	B *come up*	C *end up*
g	A *bring it about*	B *get it over with*	C *carry it out*
h	A *came down to*	B *broke down with*	C *fell out with*
i	A *do without*	B *get over with*	C *allow for*
j	A *come off*	B *come about*	C *come up*

2 Choose the best ending 1 to 10 for each sentence a to j.

a To Anna's surprise, a pink stretch limousine had just drawn *6*

b Tony told the doctor that his attack had been brought ....

c A team of engineers has been carrying ....

d After searching for hours for somewhere to eat, we ended ....

e I think I can change my meeting to Tuesday, so I can fit ....

f After a great deal of discussion, we believe we have come ....

g I don't really know what you two have been getting ....

h The tense situation on the border has come ....

i I haven't looked at your project yet, but I'm hoping to get ....

j Latest research in the hospital medical school bears ....

1 ... up with a solution to the parking problem in this area.

2 ... out the claim that the condition is caused by exposure to high levels of noise.

3 ... in with your plans for the visit to Leeds on Monday.

4 ... out emergency repairs on the bridge since early this morning.

5 ... up to, but I'll find out sooner or later, believe me!

6 ~~... up outside the front door, and someone who looked like Johnny Depp was getting out.~~

7 ... round to it later on this afternoon.

8 ... about as a result of rocket attacks from both sides in recent weeks.

9 ... up buying some fruit from a street market behind the bus station.

10 ... on by a meal he had eaten in a hotel.

3 Complete the sentence with a phrasal verb from the list.

> break off   ~~break out~~   bring round   come about   come into
> come off   come out   do away with   fall back on   get off

a Police feared that after the match, fighting between rival fans would _break out_ .

b Nobody is sure whether the revised plan will ....

c Most scientific developments .... as a result of team-work.

d You need some savings to .... in case you run into financial difficulty.

e The lecturer was forced to .... and drink a glass of water before resuming.

f Despite the evidence, the accused man managed to .... , much to everyone's surprise.

g Alan will .... a fortune when he reaches the age of 21.

h David's new album is expected to .... at the end of the year.

i The party is proposing to .... with council tax and replace it with local income tax.

j The prime minister said he hoped to .... the rest of the cabinet to his point of view.

4 Write a new sentence with the same meaning, using the correct form of a phrasal verb from the list. Use a dictionary if necessary.

> bear out   bring about   bring up   call up   come up with
> count on   draw up   fall for   get at   ~~get on~~

a It's nearly 8.00, so you'd better get ready to leave.
   It's getting on for 8.00, so you'd better get ready to leave.

b I couldn't really understand what she was suggesting.
   ....

c I don't think we can rely on Johnson to support us.
   ....

d There's an important point I think I should mention.
   ....

e In 1939, Jim was conscripted into the army.
   ....

f The director is preparing a list of suitable candidates for the job.
   ....

g The statement of the accused was corroborated by other witnesses.
   ....

h Carol has thought of a really good solution to the problem.
   ....

i The stranger offered to sell Harry the Eiffel Tower, and Harry was taken in.
   ....

j A lack of marketing expertise eventually led to the downfall of the entire motor industry.
   ....

EXTENSION ACTIVITY

A Choose twenty phrasal verbs and look them up in a dictionary, noting any other meanings and whether these are transitive or intransitive.

B Choose ten examples from the explanation pages and translate them into your language.

*Need more practice? Go to the **Review** on page 208.*

phrasal verbs (2)

give (something) away (something)
betray
I'm not giving away any secrets if I tell you this!

give in to (something), give in (intransitive)
yield, surrender
The company said **it would not give in** to blackmail by the workforce.
'
give off (something)
produce a smell, gas, heat etc
The glass globe **was giving off** a pale green light.

give out (intransitive)
become exhausted
When John's money **gave out**, he had to take another job.

give over to (usually passive)
use time for a particular purpose
The afternoon **is given over** to sports activities.

give (oneself) up
surrender
The two gunmen **gave themselves up** when more police arrived.

give (someone) up (for)
stop looking for because lost or dead
The dog **had been given up for lost** before he was found 200 miles away.

go about (something)
do what is normally done
I'm not sure **how to go about** removing the old boiler.

go back on (something)
break a promise
MPs accused the government of **going back on** earlier promises.

go for (something)
like something (informal)
Anna says she **doesn't really go for** that type of boy.

go in for (something)
make a habit of
Peter doesn't **go in much for** sport.

go in for (something)
enter a competition
Are you going in for the Advanced English Test this year?

go off (intransitive)
when food becomes bad
This fish smells awful. It must have **gone off**.

go on (intransitive)
happen
There's something strange **going on** here!

go round (something)
be enough
Are there enough books **to go round the class**? If not, you'll have to share.

go through with (something)
complete a promise or plan (often negative)
David says he's going to resign, but I don't think **he'll go through with it**.

go without (something)
manage without something
We had **to go without** water for a week after a pipe burst.

grow on (someone)
when someone begins to like something
I didn't like this book at first, but **it is growing on me**.

hang around
spend time doing nothing
There were several teenagers **hanging around** at the end of the street.

hang onto (something)
keep
I'm going **to hang onto** this painting. It might be valuable in a few years.

have (got) it in for (someone)
be deliberately unkind to someone (informal)
My boss is always telling me off. **He's got it in for me**

hit it off (with someone)
get on well with someone (informal)
I don't really **hit it off** with my new neighbour.

hit on / upon (something)
discover by chance, have an idea
We **hit upon** the answer to the problem completely by chance.

hold (something) up (something)
delay
Sorry I'm late. **I was held up** at my office.

hold with (something)
agree with (usually negative)
I don't hold with the idea of people borrowing more than they can afford.

impose (something) on (something / one)
force people to do accept something
It's wrong that some people should **impose** their viewpoint **on** everyone else.

keep (something) up (something)
continue to do something
Don't relax the pressure. We must **keep it up** until we finish the job.

keep to (usually passive)
be limited to
Make sure you **keep to** the deadline. It's vital to finish the job in time.

lay down (especially the law) (or + that-clause)
state a formal rule
In the constitution **it is laid down that** all accused are innocent until proved guilty.

let (someone) down (someone)
disappoint
*Jim was supposed to help me yesterday, but **he let me down**.*

let (someone) in on (something)
tell someone a secret
*Don't **let** Helen **in on** any secrets, because she'll tell everyone.*

let (someone) off
excuse from punishment
*Luckily the police **let** Maria **off** with a warning, and didn't give her a fine.*

let on (intransitive) (+ that-clause)
talk about a secret
*Don't **let on** that I told you about Mike's surprise party.*

live up to (something) (expectations)
reach an expected standard
*My holiday in China certainly **lived up to** my expectations. It was fantastic.*

look into (something)
investigate
*The airline is **looking into** my complaint about my missing baggage.*

look on / upon (something)
consider
*George **looked upon** his new job **as** an opportunity to prove himself.*

look (someone) up
visit
*Why don't you **look us up** the next time you're in London.*

look up (intransitive) (usually progressive)
improve
*Since we won the lottery, **things have definitely been looking up** for us!*

make for (comparative + noun)
result in
*The new stainless steel body **makes for easier cleaning**.*

make off with (something)
take (something stolen)
*While my back was turned, someone **made off with** my suitcase.*

make out (+ that-clause)
pretend
*When the security guard challenged him, the man **made out that** he was a customer.*

make out (something)
manage to see, hear, understand etc
*I **could just make out** some writing across the top of the door.*

make (someone) out
understand someone's behaviour
*David is a strange boy! I just **can't make him out**!*

make (something) up (something)
invent
*It turned out that Joe **had made up** the whole story, and wasn't a journalist at all.*

make up for (something)
compensate for
*Joe's silver medal in the 200 metres **made up for** his disappointment in the 100 metres.*

miss (something) out (something)
fail to include
*You've **missed out** the full stop in this sentence.*

miss out (on something)
lose a chance
*All her friends won prizes, but Karen **missed out** again.*

own up (to something)
admit
*When the teacher asked the class who had started the fire, Chris **owned up**.*

pack (something) in (something)
stop (informal)
*Sue decided to **pack in** her job and travel abroad for a while.*

pay (someone) back (for)
take revenge (informal)
*I'll **pay him back** for all the rude things he's said about me!*

pick up (intransitive)
improve (informal)
*A lot of people think that the economy **is picking up** again after a slack period.*

pin (someone) down
force someone to make a decision
*He says he'll call round and do the job, but **I can't pin him down** to an exact date.*

play up (intransitive)
act badly
*The washing machine **is playing up** again. It's making a horrible noise!*

point out (+ that-clause)
draw attention to a fact
*Can **I point out that** I did suggest that idea in the first place!*

pull (something) off (something)
succeed in doing
*United nearly won the match, but just failed to **pull it off**.*

push on (intransitive)
continue doing something
*I don't think we should wait here. Let's **push on** and try to get there tonight.*

1 Choose the best phrasal verb, A, B or C, to complete the sentence.

a It's a bit hard to ___B___ what the sign says from here.

b Tina doesn't _____ expensive fashion items.

c I didn't like this place when I first came here, but now it is _____ me.

d The police are _____ complaints from other shoppers at the store.

e How do you think we should _____ finding somewhere to live?

f The president is still _____ power, even though he was voted out.

g This cheese smells as if it's _____!

h My teacher always blames me for everything. I think she's _____ for me.

i The authorities repeated that they would not _____ to the demands of the armed group.

j Smith has since _____ deceiving more than twenty other customers.

a	A *hold with*	B *make out*	C *pin down*
b	A *go in for*	B *make off with*	C *keep to*
c	A *going back on*	B *looking upon*	C *growing on*
d	A *looking into*	B *going in for*	C *making off with*
e	A *go about*	B *hit upon*	C *make for*
f	A *going in for*	B *making up for*	C *hanging on to*
g	A *gone off*	B *packed in*	C *pinned down*
h	A *packed it in*	B *got it in*	C *given it in*
i	A *go in*	B *own up*	C *give in*
j	A *lived up to*	B *owned up to*	C *made off with*

2 Choose the best ending 1 to 10 for each sentence a to j.

a Well done. Make sure you keep ___6___

b Oh dear, it seems that she has missed _____

c The company spokesperson later pointed _____

d Fifty years ago, such behaviour would have been looked _____

e It turned out in the end that Sue had made _____

f I really feel that you have let all of us _____

g After thinking about it, the survivors hit _____

h How exactly will you go _____

i There was a strange glass globe on the floor, giving _____

j It's been great seeing you – why don't you look _____

1 ... down, because we were relying on you completely.

2 ... out that the figures were only rough estimates, and had not been confirmed.

3 ... us up again the next time you're in the area?

4 ... upon as criminal, and severely punished.

5 ... about removing the old heating system?

6 ... up the good work in future!

7 ... off a mysterious throbbing light.

8 ... upon the idea of using pieces of wood to spell out S.O.S. on the sand.

9 ... up the whole story, and had never actually studied at university.

10 ... out on beating the record once again.

3 Complete the sentence with a phrasal verb from the list.

> give away   give out   go about   go round   keep to
> ~~look into~~   make up for   pack in   play up   point out

a The government has agreed to _look into_ the claim that £2 billion has been wasted.

b Don't worry, there are plenty of life jackets to ....

c The doctors are afraid her heart will .... unless she has an operation.

d The computer used to .... a lot so we decided to get a new one.

e Paula decided to .... her teaching job and work in a bar.

f I'd like to .... that I haven't actually received any payment yet.

g I hope this award will .... your disappointment at not winning first prize.

h Try to .... the announced topic. You're going off the subject slightly.

i How exactly do I .... applying for a student grant?

j Don't say too much, or you'll .... the answer without meaning to!

4 Write a new sentence with the same meaning, using the correct form of a phrasal verb from the list.

> go on   grow on   hang around   miss out   let down
> let on   pay back   ~~pick up~~   pull off   make up

a The government expects the economy to improve in the later part of the year.
  The government expects the economy to pick up in the later part of the year.

b You've forgotten to put a question mark at the end of the line.
  ....

c There are a lot of people doing nothing in the street outside our house.
  ....

d I think it's time we took revenge on him for all the awful things he has done!
  ....

e Ann was supposed to look after my dog, but she disappointed me.
  ....

f What on earth is happening here?
  ....

g Frankie nearly won both races but just failed to manage it.
  ....

h I didn't like the film at first, but then I started to like it more.
  ....

i Don't tell anyone that I put that notice on the door!
  ....

j Tony invented a story about meeting Bob Dylan in a café.
  ....

EXTENSION ACTIVITY

A Choose twenty phrasal verbs and look them up in a dictionary, noting any other meanings and whether these are transitive or intransitive.

B Choose ten examples from the explanation pages and translate them into your language.

*Need more practice? Go to the **Review** on page 208.*

phrasal verbs (2)

39 phrasal verbs (3)

put (something) across (to something)
explain an idea
*I can understand you, but can you **put these ideas across** to the general public?*

put (something) down (to something)
explain the cause of
*The team's poor performance **was put down** to insufficient training.*

put in for (something)
apply for
*Mark **has put in for** the post of assistant director.*

put (someone) off (something)
discourage, upset
*I can't sing if people stare at me. **It puts me off**.*

put (someone) out
cause problems (negative / question)
*Sorry we can't come to dinner. I hope this doesn't **put you out** at all.*

put (someone) up (someone)
let someone stay in your house
*Why don't you come and stay? We can easily **put you up** for a few days.*

put up with (something / someone)
tolerate, bear
*After a while the noise became so loud that Brian **couldn't put up with it** any longer.*

rip (someone) off
charge too much, cheat (informal)
*€250 a night in that hotel? **You were ripped off!***

run (someone) down (someone)
criticize
*Why do you keep **running yourself down** so much? You're fantastic!*

run into (someone)
meet by chance
*You'll never guess who I **ran into** the other day! Your old friend Marianne.*

run to (something)
reach an amount or number
*The cost of the Olympic building programme now **runs to** over £5 billion.*

run over / through (something)
check, explain
*Could you just **run over** the details again? I'm not sure I understand.*

see (someone) off (someone)
go to station with someone etc to say goodbye
*Anna is coming with me to the airport **to see me off**.*

see through (something)
understand dishonesty, pretence
*He pretended to be busy, but **I saw through** his deception at once.*

see to (something)
deal with
*The fridge has broken down, but someone is coming **to see to it** tomorrow.*

set about (something)
begin doing something
*We know what we have to do, but we're not sure how **to set about it**.*

set (something / someone) back
delay progress
*The cold weather **has set back** the work, and the building won't be finished on time.*

set in (intransitive)
when something unpleasant starts and will probably continue
*It looks as if the rain **has set in** for the day!*

set out (something)
give in detail
*This document **sets out** exactly how much you have to pay, and when.*

set out (+ to-infinitive)
intend to
*The court heard that the two men deliberately **set out to** deceive customers.*

set something up (something)
establish, arrange (a meeting)
*The police **have set up** an inquiry into the complaints.*

set upon (someone)
attack
*The security guards **were set upon** by three armed men.*

shake (something) off
get rid of
*I can't seem to **shake off** this flu. I've had it for ten days.*

sink in (intransitive)
be understood
*I had to read the letter several times before the news finally **sank in**.*

slip up (intransitive)
make a mistake
*I think someone **has slipped up**. These are not the books I ordered.*

sort (something) out (something)
do something to solve a problem
*I'm sorry about the mistake. We'll **sort it out** as soon as we can.*

stand by (something)
keep to (especially an agreement)
*The leader of the party said **they would stand by** the agreement they made last year.*

stand for (something)
represent
In this sentence, i.e. **stands for** *id est, the Latin for 'that is'.*

stand for (something) (usually negative)
tolerate
I won't stand for *any more shouting and swearing!*

stand in for (someone)
take the place of
As Mr Davis is in hospital, Jill Cope **will be standing in for** *him for the next two weeks.*

step down (intransitive)
resign
At the end of this month, Helen **will be stepping down** *as union representative.*

step (something) up (something)
increase
The report **has stepped up** *the pressure on the director to resign.*

stick up for (someone / something)
defend (informal)
Don't just say nothing! **Stick up for yourself!**

sum up (intransitive)
give a summary
Let me **sum up** *by repeating the main points.*

sum (something) up (something)
show what sth is like
I think that what he has done **sums up** *his behaviour in general.*

take (someone) in (someone)
deceive
He **took me in** *at first, but then I realized what he was really like.*

take (someone) off (someone)
imitate
Jack can **take off** *all the teachers really well.*

take (something) on (something)
acquire a particular characteristic
Her words **have taken on** *a different meaning since the accident.*

do extra work
Pat **has taken on** *too much work and is exhausted.*

take (something) over (something)
gain control of
A small group of determined men **took over** *the country.*

take to (someone / something)
grow to like
My mother **took to** *Sarah as soon as they met.*

take to doing something
develop a habit
Sam **has taken to wearing** *his grandfather's old suits.*

talk (someone) into / out of (something)
persuade
I didn't want to buy the car, but the salesman **talked me into it.**

tell (someone) off (someone)
criticize angrily
Ted's teacher **told him off** *for being late.*

tie (someone) down to (something)
force to do or say something definite
Anna says she will visit us, but **I can't tie her down to** *a date.*

track (someone / something) down
find after a long search
(someone / something)
The police finally **tracked the robbers down** *in South America.*

try (something) out (something)
test to see if it works
They **tried out** *the new drug* **on** *animals before using it on humans.*

turn (something) down (something)
reject
The council **has turned down** *our application for planning permission.*

turn out (+ *to*-infinitive) or (*that*-clause)
happen to be in the end
The girl in red **turned out** *to be Maria's sister.*

turn up (intransitive)
arrive or be discovered by chance
Guess who **turned up** *at our party? Your old friend Martin!*

wear off (intransitive)
lose effect
When the drugs begin **to wear off**, *you may feel some pain.*

work (something) out (something)
calculate
I can't **work out** *the answer to this maths problem. Don't worry about the money you owe.* **We'll work something out.**

deal with a problem
work out (intransitive)
be successful, have a happy ending
I'm sure that everything **will work out** *fine in the end.*

1 Choose the best phrasal verb, A, B or C, to complete the sentence.

a It's easy to ___A___ the deceptions of people like George.

b The unusual test results were _____ a fault with the computer.

c You have to learn to _____ yourself or no-one will respect you.

d Mrs Andrews _____ the children who climbed into her garden.

e The pain in my leg began to _____ after a couple of hours.

f The letters BBC _____ British Broadcasting Corporation.

g The project has been _____ by technical problems, and won't be ready on time.

h Don't look over my shoulder while I'm writing. It _____ .

i Tom's parents managed to _____ of buying motorbike by offering to buy him a car.

j At the end of the film, it _____ that the police chief was actually the murderer.

a	A *see through*	B *take in*	C *sum up*
b	A *put down to*	B *tracked down*	C *slipped up*
c	A *put up with*	B *tied down to*	C *stick up for*
d	A *put out*	B *turned down*	C *told off*
e	A *wear off*	B *set in*	C *step up*
f	A *put in for*	B *take over*	C *stand for*
g	A *set back*	B *put out*	C *worked out*
h	A *sums me up*	B *ties me down*	C *puts me off*
i	A *saw him off*	B *talk him out*	C *put him out*
j	A *took in*	B *set out*	C *turned out*

2 Choose the best ending 1 to 10 for each sentence a to j.

a It has been announced that the prime minister will step   _6_

b Sue is looking for a new job and has decided to put   _____

c The government has promised to set   _____

d I'm sorry, but I won't put   _____

e We apologize for the mistake, and we are doing our best to sort   _____

f Quite honestly, I think you've taken   _____

g I was walking through the park the other day, when who should I run   _____

h Do you think that the government set   _____

i Mrs Watson will be standing   _____

j I only heard the news an hour ago and it hasn't really sunk   _____

1 … on far too much, and you really ought to get an assistant.

2 … in for the position of assistant director.

3 … out to deliberately deceive people about this matter?

4 … up with such rude behaviour.

5 … in completely yet.

6 … down at the end of June, and take up a post with the UN.

7 … in for Mr Dobbs while he is in hospital.

8 … things out as quickly as we can.

9 … into but my old French teacher, carrying a baby.

10 … up an inquiry into the sale of armaments.

3 Complete the sentence with a phrasal verb from the list.

> ~~put down~~   put out   see off   set about   set out   stand for
> step up   track down   turn down   work out

a The managing director ___put down___ the company's poor performance to high interest rates.
b The police were able to _____ the car thieves using satellite technology.
c This is a sensitive matter, and we have to _____ dealing with it very carefully.
d Paula seemed rather _____ when we brought so many other people to her party.
e All the points for and against are _____ clearly in the report.
f The company has decided to _____ production of cars at its factory in Hull.
g You might need a calculator to _____ this problem.
h Claire decided to _____ the job, because it would have meant more travelling.
i Our maths teacher simply won't _____ any talking in class.
j Helen is going to the airport to _____ some friends.

4 Write a new sentence with the same meaning, using a form of the phrasal verb from the list.

> put across   rip off   run down   run through   run to   see to
> set upon   step down   take in   take over   ~~turn down~~   turn up

a The local planning office has rejected the company's application to build flats on the site.
   The local planning office has turned down the company's application to build flats on the site.

b The lawyers made notes as the judge went over the details of the case. _____

c The security guard was fooled by the thief's disguise. _____

d Carol arrived at the party unannounced, much to everyone's surprise. _____

e Harry has very good ideas, but he can't explain them to an audience. _____

f I don't think you should keep criticizing yourself. _____

g Someone has to fix the children's lunch at 12.30. _____

h Mr Johnson will be leaving the job of company spokesperson at the end of the month.
   _____

i A group of foreign investors is now in control of the company. _____

j Jim was attacked by three muggers in the street. _____

k €500 for that? I think you've been cheated! _____

l The report has got over five hundred pages. _____

5 Write a new sentence with the same meaning, containing the word in capitals.

  a I can't seem to get rid of this pain in my left leg.   SHAKE
     I can't seem to shake off this pain in my left leg.

  b Tina is really good at imitating the accounts manager.   TAKING

  c You can stay at our house for a few days.   PUT

  d I think someone has made a mistake, because I'm not owed any money.   SLIPPED

  e I think this bad weather is going to last all day.   SET

  f The foreign minister promised that his country would honour the agreement.   STAND

  g David has started running up and down the stairs for exercise.   TAKEN

  h That really defines what sort of person she is!   SUMS

The following exercises practise grammar from **Units 37** and **38**.

6 Write a new sentence with the same meaning, using the correct form of a phrasal verb
from **Units 37, 38** and **39**.

  a I was worried about the examination and didn't manage to fall asleep for ages.
     I was worried about the examination and didn't manage to drop off for ages.

  b I'm slowly beginning to like that song.

  c The prime minister and the finance minister have quarrelled again.

  d Three young boys committed the robbery on their way home from school.

  e We waited for a bus for ages, and in the end we walked.

  f I don't understand exactly how much this is going to cost.

  g The Mexican restaurant we tried wasn't as good as we thought it would be.

  h The spare parts we have been waiting for have been delayed in the post.

  i Helen didn't quite understand what Ben was trying to say.

  j I don't like the way he talked to you! I wouldn't stand for it, if I were you.

k When the teacher asked who had broken the desk, two boys confessed.

....

l Fiona doesn't really like camping holidays.

....

m I'm going to use my French and see what it's like when I'm on holiday.

....

n I'll try and find the time to call you later on today.

....

7 Write a new sentence with the same meaning, containing the word in capitals.

a Make sure you keep your ticket, as you'll need it later.   HANG
   Make sure you hang on to your ticket, as you'll need it later.

b Nick says he's going to complain, but I don't think he'll actually do it.   GO

....

c I don't think you should force people to believe what you do.   IMPOSE

....

d I decided to call on my old aunt while I was in the area.   DROP

....

e The work we had done on our house was performed by a firm of local builders.   CARRIED

....

f The party finally ended after the neighbours complained about the noise.   BREAK

....

g Emily says she'll visit us one day, but I can't get her to give a definite date. PIN

....

h Our luxury cruise holiday wasn't really as good as we expected it to be.   LIVED

....

i When there was no food left, the two men were forced to eat insects.   GAVE

....

j Rita is a strange person, I really don't understand her.   MAKE

....

k George got on really well with his mother-in-law.   HIT

....

l I don't think the gunmen will surrender without a fight.   GIVE

....

m I'd like to make it clear that I'm not in fact English, but Scottish.   POINT

....

EXTENSION ACTIVITY

A Choose twenty phrasal verbs and look them up in a dictionary, noting any other meanings and whether these are transitive or intransitive.

B Choose twenty phrasal verbs which you think are useful or interesting from **Units 37, 38** and **39**, use each one to write a new example.

40 organizing text (1)

This unit includes a variety of words and phrases which can be used to organize text. Not all their uses are given here, and many can be used in other ways.

By *connector* is meant any word or phrase that can stand alone at the front of a sentence, often followed by a comma.

adding a point

- *Also* is used to add a point within a sentence. It is not normally used as a connector at the beginning of a sentence in formal speech and writing.
  *Cars use up valuable energy resources, and **also** pollute the environment.*

- *As well as* is followed by a noun or *-ing*, and can be used in an introductory clause.
  *Cars use up valuable energy resources, **as well as polluting** the environment.*
  ***As well as polluting** the environment, cars use up valuable energy resources.*

  As well as this can be used as a connector, referring to a previous sentence.
  *Cars use up valuable energy resources, and also pollute the environment. **As well as this**, they make life unpleasant in big cities.*

- *In addition* can be used as a connector.
  *Cars use up valuable energy resources, and also pollute the environment. **In addition**, they make life unpleasant in big cities.*

- *Moreover, furthermore, what is more* are formal connectors which emphasize that there is an additional point to be made.
  *Cars use up valuable energy resources, and **also** pollute the environment. **Moreover / Furthermore / What is more**, they make life unpleasant in big cities.*

- *Above all* is a connector which adds a point, and stresses that this point is the most important one.
  *Cars use up valuable energy resources, and also pollute the environment. **Above all**, they make life unpleasant in big cities.*

- *Besides* is an informal connector: it has the same meaning as *anyway* or *in any case*.
  *This car is too big for me. **Besides**, I can't really afford it.*

contrast or concession

- *However* can be used as a connector at the beginning or end of the sentence. Note that there is always punctuation on both sides of it, ie a full stop or comma. It cannot be used to connect two clauses.
  *Wind turbines are another source of renewable energy. **However**, they are not without drawbacks.*
  *Wind turbines are another source of renewable energy. They are not without drawbacks, **however**.*

  Compare the use of *although*:
  *Wind turbines are another source of renewable energy, **although** they are not without drawbacks.*

- *Despite (this)* introduces a point which contrasts with a previous statement. Note that *despite* is followed by a noun or *-ing* form of the verb.
  *Wind turbines are an increasingly popular source of renewable energy. **Despite being easy to build**, they do have some drawbacks.*

- *Nevertheless, none the less* are more formal connectors referring back to the previous point: they can also come at the end of the sentence.
  Wind turbines are an increasingly popular source of renewable energy.
  ***Nevertheless / Nonetheless**, they do have some drawbacks.*
  *They do have some drawbacks, **nevertheless / nonetheless**.*

degree

● *To some extent / to a certain extent* are used as a way of saying 'partly'. It can come at the beginning, in the middle or at the end of a sentence.
*Most people would accept this argument **to some extent**.*
***To a certain extent**, I agree with you.*
*This solution is, **to a certain extent**, easy to understand.*

● *In some respects / ways* are used as a connector limiting what comes before or after.
Some people argue that the only solution to the problem of global warming is new technology.
***In some respects, this is true**.*
Some people argue that the only solution to the problem of global warming is new technology.
***In some respects**, the development of non-polluting fuels might solve part of the problem.*

comparing and contrasting

● *On the one hand … (but / while) on the other hand …* introduce contrasting points.
***On the one hand**, nuclear power does not add carbon to the atmosphere, but **on the other hand** it presents other more serious pollution risks.*

We can also use *on the other hand* to introduce a contrasting paragraph.

● *On the contrary* introduces a contrasting positive point after a negative statement.
*The cost of electricity produced by nuclear power does not go down. **On the contrary**, clean-up costs mean that in the long term the cost increases substantially.*

● *Compared to, in comparison to / with* are used as an introductory phrase, or at the end of the sentence.
***In comparison to / Compared with** last year, there has been some improvement.*
*There has been some improvement **in comparison to / compared with** last year.*

● *In the same way* introduces a point which is similar to the previous one.
Wave power generators use the constant movement of the waves to produce electricity.
***In the same way**, tidal generators use the back and forward motion of the tides.*

The sentence adverb *similarly* can also be used.
***Similarly**, tidal generators use the back and forward motion of the tides.*

● *(But) at least* is used to emphasize that there is an advantage, despite a disadvantage just mentioned.
*Wind turbines are noisy, **but at least** they do not create air pollution.*

results and reasons

● *consequently, as a result (of)*
*The house was left empty for several years and no maintenance was carried out. **Consequently / As a result**, it is now in a poor condition.*
***As a result of** this neglect, it is now in a poor condition.*

● *thus* (formal)
*The locks on the front door had been changed. **Thus**, it was impossible for the estate agent to gain entrance to the house.*
*It was **thus** impossible to gain entrance to the house.*

● *accordingly* (formal)
*Smith was away in Italy at the time of the attack. **Accordingly**, he could not have been responsible.*

● *Hence* explains how the words following it are explained by what has gone before.
*The city is the site of ancient spring and Roman bath; **hence** the name Bath.*

● *On account of, owing to* have the same meaning as *because of* and are both prepositions.
*Maria had to retire from professional tennis **on account of / owing to a foot injury**.*

● *Due to* is a preposition with the same meaning as *owing to*, but which can follow *be*.
*Her retirement from professional tennis **was due to a foot injury**.*

1 <u>Underline</u> the best word or phrase.

a Flights abroad are becoming cheaper, <u>*although*</u> / *however* most people are aware of the damage they cause to the environment.

b The beach is mainly pebbles, but *at least* / *in the same way* it is fairly clean.

c Wilson was dismissed from his job, *in addition to* / *on account of* the seriousness of his offence.

d Huygens' astronomical observations required an exact means of measuring time, and he was *thus* / *nevertheless* led in 1656 to invent the pendulum clock.

e Students are often not taught to think effectively. *However* / *As a result*, they can become overwhelmed with information, as they cannot see the wood for the trees.

f Alcohol drinking is strongly associated with the risk of liver cancer. *Moreover* / *None the less*, there is some evidence suggesting that heavy alcohol consumption is particularly strongly associated with liver cancer among smokers.

g Patience is not passive; *on the other hand* / *on the contrary*, it is active; it is concentrated strength.

h This Mary Louisa Smith's marriage certificate is dated 4 June 1867. *Accordingly* / *In the same way*, she cannot be the Mary Louisa Smith born in Liverpool on 12 November 1860.

i Doctors concluded that the patient's erratic behaviour was probably *besides* / *due to* the mild concussion she suffered in the accident.

j Red dwarf stars fuse hydrogen and helium, but the fusion is slow because of the low temperature at the core of the star. *Consequently* / *In some respects*, these stars give off very little light.

2 Complete the text using one word in each space.

Genetically modified food

Genetically modified (or GM) foods are foods from plants (eg cotton, maize, tomatoes) which have been modified in a laboratory by inserting DNA from another organism. As a
a <u>result</u> of this process, the new plant variety will have some new quality (eg resistance to certain pests, improved flavour) which makes it, in some b _____ , more valuable.
c _____ all, a GM plant can be specially developed to suit certain conditions, and although the process produces similar results to normal plant selection to some d _____ , genetic modification is quite a different way of creating new varieties of plants, e _____ to the range of possible modifications.
f _____ to natural breeding techniques, which take place over a long period and may require thousands of plantings, genetic modifications can be made more efficiently, and targeted precisely at a specific need. g _____ , the GM industry has come in for a great deal of criticism. Many people argue that it is dangerous to release GM plants into the environment on
h _____ of their unusual characteristics. i _____ , critics stress that such plants are unnecessary. They argue that rather than creating potentially dangerous new varieties, we should be distributing food more efficiently.

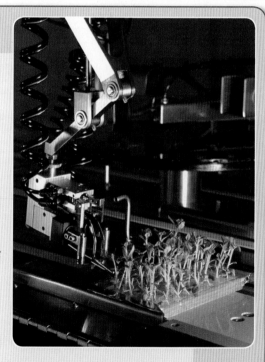

GLOSSARY

3 Write a new sentence with the same meaning, leaving out the words <u>underlined</u>, and including the words in capitals. You may need to write more than one sentence.

a Regular exercise keeps you fit, <u>and</u> it gives you a feeling of well-being.   FURTHERMORE
   Regular exercise keeps you fit. Furthermore, it gives you a feeling of well-being.

b <u>Although</u> she suffered a serious leg injury in 2005, Henderson has come back to dominate
   the 400 m this season.   DESPITE THIS

c <u>As well as</u> providing lonely people with company, pets have been proved to have a
   beneficial effect on many common medical conditions.   WHAT IS MORE

d <u>Despite</u> lower consumer demand, the company has increased profits by 6%.   HOWEVER

e Bicycles are pollution-free and silent, <u>and</u> take up very little parking space.   AS WELL AS THIS

f The heater has been tested for safety, <u>but</u> must be used according to the instructions.   NEVERTHELESS

g I don't really like the design of this sofa, <u>and in any case</u> it won't fit into the living room.   BESIDES

---

4 <u>Underline</u> the best word or phrase.

Globalization

What exactly is globalization? **a** *To some extent / Moreover* the term means whatever people want it to mean. In economics, the term usually refers to the way the world has become one market, with free exchange of goods and capital. **b** *At least / However*, it is also used to describe cross-cultural contacts. **c** *Furthermore / As well as* being part of the same economic system, countries in different parts of the world share entertainment, food, and, **d** *in some respects / owing to*, similar attitudes to life. **e** *Above all /*

Thus, globalization often refers to the way TV and the Internet have created a unified world in which information can be exchanged very rapidly. In fact, a 'global economy' is only possible **f** *as a result of / however* modern information technology. **g** *Despite / Furthermore*, politics has also become 'globalized', creating co-operation between countries. **h** *However / Although*, there are many critics of globalization who point out that while business has become global, there are still winners and losers: **i** *consequently / nevertheless*, the richer nations grow richer, and the poorer nations grow poorer. They also argue that **j** *above all / as a result of* the global power of large corporations and international financial institutions, many countries no longer control their own economies.

GLOSSARY

EXTENSION ACTIVITY

A Write a short text comparing further education with getting a job, or using public transport with using a car.

B Choose ten examples from the explanation page and translate them into your language.

geography

organizing text (1)

187

41 organizing text (2)

exceptions and alternatives

- *except (for)*
  *Everyone chose a new book, **except for Helen**, who was still reading her old one.*
  ***Except for Helen**, who was still reading her old one, everyone chose a new book.*

- *Apart from* can be used to mean the same as *except for*.
  *Everyone chose a new book, **apart from Helen**, who was still reading her old one.*

  It can also mean *in addition to*.
  ***Apart from** the dent in the front bumper, the car had scratches all along one side.*

- *Instead (of)* means that one thing replaces another.
  *I decided not to take the bus, but walked **instead**.*
  *I decided not to take the bus. **Instead**, I walked.*
  ***Instead of taking** the bus, I decided to walk.*

- *Alternatively* is a more formal way of starting a sentence, meaning *or*.
  *You could take the bus. **Alternatively**, you could walk.*

sequences

- Writers often signal that they are going to make a list of points.
  ***There are a number of ways** in which this can be done.*
  ***There are several ways** of looking at this matter.*

- *First of all, secondly, thirdly* etc; *next; finally* are often used to number points in a sequence.
  ***First of all**, there is the issue of cost.*
  ***Secondly** …   **Next**, …   **Finally**, …*

- Words such as *point, issue, problem, advantage* can also be numbered.
  ***The first problem** facing the government is …*

- In an argument, there is often a conclusion, which can be introduced by *in conclusion*.
  ***In conclusion**, we could say that …*

summarizing

- *To sum up* can be used to introduce a summarizing comment at the end of an argument.
  ***To sum up**, it seems clear that …*

- *And so forth, and so on* and *etc.* are expressions used to say there are further points we do not mention.
  *Growth is also influenced by weather, water supply, position, **and so forth**.*

  Note that such phrases can imply that the writer has a lot more to say, but does not wish to go into detail.
  ***Etc** is an abbreviation from Latin **et cetera**.*

  Note also that *etc* as an abbreviation either has a full stop at the end (etc.), or this is omitted (etc). It cannot be written e.t.c.

making assertions

- *Utterly* and *simply* emphasize an adjective. *Utterly* tends to be used with negative adjectives. *Simply* can be used with positive or negative adjectives.
  *This is **simply** wonderful!   It is **simply / utterly** wrong to argue this.*

- *Utter* and *sheer* are used with nouns to emphasize the size or amount. *Utter* tends to be used with negative nouns. *Sheer* can be used with positive or negative nouns.
  *Quite honestly, I think this is **utter nonsense**!*
  *Tania's performance was **sheer delight**!*
  *It was **sheer madness** to buy so many shares!*

- *Merely* is stronger than *only / just* and is used in a similar way, to make what follows seem unimportant or small.
  *The Earth is **merely** a tiny unimportant speck in the Universe.*

  Mere is used before nouns, with the same meaning as above.
  *The Earth is **a mere** speck in the Universe.*

- *Literally* is used to emphasize that what has been said is not an exaggeration but is really true.
  *There are **literally thousands** of people without homes.*

  See intensifiers, comment and viewpoint adverbs **Unit 27**.

giving examples

- *For example, examples include, to take an example* all need punctuation before and after.
  *Some birds regularly migrate over long distances. **For example**, swans fly several thousand kilometres …*
  *Swans, **for example**, fly …*   ***Examples include swans**, which fly …*
  ***To take an example**, swans fly …*

- *eg (e.g.)* is an abbreviation from Latin *exempli gratia*.
  *Some islands, **eg** Naxos, Milos, Santorini etc have airports.*

- *Such as* introduces an example.
  *Many birds, **such as swans**, migrate over long distances.*

- *As far as* (subject) *(be) concerned* is a way of introducing a specific example.
  *Some birds regularly migrate over long distances. **As far as swans are concerned**, this can involve crossing wide expanses of water.*

- *Namely* introduces a more specific reference after a general one.
  *Some groups of birds, **namely swans, geese and ducks**, tend to fly in a V-shaped formation.*

making clear

- *In other words* is used to introduce a point we want to make clearer by repeating it in a different way.
  *I think you should go out more with friends, or perhaps take a part-time job. **In other words**, make more of an effort to be sociable.*

- *to put it another way*
  ***To put it another way**, I think you should try to be more sociable.*

- *That is to say* and *ie* (or *i.e.*) are used to explain exactly what you mean: *ie* means *that is* and is an abbreviation from Latin *id est*.
  *A number of others are usually referred to as 'ballroom dances', **ie / that is to say** the waltz, foxtrot, quickstep, and so on.*

introducing one side of an opinion

- *In a way, in some ways, in some respects* mean 'from one point of view' and introduce one side of an opinion.
  ***In a way**, the film makes the bank-robbers seem really nice guys!*
  ***In some respects**, losing the job was a blessing in disguise.*

describing types

- *A kind of, a sort of* can describe a type of something.
  *An okapi is **a kind of** small giraffe.*

  Kind of and *sort of* are also used with adjectives or verbs informally to mean *rather*.
  *This is **kind of** interesting.*   *It **sort of** worries me.*

1 <u>Underline</u> the best word or phrase.

a   There are a number of advantages to consider. *In a way / <u>First of all</u>*, there is the lower cost.

b   *Apart from snakes / As far as snakes are concerned*, Spain has five poisonous ones.

c   Amphibians, *as well as / such as* frogs and toads, can live on land and in water.

d   You could get it photocopied. *Alternatively / Instead*, I could scan it into my computer.

e   Don't be silly! What you are saying is *utterly / mere* ridiculous!

f   I'm sorry, but this is *simply / sheer* wrong!

g   The Chinese restaurant turned out to be closed, so we went for a pizza *in other words / instead*.

h   Everyone attended the meeting, apart *for / from* Mrs Deacon, who was ill.

i   *In a way / Sort of*, the damage caused by the storm was a good thing, as it brought down a lot of weak trees, which benefits woodland in the long term.

j   A bat looks like a bird, but actually it's *kind of a / a kind of* mammal.

2   Use a phrase from the list to complete the sentence.

> 1 a kind of   2 as far as the economy is concerned   3 to put it another way   4 and so forth
> 5 in some respects   6 apart from   7 namely   8 utterly   9 in conclusion   ~~10 the first task~~

a   _10_   facing the new management will be to reassure staff that jobs will not be lost.

b   .... the second half of the book is not as good as the first half.

c   The country is moving in the right direction ....

d   .... the ending, this is a really interesting film.

e   You will also need money for notebooks, pencils, pens ....

f   Education, it is said, is .... continuing dialogue.

g   The activity on a site is the amount of bandwidth used, or ...., the amount of data that has been transferred.

h   In the last section, we also suggest other topics that need to be researched, and .... emphasize the importance of teamwork.

i   I read the book you lent me, but I'm afraid to say I found it .... incomprehensible.

j   For some companies, the IT assets, ... hardware and software, account for the largest proportion of money spent.

3   Complete the text using one word in each gap.

Early experiments in town planning

As far as Britain is a   _concerned_   , the first modern examples of town planning were the 'garden cities',
b .... as Letchworth and Welwyn Garden City, built in the early 1900s. A 'garden city' was a
c .... of idealized community, planned around large open spaces, public buildings, and
d .... forth. Letchworth, **e** .... example, had no public house, **f** .... ,
a bar selling alcohol, and included for the first time the idea of a 'green belt', that is to **g** .... an
area of countryside surrounding the town. In some **h** .... , Letchworth was ahead of its time, as
the building plan also avoided the cutting down of trees, and the town was **i** .... a 'garden', as
there were green spaces and trees everywhere. **j** .... from the attractions of the site, there was
also innovative design, as many of the houses were designed to be cheap, used modern building techniques
such **k** .... prefabrication, and had front and back gardens, **l** .... luxury for many
slum dwellers from London.

41

4 Complete the sentence with one word in each gap.

a It was _sheer_ coincidence that the two women met outside the door.

b This is _____ the best, and easily better than all the rest.

c They said that the explosion cannot be dismissed as a _____ accident.

d We have received _____ hundreds of applications for the job.

e To suggest that I had anything to do with the murder, is _____ ridiculous!

f The evening of music and dancing was one of _____ pleasure.

g I'm sorry, but as far as I'm concerned this has been a / an _____ waste of time.

h Mr Marwell has brought the company to the brink of _____ ruin.

i I'm not criticizing you, I'm _____ saying that you could have done the job differently.

j Jane was _____ shocked to discover how much money had been stolen.

social studies

5 Choose the best option, A, B, or C, for each gap.

The car and change in the 20th Century.

The car can be seen not as a **a** _C_ machine, but as an agent of social change. In the USA, **b** _____ , during the twentieth century, cars **c** _____ transformed society. First of all, more cars meant more mobility. **d** _____ , as roads became better, people could travel further for jobs. Rather than living in the city centre or near factories, people could live in suburbs **e** _____ , and drive between home and work. **f** _____ , there were new laws obliging new shops and businesses to provide parking spaces, which further encouraged a 'car-only' society. The **g** _____ pace of change was staggering: in 20 years, US roads increased in length from around 600,000 km to 1.6 million km. **h** _____ , mass production of cars transformed business, making oil and rubber into major industries, increasing demand for steel, and creating new service industries, **i** _____ filling stations, motels and insurance. **j** _____ , the car represented the American ideal of 'personal freedom' – before environmental damage and an epidemic of obesity began to force Americans to think again.

a A *utter*	B *sheer*	C *mere*
b A *for example*	B *such as*	C *that is*
c A *literally*	B *namely*	C *merely*
d A *Apart from*	B *And so forth*	C *In other words*
e A *in conclusion*	B *instead*	C *alternatively*
f A *Simply*	B *Secondly*	C *Literally*
g A *sheer*	B *mere*	C *utter*
h A *In a way*	B *Thirdly*	C *Instead*
i A *examples include*	B *etc*	C *such as*
j A *In a way*	B *For example*	C *Except for*

GLOSSARY

EXTENSION ACTIVITY

A Write a short text about the town or city you live in, using these phrases:

there are a number ... first of all, ... secondly ... apart from ... such as ... a kind of ... to sum up ...

B Choose ten examples from the explanation pages and translate them into your language.

42

organizing text (3)

replacing words (substitution)

- Pronouns often replace nouns or noun phrases, to avoid repeating the same words.
  *I put down my coffee, and gave Helen **hers** (her coffee). **She** (Helen) took one sip of **it** (the coffee) and said, 'This (this coffee) is awful. What did you put in **it** (this coffee)?'*

- *one* and *ones*
  We can use *one* in the place of a noun or when we want to avoid repeating a noun.
  *'I've got three bikes, but I like **this one** best. It's **the fastest one**.'*
  *'Yes, that's **a good one**.'*

  The plural form is *ones*.
  *The **most expensive ones** are not always the best.*

- *mine, yours* etc
  We do not normally use possessive adjectives (*my, your* etc) with *one / ones*, but use only a pronoun (*mine, yours* etc) instead.
  *This is **mine**.   This one is **mine**.*

- *some, any*
  We use *some* and *any* on their own to avoid repeating plurals or uncountables.
  *Where are the stamps? I need **some** (stamps). Have you got **any** (stamps)?*

- *so*
  After verbs *believe, expect, guess, hope, imagine, suppose, think* etc, and after *be afraid*, we use *so* instead of repeating a clause.
  *'Is Jill coming tomorrow?'   '**I hope so**'. (= I hope that she is coming)*
  *'Will you be long?'   '**I don't think so**'. (= I don't think that I'll be long.)*

  We can use *not* as the negative form.
  *'Is Jill coming tomorrow?'   '**I hope not**'. (= I hope that she isn't coming)*

  After *say, tell* we can use *so* instead of repeating all the words used.
  *'I didn't really want to see that film.' 'Why didn't you **say so**?'*
  (= Why didn't you say that you didn't want to see the film?)
  *I don't think Anna did the right thing, and **I told her so**.*
  (= I told Anna that I didn't think she had done the right thing.)

  We can also use *so* in an inverted form with *say, tell, understand* to mean 'that is what'.
  *Jack is a genius. Or **so** his teachers keep telling him.*
  (= Or that is what his teachers keep telling him.)

  After *if*, *so* can be used instead of repeating information as a conditional clause.
  *There may be heavy snow tomorrow. **If so**, the school will be closed.*
  (= If there is heavy snow ...)

  With *less, more, very much so* can be used to avoid repeating an adjective or adverb.
  *Everything is running smoothly, **more so** than usual in fact. (= more smoothly)*
  *'Are you interested in this job?'   '**Very much so**.' (= very much interested).*

- *do so*
  We can use a form of *do* with *so* to avoid repeating a verb phrase.
  *They told Terry to get out of the car, and he **did so**. (= he got out of the car)*
  *Janet left her wallet in the shop, but didn't remember **doing so**. (= leaving it)*

- *do*
  Informally we often use *do* or *do that* to refer to an action.
  *'I promised to collect the children from school, but **I can't do it**.'*
  *'Don't worry, **I'll do it**.'*

- *so do I* etc
  When we agree with another person's statement we can replace a verb with *so* (when the statement is positive) or *neither / nor* (when the statement is negative) followed by *do* or a modal auxiliary before the subject.
  *'I **like** this film.'*   *'**So do I.**'*
  *'I **don't** like seafood.'*   *'**Neither / Nor do we**.'*
  *'I **can't** hear a thing!'*   *'**Neither / Nor can I**.'*

  We can use *too* and *not … either* without inversion to mean the same thing.
  *'I **like** this film.'*   *'**I do too.**'*
  *'I **don't** like seafood.'*   *'**We don't either.**'*

leaving things out (ellipsis)

- In clauses joined by *and* or *but*, we do not have to repeat the subject in the second clause.
  *Maria **went** into the room and (she) **opened** the cupboard.*
  *I **stood** on a chair but (I) still **couldn't** reach the top.*

- In clauses joined by *and, but, or,* we can leave out a repeated subject and auxiliary, or subject and verb.
  *I've **read** the article, and (I have) **summarized** the main points.*
  *David **likes** rock music, (he likes) **going** to parties, and (he likes) **tennis**.*

  Note that it is not possible to leave out subjects, auxiliaries or verbs after words like *because, before* etc.

- When a second clause repeats a verb phrase, we can use the auxiliary part only.
  *I've **been to Russia**, but Tina **hasn't** (been to Russia).*
  *Jane says **she's coming to the party**, but **Martin isn't** (coming to the party).*

- When a phrase with *be* + adjective is repeated, we can leave out the second adjective.
  *I'm interested in this, but Harry **isn't** (interested in this).*

- We can leave out a repeated verb phrase after *to*-infinitive or *not to*-infinitive.
  *Anna **doesn't play tennis** now, but she used **to** (play tennis).*
  *He'll **throw things** out of the window, unless you tell him **not to** (throw things out of the window).*
  *Jack felt like playing football, but his friends **didn't want to** (play football).*

Jack felt like playing football, but his friends didn't want to.

- In reported questions, we can leave out repeated words after question words.
  *He said he would meet us soon, but **he didn't say when** (he would meet us).*

1 Underline the best option.

a I'm supposed to be writing a project, but *I do too / I haven't done it yet.*

b I don't really like this area, and *nor my friends do / neither do my friends.*

c The news is awful. Did you see *it / them* on TV?

d Everyone thought Helen had chosen the wrong job but nobody *told it her / told her so.*

e The prime minister may call an election this year, and *if so he is / neither is he* certain to win.

f Taxing petrol is unpopular, and never *to do so / more so* than now when prices are hitting record levels.

g I was told to report to office 101, but before *it / doing so* I went to the cafeteria.

h The world is getting hotter, or *so do / so* many people would have us believe.

i They are all more or less the same quality, but *this is the most expensive one / this one it's the most expensive.*

j I ate my sandwich, but Emma didn't eat *her / hers.*

2 Replace the words underlined with a suitable word or words.

a I like horror films, but I didn't enjoy that <u>film</u>.   *one*

b 'Did you enjoy the play?' 'Yes, <u>I enjoyed it very much indeed</u>.'   ....

c The museum may be closed tomorrow. If <u>so</u>, we'll go on Tuesday.   ....

d We sell a lot of jeans, and these are the most popular <u>jeans</u>.   ....

e I've finished my project but Maria hasn't finished <u>her project</u>.   ....

f The officer told Paul to get out of the car, and he <u>got out of the car</u>.   ....

g I can't skateboard and <u>Brian can't skateboard either</u>.   ....

h Valerie has been appointed finance director, or <u>that is what</u> I understand.   ....

i 'Are we starting early tomorrow?' 'I hope <u>we aren't starting early</u>!'   ....

j 'I really wanted to leave earlier'. 'Why didn't you say <u>you wanted to</u>?'   ....

3 Choose the best option, A, B or C, to complete the sentence.

a David says he'll be arriving on Monday, but he doesn't know   *C* ....

b I didn't believe what Jane had said, and I told   ....

c Kate has completed her project, but   ....

d I tried to repair the washing-machine   ....

e Danny didn't accept Helen's invitation, though   ....

f Mary used to like horror films but   ....

g Now you've finished your lunch, could you give the twins   ....

a A *when he will.*   B *very much so.*   C *exactly when.*

b A *her so.*   B *so.*   C *that so.*

c A *neither have I.*   B *I haven't.*   C *I hope so.*

d A *but it couldn't do.* B *so I couldn't.*   C *but couldn't do it.*

e A *he wanted to.*   B *he thought so.*   C *nor did he.*

f A *nor does she.*   B *she doesn't now.*   C *they don't like her now.*

g A *theirs.*   B *their.*   C *it.*

4 <u>Underline</u> the words that can be left out. Leaving out words may be impossible in some sentences.

   a I don't have a bike now but I used to <u>have one</u>.

   b Tony will be going to the shops and he'll get you some stamps.

   c Harry likes listening to music and he likes playing computer games.

   d I'm worried about the exam, but my friends aren't worried about it.

   e Mary used to make her own clothes, but she doesn't make her own clothes any more.

   f Kate says she's not interested, but Rita might want to.

   g I've been to Brazil, but Theresa hasn't been there.

   h Jack said he would bring someone to the party, but he didn't say who he would bring to the party.

   i Jim wanted to go swimming, but none of his friends felt like it.

   j I've done the shopping and I've cleaned the house.

5 Rewrite the sentence or one of the sentences so that it contains the word in capitals.

   a 'Do you think you'll be late tonight?' 'I don't suppose I will'.   SO
     'Do you think you'll be late tonight?' 'I don't suppose so'.

   b Bond started to disconnect the red wire, but as he started disconnecting it, something
     told him he had made a mistake.   SO

   c If you wanted to stay at home, why didn't you say you wanted to stay at home?   SO

   d Sue tried to reach the top shelf but it was impossible.   DO

   e I can't stand folk music, and David can't stand folk music.   CAN

   f Laura left her bike outside the cinema, but she didn't remember leaving it there.   SO

   g The robbery was committed by two people, or that is what we believe.   SO

The following exercises practise grammar from **Units 40, 41** and **42**.

6 Rewrite the sentence or one of the sentences so that it contains the word in capitals.

a There is no problem with money.   AS FAR

b From one point of view, I think you're absolutely correct.   IN

c Jim wasn't there, but everyone else was.   APART FROM

d Those are your cards and these are my cards.   YOURS

e Lastly, I would like to thank the organizers of this conference.   IN

f This country has higher youth unemployment than other European countries.   COMPARISON

g Tom has been ill and so has been absent from college.   DUE

h Tony thinks it was a terrible film, and I think it was a terrible film too.   DO

i Although United played badly, they won the match.   LEAST

j The tennis tournament has been postponed because of bad weather.   OWING

k 'Will you be here next year?' 'I doubt it.'   SO

l The scheme has been fairly successful.   EXTENT

m The earthquake has caused the closure of many roads in the area.   RESULT

n The two artists appear to be different but share similarities.   RESPECTS

o Poor eyesight forced her to give up driving.   ACCOUNT

p I didn't take the bus, I went on foot.   INSTEAD OF

q To begin with, write down a list of your ideas.   ALL

r Many animals, eg bears, sleep for much of the winter.   AS

s No artefact which is alien, ie not from our planet, has ever been discovered.   SAY

7 Choose the best option, A, B or C, to complete the sentence.

a Sorry, I haven't got any change. _C_, I don't really think you should be eating more ice cream.

b The prices of some holidays have fallen on average .... last year.

c The high winds uprooted many trees, ... damaging buildings.

d ...., the second film in the *Space Wars* series is more exciting than the first, but overall it is less entertaining.

e .... the water shortage, Southern Water has introduced a ban on garden hosepipes.

f Look over your notes and think about likely questions. But ...., make sure you have a realistic revision timetable, and stick to it.

g I enjoyed Johnny's last film, but I'm not so keen on ....

h Accident investigators were unable to recover the aircraft's black box data recorder. .... the exact cause of the crash remains unknown.

i Sails use the power of the wind to produce forward motion. ...., windmills use it to produce a circular movement.

j Peter says he can come back tomorrow, but his brother ....

k The Millennium Bridge was opened on 10 June 2000. .... technical problems, it was forced to close for repairs, and did not open again until February 2002.

l There has been trouble at previous matches between the two sides; .... the need for extra policing this time.

m Nothing should go wrong, but if ...., give me a ring on this number.

a	A *Thus*	B *Nevertheless*	C *Besides*
b	A *in comparison to*	B *as a result of*	C *owing to*
c	A *compared to*	B *in addition*	C *as well as*
d	A *Above all*	B *None the less*	C *In some respects*
e	A *Despite*	B *Owing to*	C *compared to*
f	A *to a certain extent*	B *above all*	C *in some ways*
g	A *this one*	B *it*	C *more so*
h	A *On the contrary*	B *Thus*	C *At least*
i	A *As a result*	B *Hence*	C *In the same way*
j	A *can't*	B *doesn't say*	C *won't do*
k	A *As a result of*	B *Despite*	C *As well as*
l	A *hence*	B *as a result*	C *owing to*
m	A *so*	B *they should do*	C *it does*

EXTENSION ACTIVITY

A a Write some questions which could be followed by these answers.

   I hope so!   *I don't expect so.*
   It's not mine.   *I think I'd rather have that one.*

   b Write some statements which could be followed by these responses.

   So do we.   *Neither can I.*
   So do you!   *Neither does mine.*

B Choose ten examples from the explanation pages and translate them into your language.

43 inversion and fronting

inversion

This involves using question word order after an adverbial with a negative or restrictive meaning comes at the beginning of the sentence. These structures are normally only used in formal speech and writing. Note that all of these adverbials can be used without inversion if they come in the normal position.

- *never*
  *I have **never** seen a more obvious case of cheating!* (normal position)
  ***Never have I seen** a more obvious case of cheating!*

- *rarely*
  ***Rarely does such a rare painting come** on the market.*

- *seldom*
  ***Seldom has a scientific discovery had** such an impact.*

- *No sooner ... than*
  ***No sooner had I shut the door than** I realized I had left my keys inside.*

- *Hardly ... when*
  ***Hardly had the play started when** there was a disturbance in the audience.*

- *Scarcely ... when (than)*
  ***Scarcely had they entered the castle when** there was a huge explosion.*

- *Only after, only when, only later, only then, only*
  ***Only Jane** managed to finish the project on time.* (no inversion)
  ***Only in a city as large as this can you** find so many foreign restaurants.*
  ***Only after we had left the ship did we** realize that the captain had remained.*

- *On no condition, under no circumstances, on no account, at no time, in no way*
  ***Under no circumstances is this door** to be left unlocked.*

- *Not until*
  *Not until he stopped to rest **did Jack realize** that he had been wounded.*
  *Not until the building had been made safe **could anyone go** back inside.*

- *Not only ... but also*
  ***Not only did he lose** all the money, **but he also** found himself in debt.*

- *Little*
  ***Little did anyone suspect** what was about to happen.*

No sooner had I shut the door than I realized I had left my keys inside.

REVISED
9:37 am, Feb 27, 200

fronting

This involves putting first a clause not normally at the beginning of the sentence. It may also involve putting the verb in an inverted position.

- Relative clauses can be placed first when they normally follow negative verbs of understanding, knowing, etc. This is normally a spoken form.
  I have no idea who he is. **Who he is**, *I have no idea.*
  I really don't know what you mean. **What you mean**, *I really don't know.*

- *Here, there, back, out, up, down, on, off* etc can begin a sentence or a clause, followed by a verb. This is usually *come* or *go*. The sentence is often an exclamation.
  A messenger came back with the answer. **Back came** *a messenger with the answer.*
  Here *comes the rain!* **Out** *went the lights!*
  Down *went the ship to the bottom of the sea.*
  As we were walking home, **down came the rain***, and we had to run for it.*

- In the same way, an adverbial phrase can begin a sentence or a clause, followed by a verb. This kind of sentence is common in literary writing.
  A group of armed men came along the street.
  Along the street came *a group of armed men.*
  While we were waiting to see what would happen next, **along the street came** *a group of armed men, waving their guns in the air and shouting.*
  Up the hill went *the bus, creaking and groaning.*
  Through the window jumped *a masked man.*

conditional sentences

- *as, though* with *may, might*
  It may sound unlikely, but it's true.
  Unlikely as it may *sound, it's true.*
  The car may be cheap, but it's in terrible condition.
  Cheap though the car may be*, it's in terrible condition.*

- *try as (someone) might*
  This construction is used to mean that although someone tried hard, they couldn't succeed in what they were trying to do.
  She tried hard, but couldn't move the wardrobe.
  Try as she might*, she couldn't move the wardrobe.*
  Try as he might*, he couldn't pass his driving test.*

- *were, had, should* conditional sentences
  These are highly formal, and omit *if*, putting the auxiliary at the beginning of the sentence.
  If the government were to resign, the situation might be resolved.
  Were the government to resign*, the situation might be resolved.*
  If proper measures had been taken, this situation would not have occurred.
  Had proper measures been taken*, this situation would not have occurred.*
  If an outbreak of flu should take place, special measures will be introduced.
  Should an outbreak of flu take place*, special measures will be introduced.*

1 <u>Underline</u> the best word or phrase.

a *Not only / Rarely* do you see top-rate cameras which are also easy to use.

b *Should / Were* the strike go ahead, it could severely damage the company.

c *Never I have seen / Never have I seen* such a dramatic end to a football match.

d *What he is talking about / What is he talking about*, I have no idea.

e Only the two members of the French team *managed / did they manage* to finish the race.

f *As it may seem strange / Strange as it may seem*, he is actually one of the richest men in the world!

g Hardly had the train pulled out of the station *when / than* there was a loud screeching sound.

h Suddenly, *ran into the room / into the room ran* a huge dog.

i *Had we known / Had we to have known* in advance, we could have done something about it.

j Not until the wreckage had been examined *could / was* terrorism be ruled out.

k *Hardly / Little* did I know that it would be another three years before I saw her again.

l *Should / Were* the alarm to ring, leave the building immediately.

2 Choose the best option, A, B or C, to complete the sentence.

a *..C..* how serious the situation was.

b Just as the players took their places on the court, ...

c .... my bag I really can't remember.

d .... , everyone would probably have escaped from the building.

e At no time .... on the plane in any danger.

f .... second thoughts, don't hesitate to phone me.

g Strange .... , I actually enjoy working underground.

h Jane .... the train but also lost her luggage.

i .... , we might consider making another offer.

j Without warning, onto the stage .... brandishing a knife.

k Suddenly the sky went dark, and .... the rain.

l .... is this piece of equipment to be removed from the building.

a A *Little anyone did realize*	B *Little realized anyone*	C *Little did anyone realize*
b A *did the rain pour down*	B *down poured the rain.*	C *did pour down the rain*
c A *Where I've left*	B *Where have I left*	C *Where left I*
d A *Had it not been locked the fire door*	B *Had not been locked the fire door*	C *Had the fire door not been locked*
e A *were the passengers*	B *the passengers were*	C *were they the passengers*
f A *Should have you*	B *Should you have*	C *Should you had*
g A *as does it sound*	B *sound though it is*	C *as it may sound*
h A *not only did she miss*	B *not only missed*	C *not only did miss*
i A *Were it the situation to change*	B *Were a change in the situation*	C *Were the situation to change*
j A *did jump a man*	B *jumped a man*	C *did a man jump*
k A *there down came*	B *came down*	C *down came*
l A *On no account*	B *Hardly*	C *Rarely*

3 Write a new sentence with the same meaning, containing the word in capitals.

a If we took no action, the situation would only become worse.   WERE
   Were we to take no action, the situation would only become worse.

b A member of the government rarely admits to making a serious mistake.   DOES

c You are not to leave this room under any circumstances.   NO

d The police only later revealed the true identity of the thief.   DID

e Although Andrew tried hard, he couldn't pass his driving test.   MIGHT

f If you'd consulted me at the outset, I could have given you the right advice.   HAD

g If you offered me a higher salary, I would take the job.   WERE

h If the weather worsens, the match will probably be cancelled.   SHOULD

i It was only after checking the accounts that they realized money was missing.   DID

j The breach of security has not affected the examination results in any way.   NO

4 Complete the text using one word in each gap.

Last year, we visited Brazil and saw the carnival in Rio. Strange
as it may a ___seem___ , we just hadn't thought of visiting Brazil
before, and we couldn't believe how fantastic it was. Rio is a great
city, and it's sometimes hard to believe it's real! We really enjoyed
the carnival. We had booked some events before we arrived, and
b _____ did we realize how lucky we were to have tickets for
the Samba show. No c _____ had we taken our seats, than
the show began. d _____ the stage came groups of dancers,
one after the other, for hours! That was exhausting but there was
more to come. Not e _____ we stood and watched the carnival
parade did we realize how many people were taking part! Along
the street f _____ dancers and musicians, and everyone
clapped and cheered. g _____ anyone told me I would end
up dancing in the street all night, I wouldn't have believed them!
There were such amazing costumes and floats. h _____ in a
city as diverse as this, could you see so many unusual sights. Never
i _____ I have imagined what an amazing sight it would be.
Only j _____ we finally got home and looked at all our photos
k _____ we realize how incredible our holiday in Brazil had
been. l _____ anyone should want to go any where else for a
holiday, I really don't know!

5 Complete the sentence so that it means the same as the first sentence.

a Two armed policeman ran into the room.
Into *the room ran two armed policemen* .

b You can only really enjoy the view on a clear day like today.
Only _____ .

c If the ship collided with an iceberg, the passengers would be in no danger.
Should _____ .

d The case may be unusual, but such cases are not completely unheard of.
Unusual _____ .

e Suddenly it started raining.
Suddenly down _____ .

f A government has rarely acted with such blatant dishonesty.
Rarely _____ .

g If you asked me again, I would give you the same answer as before.
Were _____ .

h I have no idea what the matter is.
What _____ .

i If we had realized that the hurricane would hit the city, we would have evacuated the residents in advance.
Had _____ .

j Nobody had any suspicion that the police inspector was the murderer.
Little _____ .

k The theft was only discovered when the accounts were checked.
Only _____ .

l Paula had no sooner shut the door than she realized she had left her key inside.
No sooner _____ .

6 Put one suitable word in each space.

a Rarely _do_____ we find students who are willing to think for themselves.

b _____ in the polar regions does the temperature fall to such a low level.

c Little _____ anyone suppose that Mrs Robertson was an enemy agent.

d Scarcely _____ everyone left the building when there was a huge explosion.

e Seldom _____ so many people voted for such an unlikely candidate.

f Not until doctors examined Brian later _____ anyone realize that he had been shot.

g No sooner had we reached the bottom of the mountain _____ it started snowing heavily.

h _____ no circumstances are bags to be taken into the library.

i Only _____ the airline official checked again did she realize I had been given the wrong ticket.

j Not only did Harrison break into the house, _____ he also attacked one of the occupants.

k Never _____ there been a better time to buy a new car.

l Not only _____ she finish the test before the others in the class, but she also got the best mark.

7 Choose the best option, A, B or C, for each gap.

Odysseus and the Sirens

Before the ship came to the island of the Sirens, Odysseus ordered his men to plug their ears with wax and tie him to the mast. 'Under no circumstances **a** _B_ cut me free, whatever happens,' he told them. **b'** .... we are clear of the island must I be set free.' **c** .... he did this was very simple. The Sirens lured sailors to their deaths by their beautiful singing. **d** .... all the sailors to hear their songs, they would lose their will to continue on their journey. Odysseus wanted to hear the beautiful singing, but he wanted to survive. Soon **e** .... appeared the island of the Sirens. The women were sitting on a bank of flowers, holding out their arms to the ship, and singing. No sooner **f** .... them, than Odysseus became mad with longing. **g** .... not been tied to the mast, he would have leapt into the water and swum to the shore. **h** .... he might, he couldn't persuade his men to untie him. Past the island **i** .... , the crew pulling at the oars. **j** .... the singing of the Sirens had died away, and the island had passed out of sight, did Odysseus regain his proper senses. His men untied him, and they continued on their voyage.

a	**A** *you will*	**B** *are you to*	**C** *do you*
b	**A** *Only after*	**B** *Not only*	**C** *Never*
c	**A** *Little*	**B** *Try as*	**C** *Why*
d	**A** *Were*	**B** *If*	**C** *Should*
e	**A** *than he had expected*	**B** *had it*	**C** *out of the mist*
f	**A** *he heard*	**B** *had he heard*	**C** *was he hearing them*
g	**A** *Was he*	**B** *Did he*	**C** *Had he*
h	**A** *Try as*	**B** *If*	**C** *Only after*
i	**A** *did they went*	**B** *went the ship*	**C** *go Odysseus and his men*
j	**A** *Not until*	**B** *In no way*	**C** *No sooner than*

GLOSSARY

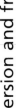

EXTENSION ACTIVITY

A Write some examples beginning:

> *Were my country …*   *Should global warming …*   *Had I known …*

B Choose ten examples from the explanation pages and translate them into your language.

44 emphasis

it-clauses

These are clauses introduced by *it is / was*, putting the clause at the front of the sentence for emphasis. Key words usually receive more stress when spoken. Stressed words are in **bold** in the examples. Sentences of this kind are also called *cleft sentences*.

- noun phrase (including *-ing*) + *that*-clause
  It's keeping your balance that matters most.
  (= What matters most is keeping your balance.)
  It was the left back who finally scored.
  (= The left back was the one who finally scored.)
  It was the last straw that broke the camel's back.

- adverbial and prepositional phrases + *that*-clause
  It was after Jane got to the office that she realized she had forgotten her keys.
  (= After Jane got to the office, she realized she had forgotten her keys.)
  It was in the middle of the night that the fire was discovered.
  (= The fire was discovered in the middle of the night.)

- *when, how, what, because* + *that*-clause
  This kind of sentence is more common in everyday speech.
  It was when I saw the police that I panicked.
  (= When I saw the police was when I panicked.)
  It was because I had no money that I had to go home.
  It's how he can put up with it that I don't understand.
  It was what she said next that surprised everyone.

what-clauses

These clauses also put more emphasis on what follows, and form another kind of cleft sentence. This kind of sentence is more common in everyday speech.

- *what* + verb phrase + *is* (+ *the fact that, the way, why, what, who* etc)
  What bothers me is the way the news was announced.
  (= The way the news was announced bothers me.)
  What upsets me is the fact that you lied.
  (= The fact that you lied upsets me.)
  What we don't really know at the moment is why the accident happened.

- instruction + imperative
  We often use a *what*-clause when we give an instruction with verbs such as *want, need*, etc
  What I want you to do is go home and rest.
  What you need to do is fill in this form.

- explanation + *that*-clause
  We often use a *what*-clause when we explain a situation.
  What we have to remember is that he's only been working here for a week.

- *what* + verb + object
  Some *what*-clauses can be put at the beginning or the end of the sentence.
  What interests me is his early paintings.
  His early paintings are *what interests me*.

emphasizing negatives

- These phrases are used to emphasize adjectives with *not*: *not at all, not in the least / the slightest, not the least / slightest bit*.
  No, don't worry, **I'm not at all cold**.
  Sorry, but **I'm not the slightest bit interested**.
  Terry **wasn't at all worried**.

44

- *No* + noun and *none* can be emphasized by: *no ... whatsoever, none at all, none whatsoever.*
  There are **none at all** in this box, as far as I can see.
  There is **no money whatsoever** available for school trips at the moment.

own

- We use *own* to emphasis possessive adjectives.
  She used **her own money** to buy the stamps.

  Common phrases include *(your) own fault, in (your) own words.*
  The accident was **his own fault**.
  Tell us the story **in your own words**.

- Note also: *on (your) own* (without anyone else)   Tim lives **on his own**.
  of (your) own (not belonging to anyone else)   I have a room **of my own**.

auxiliary *do*

- We can use *do* to emphasize a statement.
  I do like your new car! It's really cool!

- We also use *do* in polite forms.
  Do come in!   **I do hope** you enjoyed our little talk.

all

- We can put *all* (meaning *the only thing*) at the beginning of a clause for emphasis.
  All he does is watch television.   **All** I need is another €500.

very ... indeed

- We can use *very* + adjective + *indeed* to add emphasis in speech.
  Thank you **very** much **indeed**.

  Often this is in response to what another person says.
  Was the chicken good?   Yes, it **was very good indeed**!

- We can use *very* to mean *the exact* in speech.
  That's **the very book** I've been looking for!   (= the exact one)
  She's probably waiting outside **at this very moment**!   (= this one exactly)

  Very can also mean at the extreme end of something.
  Turn right **at the very top** of the stairs.
  This is **the very last time** I ask, I promise.

whatever, who ever, wherever etc

- Question words ending -*ever* make the question more emphatic, and often suggest disbelief.
  Whatever was that terrible noise!   (I really don't know)
  Wherever did you find that fantastic dress?

repetition

- A verb can be repeated for emphasis. Commonly used verbs are: *wait, try.*
  I waited and waited, but she never turned up.
  Helen tried and tried, but she couldn't reach the shelf.

- Some adverbials also use repetition for emphasis.
  They asked him the same question **again and again**.
  We are spending **more and more** each year.
  The ship was getting **further and further** away.

(See also **Unit 27**, intensifiers.)

1 <u>Underline</u> the best phrase.

a Fiona is <u>*not the slightest bit*</u> / *none at all* interested in football.

b I'm sorry, but this is *none at all* / *nothing whatsoever* to do with you!

c I *do hope you* / *hope you do* haven't been waiting too long.

d The plane tickets arrived by messenger at *the very last moment* / *the last moment indeed*.

e What we want to know is *who did it send* / *who sent* the anonymous letter.

f That's *the very thing* / *the thing whatsoever* I was going to say!

g What you need *to do* / *that you do* is phone your insurance company.

h *Where indeed* / *Wherever* have you been all afternoon? We've all been very worried!

i It was Jim *the one who* / *who* finally found the answer.

j Marcia was not *whatsoever* / *at all* worried by her high credit-card bill.

2 Choose the best option, A, B or C, to complete the sentence.

a ...A... did you get that silly hat?

b Kate .... upset by what Frank said to her.

c .... the lights went on that we saw the jewels were missing.

d I've nearly finished. .... is another half an hour, and that'll be it.

e What you have to bear in mind .... your last chance.

f 'Do you have any regrets?' '............ .'

g What annoys me .... nobody told me about the change.

h We waited and waited, ... the letter never arrived.

i The completion date for the new stadium is getting .... away.

j What I .... do is waste time worrying.

a **A** *Wherever*	**B** *Whatsoever*	**C** *It was when*
b **A** *was none at all*	**B** *was none whatsoever*	**C** *wasn't at all*
c **A** *What happened was*	**B** *It was*	**C** *It was when*
d **A** *It's what I need*	**B** *All I need*	**C** *More and more*
e **A** *that is this is*	**B** *is this that is*	**C** *is that this is*
f **A** *No whatsoever*	**B** *None whatsoever*	**C** *Not at all whatsoever*
g **A** *that*	**B** *is the fact that*	**C** *it is that*
h **A** *when*	**B** *whenever*	**C** *but*
i **A** *further and further*	**B** *more and more*	**C** *again and again*
j **A** *want is*	**B** *don't want you to*	**C** *want you is*

3 Write a new sentence with the same meaning, containing the word in capitals.

a The police asked David the same question repeatedly.   AND

   The police asked David the same question again and again.

b There was absolutely no chance of saving the damaged ship.   ALL

c The house I was looking for was right at the end of the street.   VERY

d The only thing I want to do is sleep.   ALL

e I want to have a bike just for myself.   OWN

f I became alarmed when I saw smoke coming from under the door.   IT

g Thanks a million for your help.   INDEED

h I can't imagine what you mean!   WHATEVER

i Everyone was taken by surprise by what Robert did next.   IT

j You have no-one to blame but yourself.   OWN

---

social studies

5 Complete the text using one word in each gap.

Admitting we are wrong

Most people have trouble admitting their **a** _own_ faults, though they are more than happy to point out everyone else's. This can be useful. After all, it's usually when someone else tells us that we have done something wrong **b** _____ we learn something about ourselves. What we have to do **c** _____ take a deep breath, and face up to what we have done. Remember, when it comes to understanding ourselves, we're not on our **d** _____ . Everyone we know lends a helping hand! Of course, doing the wrong thing is easy, but it's **e** _____ we do about our mistakes that counts. Naturally we are all good at refusing to believe that we have done anything wrong **f** _____ all. As we try to justify our actions, our explanations get more and **g** _____ complicated. We try to convince the listener that we are telling the truth, but it's no use. There is no chance **h** _____ all that they will believe us. And the truth is that **i** _____ is ourselves we have deceived, not them. That's the **j** _____ point I'm trying to make. **k** _____ you do, don't get in the habit of deceiving yourself. **l** _____ is difficult is honestly admitting that we are wrong – especially to ourselves.

GLOSSARY

EXTENSION ACTIVITY

A Write some true examples beginning or ending:

I was when I started at this school …   *What interests me most is …*
… no time whatsoever …   *… very good indeed*

*Need more practice? Go to the **Review** on page 208.*

emphasis

Review

How to use this section

a   As extra practice, if you have finished the rest of the unit and the Extension Activities.

b   To test yourself. Do the exercises, check your answers, then decide if you need to have a look at the presentation page again.

c   If you need extra practice, read the presentation page(s) again, then try to do the extra exercises.

Unit 3

Complete the text with the correct form of the verb in brackets. Use past simple, past continuous, or past perfect simple.

Something wholesale
by Eric Newby

My father's office was on the fourth floor. Now he
a (sit) .... behind the large shiny desk
which he b (occupy) .... since the
departure of Mr Lane. As usual, on the top of his desk there
c (stand) .... a large jug of barley
water. My father was now seventy-five years old. A serious
operation d (reduce) .... him to a
shadow of his former self. He e (undergo)
.... it in an East End hospital while the
bombs f (rain) .... down. His former
pugnacity g (largely evaporate) ....
Previously he h (be) ....
a man of impressive physique; he was now extremely
thin and fragile, like a piece of old lace. But he was still
exceptionally handsome, and in a suit of thick flannel, with
a rose in his buttonhole and a fresh complexion, he
i (look) .... like a small boy whose
preparatory school j (give) .... him
leave to attend the wedding of an elder brother.

Unit 8

Complete the sentence so that it means the same as the first sentence.

a   People believed that the car had been stolen.
    The car *was believed to have been stolen.*

b   People thought the plane had crashed in the mountains.
    The plane ....
    ....

c   People knew that the prime minister had rejected the plan.
    The prime minister ....
    ....

d   People reported that the owner of the bank had fled to South America.
    The owner of the bank ....
    ....

e   People thought the police had found fingerprints at the scene of the crime.
    The police ....
    ....

f   People believed that the hurricane killed over a thousand people.
    The hurricane ....
    ....

g   People knew that the suspect visited the murdered man on the afternoon of his death.
    The suspect ....
    ....

h   People reported that the newspaper paid the singer $2 million in damages.
    The newspaper ....
    ....

Unit 9

Underline the best verb form, or choose both if this is possible.

a It took a long time, but I *had / got* my car started in the end.

b Sorry, I've got to rush. I have to *have / get* the evening meal prepared.

c Anna *is having / is getting* her teeth seen to.

d We'll have to work harder if we're going to *have / get* the job done in time.

e I've just *had / got* my car broken into.

f I've been trying really hard, but I haven't *had / got* my project written yet.

g Paul *had his hair / got his hair* cut yesterday, and he looks awful!

h We're going to *have / get* an electrician to check the wiring.

i Have you *had / got* your new IPod to work yet?

j Are you *having / getting* your house painted, or are you doing it yourself?

Unit 11

1 Use the prompts to make a sentence. Include the words in capitals.

a you have a camera with you at the scene of the accident / take some shots of all the vehicles involved.   HAPPEN

If you happen to have a camera with you at the scene of the accident, you can take some shots of all the vehicles involved.

b check the weather reports before you leave / you might take the wrong clothes with you. OTHERWISE

c the income from advertising / newspapers not earn enough money   WERE

d investors buy shares / they have confidence in the market   UNLESS

e we guarantee to get you talking / you can't speak a word of English   EVEN IF

f permanent residents can vote / they are aged 18 or over   PROVIDED

g I accept the job / I be able to work from home some of the time?   WERE

h be a serious outbreak of bird flu in Europe / what the EU do?   SUPPOSING

i unless we do something now, the situation get worse   IF

2 Complete the text with one word in each gap.

Why are some people so difficult about money? 'Lend me €100, a ___or___ I won't be able to go out on Saturday,' you say on Friday morning. 'Ah, b _____ only you c _____ asked me yesterday. I really haven't got enough myself this week. And d _____ if I did have some, I don't think you'd pay it back.' You try another line of attack. 'If it hadn't e _____ for that meal I bought you, I f _____ need to borrow any money. And I'll have some money by next weekend. What if I g _____ to promise to pay it back next Saturday?' There is a moment's silence. 'Well, I might lend you €50, h _____ you pay it back on Monday.'

Unit 12

Rewrite the sentence so that it contains the word in capitals and has same meaning.

a I advise you not to make any hasty decisions. WERE

I wouldn't make any hasty decisions, if I were you.

b He pretends to be in charge of the office. BEHAVES

c Please don't bring the dog with you. SOONER

....

d I regret selling my old car. WISH

....

e Do have a good time at the party! HOPE

....

f Please don't call me again. RATHER

....

g It's a pity you're leaving in the morning. WISH

....

h I don't think you should drink any more. WERE

....

i I'd like to find the answer to this problem. WISH

....

Unit 14

Underline the best verb form to complete the sentence.

a There's someone outside, but it <u>can't be</u> / mustn't be
   Tony. He's in New York.

b Hello, you could be / must be Helen. I'm Peter's
   brother, George.

c I'm not quite sure where Anna is. She might have gone
   / must have gone to the shops, I suppose. Or perhaps
   she's upstairs.

d I don't know what's happened to Sue. She should have
   got here / must have got here by now.

e My wallet isn't in my pocket. I should have left / must
   have left it in my other jacket.

f Professor James never has any idea about time, so
   she's bound to be / she must be late.

g It's strange that Brian didn't even stop and say hello.
   He can't have recognized / shouldn't have recognized us.

h Little David isn't usually much of a problem, but he
   could get / can get difficult when he's tired.

i All flights are cancelled until Monday, so we may as
   well go / can hardly go back to the hotel until then.

j You might have told / can't have told me there was a
   test today. I haven't done any revision at all.

Unit 16

Rewrite the sentences about medicine in the past, using
would or wouldn't.

a In the past, surgeons operated on patients without
   any kind of anaesthetic.

....

b They tried to work as quickly as possible to minimize
   the patient's suffering.

....

c Such operations often took place in the patient's own
   home.

....

d In some countries, religious authorities refused to
   allow surgeons to study anatomy using dead bodies.

....

e Surgeons often learned about anatomy by treating
   soldiers in battle.

....

f Doctors were also expected to follow the explanations
   of ancient writers.

....

g When new medical discoveries were made in the
   Renaissance, traditional doctors refused to believe
   that the old methods were wrong.

....

h Some ancient ideas – such as that of removing
   blood from patients (bleeding) – survived in medical
   practice until the late nineteenth century.

....

Unit 18

Rewrite what each person said as direct speech, and include the word in capitals.

a Carol invited me to stay to lunch. WOULD
   'Would you like to stay to lunch?'

b Peter reminded me to take my keys with me. FORGET
   ....

c Sue suggested we all met outside the cinema. DON'T
   ....

d Martin denied having anything to do with the burglary. HAVE
   ....

e Paula apologized for taking so long over the phone call. TOOK
   ....

f Mrs James accused the boy of breaking her kitchen window. YOU
   ....

g Tony refused to give his name to the police. NO
   ....

h Claudia offered them tea and cakes. YOU
   ....

i Bill promised to return the money as soon as he could. CAN
   ....

j Laura regretted not having studied harder at university. WISH
   ....

Unit 19

Choose the best option, A, B or C, to complete the dialogues.

a '...A...?' 'Yes, it certainly is.'
   A *It's a lovely day, isn't it*   B *Is it a lovely day*
   C *It isn't a lovely day, is it*

b Yes, we have a choice of rooms. ....?
   A *You want a single, don't you?*   B *You don't want a single, do you?*   C *Do you want a single or a double?*

c ....? The last time I saw you, you were a little girl in a pushchair!
   A *You can be Annie, can't you*   B *Aren't you Annie, are you?*   C *You can't be Annie, can you*

d Do you really travel 150 km to work every day? That's a long way! ....
   A *You don't get tired of it, do you?*   B *Don't you get tired of it?*   C *You get tired of it, do you?*

e 'I'm still worried about burglars while we are away. ....?' 'Yes, stop worrying!'
   A *Didn't you lock all the doors and windows?*
   B *You didn't lock all the doors and windows, did you?*
   C *You did lock all the doors and windows, didn't you?*

f 'I've got some surprising news! I'm getting married next week!' '............'
   A *You aren't, are you?*   B *Aren't you?*
   C *You are, aren't you?*

g '............?' 'Yes, that's right, it was.'
   A *Didn't Jack Nicolson win the Oscar for best actor*
   B *It wasn't Jack Nicolson who won the Oscar for best actor, was it*   C *Wasn't it Jack Nicolson who won the Oscar for best actor*

Unit 20

1 Complete the text with *a / an* or *the*, or leave blank for zero article.

a The...... Hubble Space Telescope (HST) is b .... large, space-based observatory in orbit around c .... Earth, named after d .... astronomer Edwin Hubble.
e .... position of f .... telescope outside
g .... Earth's atmosphere gives it h .... number of advantages over telescopes based on i .... ground.
j .... main advantage is its clearer images, as they are not blurred by k .... atmosphere. It can also observe using l .... ultra-violet light.
m .... Hubble was launched into n .... space in 1990, and since then it has become one of o .... most important instruments in p .... history of q .... astronomy. At r .... moment, s .... future of t .... telescope is uncertain. Without servicing by u .... manned space mission, v .... telescope will slowly stop functioning, and will re-enter w .... Earth's atmosphere sometime after x .... 2010.

2 Write a new sentence with the same meaning containing the word in capitals.

a We use telescopes to view distant objects.　A
　We use a telescope to view distant objects.

b The monthly rent for this flat is €500.　A

c My right arm hurts.　GOT

d This meal is really wonderful!　A

e Sandy comes from Australia.　AN

f Sports utility vehicles (SUVs) are becoming less popular.　IS

g The answer seems to be $2^2/_3$.　TWO

h Is there someone here called Steve Jenkins?　A

i Do you want to come and see a film?　CINEMA

j Everyone stopped fighting in 1918.　WAR

Unit 21

1 Complete the text with *a / an* or *the*, or leave blank for zero article.

The Bunsen burner

a ......*A*...... German chemist Robert Bunsen invented **b** .... Bunsen burner in 1855 when he started working at **c** .... University of Heidelberg, and demanded **d** .... new laboratory with **e** .... gas piping. He had been trying to find **f** .... way of lighting his laboratory and also producing **g** .... more efficient way of heating **h** .... equipment. **i** .... problem with **j** .... burners already in use was that they produced **k** .... smoky flame and did not produce very much heat. Bunsen had **l** .... idea of mixing **m** .... gas with **n** .... air before **o** .... combustion took place. He asked Peter Desaga, who was **p** .... university engineer, to design and build **q** .... burner. It was probably Desaga who came up with **r** .... idea of controlling **s** .... amount of **t** .... air mixed in **u** .... burner by **v** .... means of **w** .... metal sleeve that fits over **x** .... vertical pipe of **y** .... burner. **z** ....

mixture of **1** .... gas and **2** .... air burns with **3** .... blue flame and produces intense heat. By turning **4** .... sleeve, **5** .... openings are gradually closed, and **6** .... power of **7** .... flame can be reduced, until **8** .... mixture is **9** .... pure gas and burns yellow and with less intensity.

2 Complete the text with *a / an* or *the*, or leave blank for zero article.

Floods

a .... flood occurs when **b** .... area of **c** .... low-lying land is covered by **d** .... water. There are various kinds of flood. During **e** .... period of **f** .... heavy rainfall, **g** .... soil and **h** .... plants which grow in it are unable to absorb all **i** .... water, and so **j** .... excess water finds its way into **k** .... streams, rivers, lakes and so on. If **l** .... amount of **m** .... water is too great then **n** .... flood will follow. **o** .... river may flood from time to time naturally, and so forms **p** .... area known as **q** .... flood plain. **r** .... flash flood is **s** .... flood that occurs after **t** .... sudden downpour. **u** .... coastal areas may also be flooded by **v** .... high tide caused by **w** .... strong ocean winds. **x** .... tsunami is **y** .... flood caused by **z** .... underwater earthquake.

Unit 23

Read these sentences about William Shakespeare. Change the <u>underlined</u> words in each sentence, using the clue in brackets.

a Shakespeare was the son of an <u>official of the town</u> in Stratford on Avon.   (compound)

Shakespeare was the son of a town official in Stratford on Avon.

b The <u>plays of Shakespeare</u> were published in a collected edition after his death.   (apostrophe)

c He is usually judged to be the <u>greatest English playwright</u>.   (apostrophe)

d He <u>held shares</u> in an acting company known as the Lord Chamberlain's Men.   (compound)

e He was also an actor and <u>wrote narrative poems and sonnets</u>.   (of)

f He was successful enough to become <u>an owner of property</u>.   (compound)

g When he died he was fifty two.   (of)

h <u>Audiences in the theatre</u> have enjoyed his plays for over four hundred years.   (compound)

i His plays are often changed to suit <u>what modern audiences are interested in</u>.   (of)

j There are also many famous <u>versions of the plays as films</u>.   (compound)

Unit 24

Complete the text with one word in each gap.

Left hand or right hand?

a _Someone_ who uses **b** _____ hands equally well is known as ambidextrous. The fact that **c** _____ is a special word for this ability only proves that for most of us **d** _____ seems more natural to be right-handed or left-handed. Of course we all use **e** _____ hands to some extent. A left-handed male, for example, might shave **f** _____ with the left hand, but write with the right. However, as we know, in many cultures **g** _____ who uses the left hand more than the right is often stigmatized. **h** _____ is even an assumption built into many languages that right means 'correct'. Similarly, **i** _____ is some prejudice against using the left hand, which is seen as 'clumsy' or 'wrong.' Although **j** _____ clearly does not matter whether **k** _____ uses the right or the left hand, **l** _____ are many disadvantages in being left-handed. **m** _____ who has tried to use scissors or a computer mouse with **n** _____ left hand will understand this. **o** _____ are very few tools and instruments designed to be easily used by left-handed people. **p** _____ is even dangerous in some cases for the left-handed to use equipment designed for the right-handed, and so **q** _____ is important for factories with such equipment to understand that not **r** _____ is right-handed.

Unit 26

Write a new sentence with the same meaning, beginning as shown.

a I can't carry all these bags on my own.
It's hard *for me to carry all these bags on my own.*

b I didn't know I had to hand in my work today.
I wasn't ....

c I feel nervous when I think about starting my new job.
It makes ....

d You can easily miss the turning if you're not careful.
It's ....

e When I heard that Kevin was ill, I was shocked.
I was shocked to ....

f Please stay here whenever you like.
You're ....

g I definitely left my wallet on the table.
I'm ....

h Don't bother going to see the new Larry Jotter film.
It's ....

i Now I know you believe me, I'm happy.
It ....

Unit 27

1 Underline all the words which are appropriate.

a It was a *quite / rather / <u>fairly</u>* good film I suppose, but I didn't think it was as good as you said.
b The students walked out *quite / rather / fairly* unenthusiastically to start the race in the pouring rain.
c Sorry, but I can't *quite / rather / fairly* see what you're getting at.
d That was a *quite / rather / fairly* horrible thing to say! Thanks a lot!
e That's *quite / rather / fairly* the most enjoyable meal I've ever had!
f Be careful when you go in the pool because the water is *quite / rather / fairly* deep.
g I don't agree with this article at all. I think it's *quite / rather / fairly* inaccurate too.

h After we examined the evidence, it was *quite / rather / fairly* obvious who the culprit was.
i I *quite / rather / fairly* think I'm going to enjoy this party!

2 Complete the text with a word or phrase from the list in each gap.

> **1** absolutely key   **2** completely free
> **3** entirely financed   **4** extremely expensive
> **5** financially speaking   **6** generally speaking
> **7** naturally   **8** ~~quite clear~~   **9** quite unable
> **10** quite usual   **11** totally private   **12** very basic

Health services

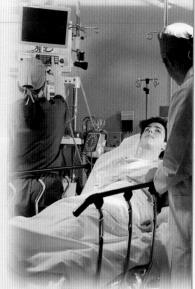

In recent years it has become a __8__ that the provision of health care is one of the **b** .... issues in modern society. In some countries the provision of health care is **c** .... at the point of use. **d** .... this means that people who visit the doctor, or have to go into hospital, do not hand over money to the people who treat them. Instead, the system is **e** .... by central government, and paid out of revenues (taxes) collected from everyone. In some health systems everyone is treated free, regardless of their ability to pay, while in other systems, patients pay a standard charge, even for **f** .... drug treatments, while those who are **g** .... to pay receive free treatment. In other countries the system is **h** .... and everyone has to pay for their treatment. **i** .... this means that patients either have to pay for their own insurance, which will pay for their bills when they are ill, or pay bills from their own pockets. In many countries it is **j** .... for both systems to exist side by side, with the state providing **k** .... services, and the better off, naturally, paying for services of a higher quality. This is sometimes known as a 'two-tier' system.

Unit 28

1 Write a new sentence with the same meaning, beginning as shown.

a I've never read a better book than this one.
This *is one of the best books I've read.*

b Staying at home watching television is less interesting than going out dancing.
It's ....

c Jane felt horrified rather than shocked.
Jane didn't ....

d The end of the universe is a very abstract concept and so it is hard to explain.
The end of the universe is too ....

e No film this year was as good as *Alien Descent*.
Alien Descent was by ....

f I can't revise any more than I have.
I've revised just ....

g We've never had worse weather in June than this.
This is ....

h I thought it was easier to speak French.
It's not ....

i Gary's last album was much better than the new one.
Gary's new album is nowhere ....

j If you keep teasing the dog, it will get more angry.
The more ....

2 Write a new sentence with the same meaning containing the words in capitals.

a I liked this film but the previous films in this series are better. **ISN'T NEARLY**
I liked this film but it isn't nearly as good as the previous films in this series.

b The best performance in the film is given by Johnny Depp. **GIVES BY**
....

c No film on release at the moment is longer. **IT'S ONE**
....

d It's increasingly hard to understand the plot of films like this. **HARDER AND**
....

e The special effects in the last film were not so impressive. **MUCH MORE**
....

f But I was scared out of my wits, rather than shocked, by some parts. **SHOCKED AS**
....

g I haven't seen a more entertaining film this year. **EASILY THE**
....

h In some ways the last film in the series was funnier. **FUNNY AS**
....

i But it is just as worth seeing this film. **EVERY BIT**
....

j You enjoy this film more if you watch it more. **THE MORE**
....

Unit 30

Write a new sentence with the same meaning containing the word in capitals.

a David's novel is still unfinished. **YET**
David hasn't finished his novel yet.

b We waited for a bus for half an hour, but eventually we gave up. **END**
....

c Nick got to the airport too late to catch his plane home. **TIME**
....

d I won't be here after any more after Friday.   UNTIL

e I'll talk to you when the lesson is over.   AFTER

f The trains here are very comfortable but they always run late!   ON

g We'll send you the certificate when we have received the fee.   ONCE

h I shouldn't be there later than 11.00.   BY

i Peter could hear loud howling noises all night long.   THROUGHOUT

Unit 31

Write a new sentence with the same meaning, containing the word in capitals.

a Luckily the fire officer managed to rescue the cat from the top of the tree.   SUCCEEDED
Luckily the fire officer succeeded in rescuing the cat from the top of the tree.

b Can I talk to you about this problem?   DISCUSS

c My parents think some of my friends are unsuitable.   APPROVE

d How much you pay will relate to the condition of the vehicle.   DEPEND

e My computer has a problem, but someone is coming to fix it tomorrow.   SEE

f Do you have fire insurance?   INSURED

g Mr Wilkins has decided to give up his job at the company.   RESIGN

h Take a seat, and I'll ask someone to help you.   ATTEND

i The runaway bus hit a parked car at the bottom of the hill.   COLLIDED

j This ice-cream really has a strawberry taste.   TASTES

Unit 32

Choose the best phrase, A, B or C, to complete the sentence.

a This is __C__ the worse novel I have ever read!
   A *for a change*   B *on purpose*   C *without doubt*

b Are you _____ the service you have received during your stay?
   A *acquainted with*   B *satisfied with*   C *free from*

c This inquiry _____ only with the legal aspects of the case.
   A *is concerned*   B *is absorbed*   C *is interested*

d For more and more families, expensive holidays abroad are _____ .
   A *by force*   B *out of reach*   C *out of order*

e _____ , although you broke the rules, we will accept your application.
   A *Without exception*   B *Under the circumstances*
   C *On average*

f This country is really _____ anywhere I have ever been before!
   A *ready for*   B *packed with*   C *different from*

g To be honest, I'm not the slightest bit _____ what you think!
   A *interested in*   B *aware of*   C *pleased with*

h Peter wasn't _____ getting up so early, and felt tired all day as a result.
   A *worried about*   B *used to*   C *addicted to*

i The students were _____ the prospect of having to write their projects all over again.
   A *faced with*   B *impatient for*   C *incapable of*

j Helen's parents were _____ that she was still in the job, but she had resigned.
   A *in theory*   B *by mistake*   C *under the impression*

Unit 33

Choose the best option, A, B or C, to complete the sentence.

a Julia is considered __B__ one of the best actresses in Hollywood.
 A *that she is*   B *to be*   C *being*

b The robbers made the bank clerk _____ the money.
 A *hand over*   B *to hand over*   C *handing over*

c Have you tried _____ to an osteopath? That should help your back.
 A *to go*   B *going*   C *go*

d We expect _____ the deal by the end of business on Friday.
 A *that we complete*   B *completing*   C *to complete*

e Maria suggested _____ a taxi to the airport.
 A *to take*   B *should take*   C *taking*

f I don't remember _____ the cooker, so we'd better go back and check.
 A *turning off*   B *to turn off*   C *that I turned off*

g If we go to the cinema on Wednesday, it means _____ the match on television.
 A *to miss*   B *miss*   C *missing*

h The school arranged _____ the oral examination on a different day.
 A *holding*   B *that they would hold*   C *hold*

i The president went on _____ new measures to combat global warming.
 A *announcing*   B *announce*   C *to announce*

j I really hate _____ to walk to work when it's raining.
 A *have*   B *having*   C *I have*

Unit 34

Choose the best word, A, B or C, to complete the sentence.

a This is the area __C__ the majority of new housing is being built.
 A *which*   B *that*   C *in which*

b You really are the most annoying person _____ I know!
 A *(blank)*   B *which*   C *whatever*

c Jane was one of several injured passengers _____ to the local hospital.
 A *taken*   B *were taken*   C *which was taken*

d Can everyone _____ name begins with S stand on that side of the room.
 A *whose their*   B *whose*   C *for whom their*

e Alex Jackson, _____ Wilkinson travelled to the South Pole, also wrote about the trip.
 A *which*   B *that*   C *with whom*

f This is not the same painting _____ you offered to sell us the last time we were here.
 A *(blank)*   B *to which*   C *for which*

g The street was full of people, most _____ were chanting political slogans.
 A *of whom*   B *of them*   C *which*

h Tina couldn't think of _____ anyone would want to threaten her.
 A *whatever*   B *a reason why*   C *for which*

i Anyone _____ through the door will be filmed by the security camera.
 A *which comes*   B *coming*   C *whatever*

j _____ you do, don't touch the red wire!
 A *What*   B *The reason why*   C *Whatever*

Unit 35

Write a new sentence with the same meaning, beginning as shown.

a I would like to help you, but I don't really have the time.
 Much as *I would like to help you, I don't really have the time.*

b I won't sell you the house however much you offer me for it.
 No matter _____ .

c House prices continue to rise in most areas, but in some areas they have actually started to fall.
 Whereas _____ .

d You have not paid the last six monthly instalments, so this contract is at an end.
 Since _____ .

e The weather conditions were atrocious but all the runners finished the race.
 Even though _____ .

f As we wanted to have a snack first, we got to the stadium early.
 We got to the stadium early so _____ .

g I thought I might get cold so I took some warm clothes.
 I took some warm clothes in _____ .

h The match went ahead despite the rain.
 Although _____ .

i I think we should hold the meeting another day as it's too late to start it now.
 Seeing that _____ .

j The rapid entrance of the gunmen took the guards by surprise.

The gunmen entered so _____

_____ .

Unit 36

Complete the sentence so that it means the same as the first sentence, using a participle clause or reduced adverbial clause.

a I lost my watch, so I had to borrow my brother's.

Having *lost my watch, I had to borrow my brother's.*

b If you press this button, you can change the size of the page.

By _____

_____ .

c Although it was cheap, the bike was in good condition.

Although _____

_____ .

d Sue didn't realize the meeting was in a different place, and went straight home.

Not _____

_____ .

e As I wasn't interested in the topic, I left the lecture before the end.

Not _____

_____ .

f Write your name where you are instructed to do this.

Where _____

_____ .

g After he was arrested and charged with theft, Tony phoned his lawyer.

Having _____

_____ .

h I phoned the company as soon as I received their letter.

On _____

_____ .

i I had to take a taxi as I missed the last bus.

Having _____

_____ .

j I've made a lot of new friends since I came to this school.

Since _____

_____ .

Units 37 and 38

The following exercises practise phrasal verbs from **Units 37** and **38**.

1 Write a new sentence with the same meaning, containing the word in capitals.

a Tim is in love with the girl he sits next to in maths. FALLEN

Tim has fallen for the girl he sits next to in maths.

b How are things going in your new school?   GETTING

_____

_____

c I agree that you had a bad time, but it was your own fault!   BROUGHT

_____

_____

d You can't have milk in your tea because we haven't got any!   DO

_____

_____

e The film wasn't as good as I thought it was going to be.   COME

_____

_____

f Your explanation just doesn't make sense.   ADD

_____

_____

g There's a point I'd like to mention before we finish.   BRING

_____

_____

2 Write a new sentence with the same meaning, using a form of a phrasal verb from **Units 37** and **38**.

a I think it's time you started working seriously.

I think it's time you got down to some serious work.

b Sorry, what did you say? I'm falling asleep!

_____

_____

c Tina's name kept coming into our conversation.

_____

_____

d In the end, the problem is a matter of a lack of proper planning.

....

e Feelings of resentment between them grew over a long period.

....

f Alan can't always explain exactly what his ideas are.

....

g Helen has thought of a really good way to cut the cost of this project.

....

h We found this hotel completely by chance.

....

i I think we should keep going until we get to the top of the hill.

....

j Are you entering for the Advanced French Test this year?

....

k Sorry to be so late, but I was delayed in my last meeting.

....

l Things have certainly been improving since I was promoted.

....

m Sue promised to come and help me but she didn't show up.

....

n Don't tell Helen about our plans, or she'll be jealous.

....

o Little Johnny admitted that he had taken Paula's sweets.

....

Unit 44

Complete the text using a word from the list in each gap. You can use any word more than once.

> at all   it   own   very   what

Monet: Japanese bridge at Giverny

The French Impressionists c1860–1880

a _What_ interested the Impressionists was an emphasis on everyday subjects. **b** .... was to avoid the traditions of studio painting that they painted in the open air. At first the public was not interested in them **c** .... In fact, the **d** .... name 'Impressionist' was given to them in an article making fun of Monet's painting *Impression, Sunrise*.
e .... they were also concerned with was the way light changes, and how this shows the passing of time. They were not **f** .... interested in reproducing a detailed photographic 'reality'. In fact, that was the **g** .... thing they wanted to avoid. Instead, **h** .... was the overall effect which was important. **i** .... they were trying to create was a different way of seeing things, using pure colours. Colours were created by looking at the painting. They did not use black, for example, because they believed there was no black **j** .... in nature.
k .... they wanted to avoid were the carefully mixed colours and hidden brushstrokes of academic artists, which they did not use in their
l .... paintings.

Wordlist

 Red words based on Macmillan English Dictionary

*** most common and basic words
** very common words
* fairly common words

Unit 1
achieve vb***
antibiotics (n)
argue (vb)***
cause (n)
fatality (n)
hairstyle (n)*
in line with
interruption (n)*
measure (n)***
nuisance (n)*
over-confident (adj)
overtake (vb)*
recent (adj)***
reckless (n)
return (n)
scheme (n)***
set about (phrasal verb)
settle in (phrasal verb)
target (n)
tear up (v)**
to tell you the truth
tough (adj)***

Unit 2
acid (n)***
adapt (vb)**
burglar (n)*
calm down (phrasal verb)
complaint (n)***
course (n)***
creep (vb)*
depend on (vb)***
expense (n)***
fatigue (n)*
fee (n)***
full-time (adj)**
guard dog (n)
inquiry (n)***
lose your temper (phrase)
parrot (n)*
point out (phrasal verb)
psychiatrist (n)*
publish (vb)***
redecorate (vb)
rottweiler (n)
section (n)***
strain (n)**
stuff (n)***
track (n)***
tuition (n)*

undergraduate (n)
wreckage (n)*

Unit 3
ceasefire (n)*
check-in desk (n)
harsh (adj)**
merchant (n)
military (adj)*
negotiate (vb)**
outrage (n)*
racing (adj)
realm (n) *
recruit (vb)**
sacrifice (vb)*
sign (vb) ***
supply (n)***
treaty (n) **
U-boat (n)

Unit 4
abroad (adv)***
alien (n)**
archaeologist (n)*
benefit (n) ***
come up with
compulsory (adj) **
controversial (adj)**
define (vb)***
delay (vb) **
disturbing (adj)*
labour (n) ***
pension (n) ***
perform (vb)***
portrait (n)**
psychologist (n)**
retirement (n) *
social security (n) *
squid (n)
trend (n) ***

Unit 5
admission (n)**
at this rate (phrase)
breakdown (n)**
circumstance (n)***
construction (n)***
flame (n)**
fortune (n)**
global warming (n)*
insist (vb)***
investment (n)***
prediction (n)**
riot (n)**
slip my mind (phrase)
source (n)***

Unit 6
accelerate (vb)*
alpine (adj)
altitude (n)*
ambitious (adj) **
baby boom (n)
barge(man) (n)
barrier (n)**

bits and pieces (phrase)
chase (vb)**
concentration (n)***
copper (n) **
critic (n)***
currently (adv)***
cycle (n)**
dealer (n) ***
disassemble (vb)
dock (n) **
downswing (n)
dramatic (adj)***
dub (vb)*
emission (n)**
explosion (n)**
feat (n)
feature (n)***
freight (n)*
get hold of (phrase)
greenhouse gas (n)
heavy goods vehicle (n)
invasion (n)***
life expectancy (n)
link (n)**
marine (adj) *
mud (n)**
neighbourhood (n)**
outspoken (adj) *
pointless (adj)
referendum (n)**
seize (vb)**
shed (n)**
shilling (n)
solar (adj)**
split (vb)**
steadily (adv)
strip off (phrasal verb)
trade (n)***
upswing (n)

Unit 7
accommodate (vb)*
assess (vb)**
beat (vb)***
blaze (n)*
block (n)***
campaign (n)***
cave in (phrasal verb)
coalition (n)**
coal miner(n)
counterfeit (adj)
crumbly (adj)
deforestation (n)
desertification (n)
disruption (n)*
drain (n)*
explosion (n)**
fault (n)***
(film) set (n)***
foot the bill (phrase)
gallery (n)**
gutted (adj)
inhalation (n)
inspiration (n)**

investigate (vb)***
issue (n)***
mobilize (vb)
moisture (n)
MP (n) **
nutrition (n)*
nutty (adj)
opposition (n)***
outset (n)*
refreshing (adj)*
seal (vb)**
shoot (vb)***
soak (vb)*
source (n)***
stage (n)***
staple (n)*
sustainable (adj)
unclear (adj)*
unconscious (adj)*

Unit 8
actual (adj) ***
along similar lines (phrase)
anaesthetic (n)
baptism (n)
beech (n)
colonial (adj)**
cut (n)***
extraction (n)
focus (vb)***
fortification (n)
guess (n) **
informed (adj)
matter (n)***
merger (n)*
meteor (n)
parish (n)**
performer (n)*
phenomenon (n)**
pit (n)**
plague (n)
playwright (n)
purgatory (n)
register (n)**
sequence (n)***
sharply (adv)**
transfusion (n)
undecided (adj)

Unit 9
alter (vb)**
amputate (vb)
bar (n)***
central heating (n)
dry cleaner's (n)
hip (n)**
install (vb)**
lock (n)**
power tool (n)
surgeon (n)**

Unit 10
alien (n)**
asteroid (n)
back-up (n)*
black hole (n)
collide (vb)*
decay (vb)*
DNA (n)*
dominant (adj)**
dominate (vb)**
endangered species (n)
evolve (vb)**
extinct (adj)*
fossil fuel (n)
goalkeeper (n)*
grind (to a halt) (phrase)
helmet (n)**
hike (n)
iceberg (n)
keyboard (n)*
lifeboat (n)
lifejacket (n)
mammal (n)*
reclaim (vb)
sample (n)***
short cut (n)
species (n)***
standstill (n)
tide (n)**
virus (n)***

Unit 11
adequate (adj)***
assistance (n)***
coexist (vb)
guarantee (vb)**
habitat (n)*
hunter (n)*
inconvenience (n)
mess (n)**
neglect (vb)**
safeguard (n)
skill (n)***
survive (vb)***

Unit 12
amount (n)***
debt (n)***
earplug (n)
faith (n)***
hindsight (n)
litter (n)*
treat (vb)***
uninhabited (adj)
vandalism (n)
wear out (phrasal verb)

Unit 13
appliance (n)*
application form (n)
calculate (vb)**
charge (n)***
chip (n)**
compulsory (adj)**

consume (vb)**
genetically modified (adj)
local (adj)***
reception (n)**
recommendation (n)**
refuse (n)
type (vb)***
waste (n)***
wireless (adj)*

Unit 14
crew (n)***
firefighter (n)
ladder (n)**
navigation (n)*
paw (n)*
profit (n)***
rivalry (n)
sunblock (n)
wire (n)**

Unit 15
adjust (vb)**
armed forces (n)*
battery (n)**
boast (vb)*
clown (n)
column (n)***
compulsory (adj)**
conquer (vb)*
forbidden (adj)*
format (n)**
insulting (adj)
irritating (adj)*
pile (n)**
scream (vb)**
stressed (adj)
track (n)***
waste (n)***

Unit 16
community service (n)
compensate (vb)**
criminal (adj)***
fine (n)**
justice (n)***
keen on (adj)***
offender (n)**
proposal (n)***
sentence (n)***

Unit 17
amount to (phrasal verb)
bloodstained (adj)
blush (vb)*
dealer (n)***
lawyer (n)***
market (n)***
on the way out (phrase)
shortcoming (n)

Unit 18
abandon (vb)**
attempt (n)***
blood pressure (n)

capture (vb)**
cheat (vb)*
conclude (vb)***
encouragement (n)**
lack (n)***
laptop (n)
lifestyle (n)**
outset (n)*
previous (adj)***
set fire to (phrase)
state (vb)***
task (n)***
warrior (n)

Unit 19
coast (n)***
contribution (n)***
enthusiastic (adj)**
pay attention (phrase)
projector (n)
what on earth (phrase)

Unit 20
broadcast (n)**
civil servant (n)
civil war (n)*
commentator (n)**
daring (adj)
daylight (adj)*
decoration (n)**
election (n)***
factor (n)***
grate (vb)
genetic (adj)**
harsh (adj)**
homeless (adj)*
migrate (vb)*
mild (adj)**
poverty (n)**
resign (vb)***
reviewer (n)
rhythm (n)**
scarce (adj)*
site (n)**
sprinkle (vb)*
struggle (vb)**
traffic jam (n)
trigger (n)*
tuberculosis (n)

Unit 21
defend (vb)***
dynasty (n)
field trip (n)
fort (n)*
invade (vb)*
ironing board (n)
location (n)
lush (adj)*
mining (n)*
mountain range (n)
notorious (adj)*
offence (n)***
peak (n)**

personal trainer (n)
plain (n)**
postpone (vb)*
scenery (n)*
temperature (n)**
tower (n)**
treatment (n)***

Unit 22
aware (adj)***
biological warfare (n)
campaign (vb)***
composition (n)**
consume (vb)**
consumption (n)**
crime (n)***
double (adj)***
earn (vb)***
epidemic (n)
evidence (n)***
flexibility (n)**
genetic (adj)**
limit (vb)***
operation (n)***
outbreak (n)*
pandemic (n)
ready-made (adj)
recommend (vb)***
reflect (vb)***
risk (n)***
solution (n)***
state (vb)***
support (vb)***
tank (n)***
treat (vb)***
war zone (n)
wiring (n)
wrapper (n)

Unit 23
avenge (vb)
award (vb)***
baffle (vb)
courtier (n)
infectious (adj)*
pitch (n)**
raid (vb)**
rampart (n)
rent (n)***
surroundings (n)**
threat (n)***
troupe (n)

Unit 24
according to (prep)***
enemy (n)***
inspection (n)**
legend (n)**
legendary (adj)
outlaw (n)
strike (n)***

Unit 25
culprit (n)
force (vb)***
gamble (vb)*
harm (n)**
headline (n)**
household (n)***
masterpiece (n)*
solution (n)***
stumble (vb)*
worthless (adj)

Unit 26
acidic (adj)
ambition (n)**
approach (n)***
astrophysics (n)
coach (n)**
crust (n)*
data (n)***
feedback (n)**
ice sheet (n)
melt (vb)**
mineral (n)*
motivated (adj)
nutritional (adj)
quake (n)
satellite (n)**
swamp (n)

Unit 27
associate (vb)***
claim (n)***
cobbled (adj)
condemn (vb)**
creative (adj)**
devastating (adj)*
dull (adj)**
explosion (n)**
-proof (suffix)
sum (n)***
thatch (vb)
urban (adj) ***

Unit 28
disorganized (adj)
drift (vb)**
fire brigade (n)*
kilt (n)
perform (vb)***
snore (vb)
temptation (n)**
verbal (adj)*
visual (adj)**

Unit 29
archway (n)
bark (vb)*
blame (vb)*
circumstance (n)***
collapse (vb)**
delivery (n)***
footpath (n)
furious (adj)
glacier (n)

link (n)***
monsoon (n)
pond (n)**
promote (vb)***
purchase (n)**
riverbank (n)
roundabout (n)*
senseless (adj)
shriek (n)
slip (vb)***
suspicion (n)**
sway (vb)*

Unit 30
accurate (adj)
ash (n)**
cubic (adj)
eruption (n)
firm (adj)***
halt (vb)*
hay fever (n)
launch (vb)***
paramedic (n)
pass (n)**
rear (n)**
receipt (n)**
report (vb)***
scout (n)*
slaughter (vb)*
super- (prefix)
urgent (adj)
vineyard (n)
warehouse (n)**

Unit 31
amorous (adj)
bravery (n)
deter (vb)
dull (adj)**
episode (n)**
expansion (n)**
head (vb)***
heal (vb)**
manufacture (vb)**
munitions (n)
outbreak (n)*
psychiatric (adj)*
range (n)***
rat race (n)
respect (n)***
safe (n)*
severe (adj)***
shortage (n)**
short-sighted (adj)
steel (n)**
suitable (adj)***
take the plunge (phrase)
tell apart (phrasal verb)
unwilling (adj)*
weld (vb)

Unit 32
catastrophe (n)
chat room (n)
complacency (n)
distant (adj)**
dwindle (vb)
face to face (adv)
genetic engineering (n)
inappropriate (adj)**
inquiry (n)***
parachute (n)
(someone likes the) sound
(of their own voice)
(phrase)
vitally (adv)

Unit 33
block (n)***
brake (n)*
casualty (n)
civilian (adj)*
demolish (vb)*
devastate (vb)*
faint (adj)**
filthy (adj)*
justify (vb)**
land (vb)***
mental (adj)***
outcast (n)
pester (vb)
precarious (adj)
pull (a muscle) (vb)***
run-down (adj)
skating (n)*
state (n)***
stuck (adj)
surrender (n)*
waste (vb)**
weapon (n)***

Unit 34
analyse (vb)**
capacity (n)***
clergy (man) (n)**
confine (vb)*
converse (vb)
discomfort (n)
excavation (n)
feature (vb)***
fit (vb)***
grey matter (n)
inferior (adj)*
innate (adj)
manners (n)***
naval (adj)**
navy (n)**
originate (vb)**
partner (n)***
perceive (vb)**
press (n)***
process (vb)**
shelter (vb)*
shepherd (n)
sketch (n)*

soaked (adj)
solely (adv)**
stereotype (n)*
suitable (adj)***
support (vb)***
swelling (n)
uneventful (adj)
warning (n)***
well-off (adj)

Unit 35
autograph (n)
challenging (adj)
circumference (n)
controversial (adj)**
crash (n)**
estimate (n)***
heresy (n)
hooligan (n)
immense (adj)**
inevitable (adj)**
lawyer (n)***
manned (adj)
require (vb)***
solar system (n)*
sphere (n)**
theory (n)***
vast (adj)**

Unit 36
anonymous (adj)*
association (n)***
blindness (n)
burst (vb)**
clubbing (n)
colonist (n)
conduct (vb)***
conductor (n)*
degeneration (n)
embryo (n)
evidence (n)***
fan oven (n)
haven (n)
implant (n)
isolate (vb)*
nuisance (n)*
philanthropist (n)
predator (n)**
set (adj)*
stagger (vb)*
stem cell (n)
stream (vb)*
therapy (n)**
tissue (n)**
trial (n)***

Unit 37
accused (the) (n)
album (n)**
cabinet (n)***
conscript (vb)
corroborate (vb)
council tax (n)
digital (adj)**

downfall (n)
expansion (n)**
expertise (n)**
exposure (n)**
resume (vb)**
rival (adj)**
rocket (n)*
snore (vb)
stretch limo (n)
tense (adj)*
wristwatch (n)

Unit 38
apply (vb)**
blackmail (n)
boiler (n)
burst (vb)**
claim (n)***
deadline (n)*
globe (n)
pipe (n)**
record (n)***
revenge (n)*
security guard (n)
slack (adj)
spokesperson (n)
survivor (n)*

Unit 39
armament (n)
deceive (vb)*
deception (n)*
define (vb)***
deliberately (adv)**
disguise (n)
fault (n)***
honour (vb)**
imitate (vb)*
insufficient (adj)**
mugger (n)
performance (n)***
satellite (n)**
spare part (n)
unannounced (adv)
union (n)***

Unit 40
astronomical (adj)
breeding (n)*
cancer (n)***
concussion (n)
consumer (n)***
core (n)**
corporation (n)*
cross-cultural (adj)
(a great) deal of (phrase)
demand (n)***
dominate (vb)**
dwarf (n)
erratic (adj)
fuse (vb)*
fusion (n)*
generator (n)*
liver (n)**

maintenance (n)**
modification (n)**
motion (n)***
neglect (n)*
observation (n)***
offence (n)***
organism (n)**
overwhelm (vb)*
pebble (n)
pendulum (n)
pest (n) *
potentially (adv) **
precisely (adv)***
resistance (n)***
selection (n)***
spring (n)***
substantially (adv)**
suit (vb)***
unified (adj)
variety (n)***
well-being (n)
wind turbine (n)

Unit 41
agent (n)***
amphibian (n)
asset (n)*
bandwidth (n)
brink (n)*
coincidence (n)*
dweller (n)
epidemic (n)
hardware (n)**
idealize (vb)
innovative (adj)*
IT (n)*
mass production (n)
mobility (n)*
obesity (n)
oblige (vb)**
pace (n)**
prefabricate (vb)
public (adj)
reassure (vb)**
rubber (n)**
ruin (n)*
scan (vb)**
slum (n)
software (n)***
speck (n)
staggering (adj)

Unit 42
appoint (vb)***
artefact (n)*
disconnect (vb)
election (n)**
genius (n)*
hosepipe (n)
shortage (n)**
tournament (n)**

Unit 43
blatant (adj)
brandish (vb)
breach (n)**
collide (vb)*
consult (vb)**
creak (vb)
crew (n)***
diverse (adj)**
float (n)
groan (vb)*
hurricane (n)
longing (n)
lure (vb)
mast (n)
oar (n)
parade (n)*
plug (vb)*
regain (vb)**
screech (vb)
survive (vb)***
wax (n)
will (n)***

Unit 44
bear something in mind (phrase)
collapse (vb)**
consideration (n)***
deceive (vb)*
fault (n) ***
jewel (n)*
justify (vb)**
point (n)***

Review

Unit 3
barley (n)
flannel (n)
fragile (adj) *
fresh complexion
leave (n) **
physique (n)
preparatory school
pugnacity (n)
a shadow of his former self (phrase)
shiny (adj) *

Unit 20
astronomer (n)
atmosphere (n) **
blur (vb)
launch (vb) ***
manned (adj)
observatory (n)
service (vb) **
ultraviolet (adj)

Unit 21
Bunsen burner (n)
combustion (n)
downpour (n)
excess (adj) *
flame (n) **
flash flood (n)
gradually (adv) ***
heat (n) ***
intense (adj) **
intensity (n)
low-lying (adj)
piping (n)
plain (n) **
sleeve (n) **
tsunami (n)
vertical (adj) **

Unit 21
assumption (n) **
clumsy (adj) *
equally (adv) ***
prejudice (n) **
prove (vb) ***
shave (vb) *
stigmatize (vb)
tool (n) ***

Unit 27
better off (adj)
charge (n) ***
point of use (see point of sale) (n)
provision (n) **
revenue (n) **
standard (adj) ***
tier (n)
treat (vb) ***

Unit 44
avoid (vb) ***
brushstroke (n)
emphasis (n) ***
open air (n)
make fun of (phrase)
overall (adj) ***
pure (adj) ***
reproduce (vb) **

Grammar index

Ex 4

a Dora was examined by a number of trainee doctors.
b Everyone has been surprised by the extent of the flood-damage.
c The security door was opened with a counterfeit key.
d Many would-be shoppers were put off by the freezing conditions.
e The window was smashed with a brick.
f Some families are being hit hard by the high cost of gas and electricity.
g The windows on nearby buildings were blown in by the force of the explosion.
h Several buildings were damaged by the high winds.
i The security guard was hit on the head with a blunt instrument.
j The sea wall was washed away by the unusually high tide.

Ex 5

a was awarded b was praised c had been cut down
d had been left e has been copied
f has been transformed g has been arrested
h was beaten i was elected j was appointed

Ex 6

a I was promised a pay rise …
b … was sent to me by courier the next day.
c … is being taken over by a multi-national firm.
d The man trying to climb in the window was noticed …
e … was awarded a medal for bravery.
f … was made to take the exam again.
g … was given the paintings by an elderly aunt.
h The case is going to be looked into …
i … rescue attempts were considered pointless.
j … was elected president for a second term.

Ex 7

a According to a statement from Pinewood Studios, the James Bond stage, which was destroyed by fire at the weekend, will be rebuilt.
b The cause of the blaze at Iver Heath, Buckinghamshire, in which the celebrated stage was left completely gutted, has not yet been confirmed.
c A spokesperson explained that shooting of the latest production had been completed and the film sets were being removed.
d The full effects of this incident have not yet been assessed, but the financial performance of the company will not be affected.
e Buckinghamshire Fire Brigade was called at 1118 BST on Sunday.
f The blaze was tackled by eight fire engines, and the smoke was visible from ten miles away.
g The roof covering the stage caved in through fire damage and special equipment was required to reach it.
h It is the second time the stage, originally built for the 1977 Bond film The Spy Who Loved Me, has been destroyed by fire.
i The building was previously rebuilt following a fire in 1984 after which six people were treated for burns, smoke inhalation, and shock.
j Since its reopening, when it was christened The Albert R Broccoli 007 Stage after the long-time producer of the series, it has been used in several James Bond films.

Unit 8

Ex 1

a In Irish mythology, a meteor was said to be a soul passing from purgatory to heaven.
b In Greek mythology, the beech tree was believed to be able to

carry messages from a worshipper to Zeus and the other gods.
c In ancient Egypt, bats' blood was thought
d In Aztec mythology, the Sun was believed the god Quetzalcoatl.
e In Norse mythology, the bravest warriors live after death in the hall of Valhalla.
f In ancient Egypt, the scarab, or beetle, was the Sun across the sky.

Ex 2

a The company's European division is said to be year.
b In contrast, the Far East division is said to have been suffering from rising costs.
c The company is believed to have been talking to a competitor about a possible merger.
d Some directors are known to have been thinking on the lines for some time.
e The CEO, Carl Graham, is believed to be making an attempt to focus the business more sharply in some areas.
f He is also said to be looking at the possibility of job cuts.
g The company is thought to be holding a top-level meeting about these matters next week.

Ex 3

a … thought to be the site of buried treasure.
b … said to be in a place called 'the money pit'.
c … thought to have buried the treasure centuries ago.
d … reported to have fallen into a hole at the foot of a large tree.
e … believed to have discovered traces of treasure in the hole.
f … said to have found a treasure chest in later excavations.
g … said to have flooded in.
h … believed to have searched for the treasure.
i … thought to have found old pieces of metal in the hole.
j … reported to be a natural phenomenon, or the remains of old colonial fortifications.

Ex 4

a I appreciate being taken to the station.
b I enjoyed being shown around the school.
c I don't remember being arrested!
d He said he liked being taken seriously.
e Tina denied having been paid to appear in the play.
f I don't remember being given the anaesthetic.
g I appreciate being given another chance.

Ex 5

a The hat sold yesterday at the auction is said to have been worn by Napoleon during the invasion of Russia in 1812.
b The earthquake in the North Sea is thought to have been caused by a release in pressure after oil and gas extraction.
c Harriet the tortoise, who has just died aged 176, is believed to have been owned by Charles Darwin.
d Three patients are now known to have been infected with the disease through blood transfusions.
e More than a hundred football supporters are thought to have been involved in the riot after the match.
f The recent forest fires in California are believed to have been started deliberately.
g Three other religious leaders are now known to have been arrested at the same time.
h The helicopter which crashed yesterday killing eighteen service personnel is believed to have been shot down.

... thought to have been arrested.
... ved to have crashed into the sea near a

... aid to be considering changing the laws on
... lic.
... ituation is reported to have improved.
... d to have been seen in the area for the first

... lieved to have broken out at 3 am.
... e company is reported to have recorded rising

... er of unemployed is thought to have fallen by

... sted answers:

... thought to have been born on 23 April, 1564.
... is believed to have started his education at the age of
seven / in 1571.
He is thought to have joined a company of actors between
1585 and 1592.
He is thought to have been both a playwright and a
performer.
He is believed to have written his first play in 1589–1590.
He is thought to have written the poem *Venus and Adonis*
while London theatres were closed because of the plague.
He is believed to have written *A Midsummer Night's Dream* for
a wedding in 1595.
He is thought to have written *Romeo and Juliet* in the same
year.
He is believed to have written *Hamlet* in 1600–1601.

Unit 9

Ex 1

a We have had the outside of our house painted.
b Martin had his hair cut yesterday.
c We are having a new central heating system installed at our
house tomorrow.
d I am going to have my eyes examined this afternoon.
e Tom had his nose altered last year.
f I had my leather coat dry-cleaned specially.
g We have had our paintings valued.
h Maria had the car looked at before she bought it.
i We had the windows in our house replaced last year.
j Julia is going to have two of her teeth taken out.

Ex 2

a Katie had her car stolen by one of her friends.
b We are going to have our photograph taken.
c Can you come quickly? I have had my house broken into.
d Laura is going to have her portrait painted by Tracey Emin,
the well-known British artist.
e They had their house designed by a well-known architect.
f I have all my suits made by a local tailor.
g Dave had his bike repaired at a shop in the High Street.
h I am having my hip replaced next week.
i Tony had one of his fingers broken while he was playing
cricket.
j Maria is going to have her flat redecorated by a local firm.

Ex 3

a One of the players got his leg broken.
b Andy wants to have his nose altered.
c Anna got arrested as she was leaving the shop.
d The patient had his leg amputated after the accident.
e I usually have my shoes repaired in the shop on the corner.
f I got Tom to check all the windows before he left.
g Jim says he'll be late because he is getting his hair cut.

h Have you got your work started yet?
i Sue has had her car stolen.

Ex 4

a had b have c had d done e didn't f got
g having h got i had j have k having l get

Unit 10

Ex 1

a … you press that button on the keyboard, you'll lose what
you've written.
b … lose your work if you make a back-up copy.
c … have virus protection you'll have problems with your
computer.
d … back and arms will ache if you sit too long at the
computer.
e … could have problems if you turn off the computer before
closing all programs.
f … you don't save your work before closing the word-
processing program, you'll lose it.
g … you learn the keyboard short cuts, you can save a lot of
time.
h … probably crash if you run too many programs at the same
time.

Ex 2

a A b B c A d A e B f C g B h C i C j A

Ex 3

a C b B c A d A e B f C g C h C

Ex 4

a disappeared b would begin c polluted
d would soon become e were f would soon begin
g would take h competed i would benefit j caught
k would eventually increase l vanished
m would not necessarily recover n would have o took
p poisoned q would go by r disappeared s ceased
t would not absorb u landed v would find

Ex 5

Suggested answers:

a stopped, would always be
b melt, will rise or melted, would rise
c recycle, will be d fell, would happen
e don't stop, will eventually grind f will happen, run out
g finally start, will need or finally started, would need
h wasn't, would the world be
i don't stop, will become j jumped, would be

Ex 6

a If Mrs Allen's neighbour hadn't searched his garden shed, he
wouldn't have found the missing cat inside.
b If one of them hadn't had her mobile phone with her, the
hikers wouldn't have been rescued quickly.
c If the boy hadn't been wearing a life jacket, he wouldn't have
survived.
d If Mr Anderson hadn't woken up because he heard the smoke
alarm, the family wouldn't have managed to escape the fire.
e If rescue workers had searched the car properly they would
have noticed the injured man.
f If most of the staff hadn't left the room, more than one
person would have been injured.
g If the goalkeeper hadn't made a mistake, United would have
won.
h If a police officer hadn't stopped Pratt for drink-driving, and
taken a DNA sample, Pratt would not have been charged
with the previously unsolved murder of Mrs Jones.

Ex 7

a would have happened b had missed
c would have continued d would probably not exist
e would be f would not have been able
g would have developed h would have grown
i existed j would not have changed k would look
l had not collided m would probably not be
n would not have stood

Unit 11

Ex 1

a provided b Supposing c but for d otherwise
e were to f if you happen to be g even if
h as long as i unless j If it hadn't been for

Ex 2

a C b B c C d A e C f B g B h C i A j B

Ex 3

a We will only refund your booking fee if you cancel 48 hours in advance.
b If only you'd told me about the cheap flights to Italy.
c If it hadn't been for the skill of the surgeon, the child would not have survived.
d If you should have second thoughts, let us know.
e But for your help, I would have made a complete mess of this.
f If I might take your coat?
g Even if you offer me more money, I still won't sell the house to you!
h Let me get a word in edgeways, and I'll tell you what I discovered.
i If you were to change your mind about the job, we'd be interested in hearing from you.
j Unless we are delayed, we'll be there by six.

Ex 4

a unless b will c were d would e provided f even
g otherwise h not i Supposing j would

Unit 12

Ex 1

a had b had listened c would d would stop
e didn't leave f had not bought g had spent h knew
i paid j wish

Ex 2

a C b A c A d A e B f B g C h B i C j C

Ex 3

a ... if more and more young people will go into higher education in future.
b ... their children studied a useful subject leading to a good job.
c ... their parents would let them make their own choices.
d ... they had chosen their courses more carefully.
e ... not to choose a subject simply because they think they are good at it.
f ... I were you, I'd think about what kind of work I want / wanted to do in the future.
g ... if they were only interested in having a good time.
h ... they had worked harder.
i ... if they will never repay their student loans.
j ... time that universities paid more attention to students' financial problems.

Ex 4

a would b were c time d it e made f were g drove
h could i were j would k as l were

Unit 13

Ex 1

a mustn't b did not have to read c we'd better not
d I didn't need to have e shouldn't have told me
f should not g shouldn't h should not have attempted
i mustn't j don't have to be

Ex 2

a have b must c have d better e should
f are g could h should i had j need

Ex 3

a ... better take an umbrella.
b ... have to go to school on Saturday morning in your country?
c ... to hand in a typed copy of their first lab report.
d ... needn't have changed ...
e ... think you ought ...
f ... shouldn't have left the windows open while it was raining.
g ... didn't have to pay.
h ... don't have to ...
i ... able to stop the car before it crashed into a wall.
j ... didn't have to connect it to a phone line.

Ex 4

a should b have c able d had e had f have
g should h have i been j will k should l ought
m have n better o have

Unit 14

Ex 1

a A b B c C d A e C f C g C h B i C j A

Ex 2

a 3 b 8 c 7 d 10 e 1 f 5 g 6 h 2 i 9 j 4

Ex 3

a ... could / might have an accident.
b ... can't be safe.
c ... must have kicked a ball against it.
d ... can be a dangerous place.
e ... must be safe to touch these wires now.
f ... might / could have told me that piece of metal was hot!
g ... should have arrived by now.
h ... can't have cleaned this bowl properly.

Ex 4

a 4 b 5 c 10 d 2 e 7 f 8 g 6 h 9 i 1 j 3

Unit 15

Ex 1

a couldn't b shall c shouldn't d needs e can't
f could g could h I'll do it i might j couldn't

Ex 2 Suggested answers:

a can't be b shall we do c might just d might have known
e could you f Could g needs h can't be

Ex 3

Suggested answers:

a Thanks, but you really shouldn't have brought me flowers!
b Shall I carry those books for you?
c You can't be serious!
d You might be taller than me, but you're not better at basketball!
e Could I open the window, please?
f I couldn't care less what you say!

Ex 4

a 8 b 5 c 3 d 10 e 1 f 7 g 9 h 6 i 4 j 2

Ex 5

a Could I try that shot again?
b Before we start playing, the net needs adjusting.
c Shall I hold the flag while you take your shot?
d Try as I may, I can't skate properly.
e I won't let the team down.
f I couldn't care less whether you run in this race or not.
g You never know, United might just win all their matches!
h No member of the club shall use insulting language to any other member.
i Now the weather has improved, things couldn't be better.
j That's kind of you, but you needn't have bought my ticket.

Ex 6

a C b B c A d B e A f C g A h B i B j B

Ex 7

a Do we have to take the final test?
b You shouldn't have put so much lemon in the cake.
c Tim's computer crashed, but he was able to save the pages he was working on.
d Passengers are not to pass beyond this point.
e I think you had better see an eye specialist about this problem.
f Paula started the class immediately, as she didn't have to take an entrance test.
g We didn't have to pay for our tickets.
h Dave had to leave before the end of the performance.
i We needn't have bought a second tin of paint.
j Kate should have taken her umbrella.

Ex 8

a By the time they leave school, most students should have understood the importance of regular exercise.
b When they start a job, or higher studies, some people can forget that time needs to be set aside for this.
c Those who don't find the time for exercise, are bound to regret this in the future.
d When they feel tired or over-stressed, for example, they think this must have happened because they have been working too hard.
e They don't realize that this might also be the result of failing to keep fit.
f When they do have any free time, they feel they might as well relax in front of the television, as in the gym or on the running track.
g Perhaps they think that the people who find time for exercise must be taking time away from doing their job properly.
h However, research shows that this couldn't be further from the truth.
i Most people could easily find the time to keep fit if they organized their time more effectively.
j In the end, we have to / must remember that someone who feels fit and well must be able to work more easily and with more energy.

Unit 16

Ex 1

a 6 b 3 c 9 d 1 e 4 f 7 g 10 h 5 i 8 j 2

Ex 2

a Would it be all right if I left now?
b The computer wouldn't work properly.
c You would say the wrong thing!
d It would be really great to see you again.
e Would you mind opening the door for me?
f What I did then would turn out to be a mistake.
g Would you like still or sparkling water?
h If you would follow me, I'll take you to the meeting room.
i We would hope to deliver the finished product in six weeks' time.
j I wouldn't worry about the results.

Ex 3

a would lend b does c refused d I'll be
e used to work f wouldn't be g will h would I do
i prefer j would you help

Ex 4

a would b would c – d would e would f would
g would h wouldn't i – j wouldn't k would l –
m – n – o would p – q would r – s would t would

Unit 17

Ex 1

a had already left b was c was d would
e didn't know f crashed g was h had been waiting
i wouldn't j is / was (both acceptable)

Ex 2

a … he wouldn't lend his car to just anyone.
b … he wasn't very satisfied with his job.
c … she wasn't going to worry about the money until she heard from the bank.
d … she didn't know where Bill was living at that moment.
e … told me she hadn't had her operation yet.
f … if I ate too much, I'd feel ill.
g … they would be writing to her later that week.
h … the prices wouldn't rise before the end of the year.
i … the police had noticed Jack's car, they would have arrested him.
j … she would let me know if she had any more problems.

Ex 3

a 'Aeroplanes are interesting toys, but do not have any military value.' 8
b 'Whatever young Einstein does, he will amount to nothing.' 4
c 'It will be years, and not in my lifetime, before a woman will become British prime minister.' 5
d 'I think there is a world market for perhaps five computers.' 7
e 'Television won't stay popular for more than six months, because people will soon get tired of staring at a wooden box every night.' 2
f 'We don't like your sound, and guitar music is on the way out.' 3
g 'The telephone has too many shortcomings and is of no value to us.' 6
h 'The horse is here to stay, but the car is only a novelty.' 1

Ex 4

a how long it took to get to the city centre.
b if I had visited the National Museum.
c what she thought of the hotel food.
d if I would be travelling by train.

e if she knew the way to the Opera House.
f how much I had paid to stay in the student hostel.
g whether / if she was thinking of changing hotels.
h whether / if I had to leave at 10.00.
i to go with me to the station / if she would go with me to the station.

Ex 5

a B b A c C d A e B f C g B h A

Ex 6

a say b asked c was d him e what f me g knew
h said i had j me k if l would m would n not o to

Unit 18

Ex 1

a congratulated b denied c confessed d remind
e regretted f apologized g volunteered h pointed out
i assured j warned

Ex 2

a B,C b A c C d B,C e A f C g B,C h A,C
i C j A

Ex 3

a on b me c that d entering e me f if / whether
g out h if / whether i of j her k to l to

Ex 4

a pointed out that b of failing c situation on a d √
e to them that high blood pressure
f to them that they should make / to make g √
h added that smoking i concluded that j √

Ex 5

a invited b announced c thanked d begged
e reminded f agreed g pointed out h persuaded
i volunteered j swore k decided l ordered

Unit 19

Ex 1

a they should give him b her plane arrives c isn't it
d Hasn't she? e He is, isn't he?
f what exactly are you waiting for
g where the Astoria Hotel is
h There isn't, is there? i You won't be long, will you?
j when the next train leaves

Ex 2

a … really love to know how old she is.
b … you tell me how much this shirt costs?
c … suppose you know where the projector is.
d … not clear which room is which.
e … wonder what time the lecture finishes.
f … not sure where I have to go.
g … you explain how this works?
h … they told you how long we have to wait?

Ex 3

a Can't you finish your work on time?
b What are we waiting for?
c Do you know what her first name is?
d This isn't your seat, is it?
e Could you tell me the time? Could you tell me what the time is?

f Good heavens, it isn't really 8.00 already, is it?
g You understand the second example, don't you?
h You haven't seen Chris, by any chance, have you?

Ex 4

a No, they don't. They call it Republika e Shqipërisë.
b No, it doesn't. It lies between France and Spain.
c Yes, that's right.
d No, it isn't. Canberra is the capital.
e No, it isn't. Dominica is a small island republic, but the Dominican Republic is the eastern half of the island of Hispaniola, so they are not the same.
f Yes, they do. Indians make up about 38% of the population.
g No, it didn't. It used to be called Basutoland.

Ex 5

a don't b are c haven't d what e don't f Don't
g Don't h there i we j for

Unit 20

Ex 1

a the, –, – b the, the, – c –, –, the d the, the, the, the
e the, the, the f –, –, –, – g –, the, –, the
h the, the, –, the i the, the, the, – j –, –

Ex 2

a The b an c the d – e the f the g the h – i –
j – k the l the m a n – o a p a q a r the s the
t a u the v the w a x a y a z a 1 – 2 – 3 the
4 the 5 a 6 a 7 the 8 – 9 the 10 – 11 the

Ex 3

a the, an, the b a, a, the c the, a, a d the, a, a
e a, a, the, a, the, a f the, the, the, a, the
g the, a, the, the, the h the, the, the, the i the, an, a
j the, a, the, the

Ex 4

a a b – c a d – e The f – g the h the i the j a
k a l – m the n a o – p – q the / – r the s – t –
u – v – w a x a y – z a 1 – 2 the 3 the 4 the

Unit 21

Ex 1

a The, a, the, the b the, a, the, a , the c –, –, a, the, the
d the / –, the, –, the, the, the e –, –, an
f –, a, the, the, – g the, a, a, the h The, –, – an, the, –

Ex 2

a The b – c the d the e a f – g the h the i a
j – k The l the m the n a o – p the q the r The
s the t the u the v the w the x the y the z a
1 – 2 an 3 a 4 – 5 –

Ex 3

a The, the, – b a, the, the c –, the, a d The, a, the, –
e a, a, – f the, the, the g –, an, – h The, –, the
i –, the, a, the j –, the, a

Ex 4

a the b a c the d the e – f the g the h The
i the j the k – l The m the n the o – p the
q the r The s – t The u the v – w The
x the y – z – 1 The 2 – 3 – 4 the 5 – 6 –

Unit 22

Ex 1

a hardly any b enough c lots of d very few
e only a little f not enough g a few h a lot of
i Too many j too much k as much as l enough

Ex 2

a B b A c A d C e C f A g B h C i C j A
k B l A

Ex 3

a many b much c of d less e hardly f lot g as
h quite i how j amount k much

Ex 4

a There's not enough time to finish now.
b None of my answers was / were wrong.
c There is no money in your wallet.
d There were very few customers this morning.
e There were fewer crimes last year.
f The green one costs twice as much as the red one.
g There was a large number of people queuing at the front entrance.
h There is more than enough food for six people.
i There isn't any paper in the cupboard.
j There was hardly any snow last night.

Ex 5

a … is too much traffic today.
b … too much sugar in this coffee.
c … twice as much as that one.
d … amount of money has been spent on this project.
e … than enough money to buy the tickets.
f … many as a thousand football fans were arrested.
g … few taxis at this time of night.
h … very few people know about it.
I … of the paintings was / were damaged.
j … is no water in the tank.

Ex 6

a of b many c every d large e as f times g few
h many i very j large k lots l no m every / each
n as

Ex 7

a 2 b 12 c 5 d 6 e 11 f 1 g 8 h 3 i 10 j 9 k 7
l 4

Unit 23

Ex 1

a is b surroundings c is d cards e have f is
g trousers h stairs i is j are

Ex 2

a customs b manner c damage d works e expenses
f custom g glass h damages i manners j work
k glasses l expense

Ex 3

a crowd b flash c cloud d team e pack f shower
g piece h bunch i item j gang

Ex 4

a seat belt b bookshelf c water softener d coffee pot
e toothbrush f shop window g mountain climbing
h office equipment i pencil sharpener
j computer network

Ex 5

Hamlet's father the King of Denmark has died, and his mother has married his <u>father's</u> brother, Claudius. Denmark is under threat of invasion by a foreign <u>prince's</u> army. Two soldiers on duty on the ramparts of the castle see <u>Hamlet's father's</u> ghost. Later, the ghost speaks to Hamlet and describes his <u>brother's</u> method of murdering him. Hamlet promises to avenge his murder, but pretends to be mad to escape his <u>uncle's</u> suspicions. Claudius asks <u>Hamlet's</u> friends to find out the reasons for his strange behaviour. <u>Claudius's</u> / <u>Claudius'</u> adviser, Polonius, the father of <u>Hamlet's</u> girlfriend Ophelia, suggests that his madness is caused by love. <u>Hamlet's</u> friends invite a troupe of actors to try to make Hamlet less unhappy. Hamlet asks them to put on a play he has written in which his <u>father's</u> murder will be acted. His <u>uncle's</u> guilt becomes clear when he stops the play and leaves with his courtiers. Hamlet kills Polonius in error and is sent to England with his friends as part of the <u>king's</u> attempt to kill Hamlet.

Unit 24

Ex 1

a anything b each c myself d either e anywhere
f else g the other ones h themselves i each other

Ex 2

a B b C c A d B e C f B g B h A

Ex 3

a The people who picked the correct number won £500 each.
b Some children in the class were throwing pieces of paper at one another.
c I've looked everywhere else.
d Have you hurt yourself?
e I blame myself for what happened.
f It doesn't matter if you can't get here by eight.
g Enjoy yourselves at the beach, children!
h A lot of people were driving too fast, but I was the one the police stopped.

Ex 4

a It, there b It, there c There, it d It, there e There, it
f It, it, it g There, There h There, it i There, it j It, it

Ex 5

a C b A c A d B e C f A g B h A
i C j B k B l A m C

Unit 25

Ex 1

a bad b two-hour c a sleeping d soaking e lost
f large g complete h freshly baked i heavy
j worried

Ex 2

a – b very c – d very e very f – g – h – i very
j – k very l very

Ex 3

a winter clothes b silk shirts c torch batteries
d spring sales e a leather overcoat f office equipment
g football supporters h a glass bowl i summer holidays
j computer software k a silver bracelet l autumn leaves

Ex 4

a a neglected masterpiece b the closing headlines
c freezing temperatures d an unlocked door
e mixed feelings f an arranged marriage
g a respected author h a damaging attack
i an unsolved crime j a leaking roof
k the opening scene l an acquired taste

Ex 5

a Italian speaking b freshly baked c fast-flowing
d newly married e open-minded f windswept
g earth-shattering h chocolate-coated i heartbreaking
j tree-covered k time-saving l newly discovered

Ex 6

a B b A c C d B e C f A g C h B i C j B
k A l C

Ex 7

a light b open c heavy d long e small f short
g wide h fine i great j high k narrow l low

Ex 8

a home-produced b much-reduced c freshly prepared
d ready-made e time-saving f hard-working
g so-called h home-cooked i far-reaching j locally grown
k traffic-clogged l large-scale

Unit 26

Ex 1

a to help b to find out c to leave d that you wanted
e to understand f to see g getting h to go
i to understand j to find out

Ex 2

a It's odd (that) you should be here at the same time.
b It makes me angry that you should talk to me like that.
c It right (that) Maria should win first prize.
d It's unfair (that) we should have to work until 10.30!
e I'm determined (that) there should be no repetition of
  today's unfortunate events.
f It's alarming (that) there should be no security at all in the
  building!
g It's only natural (that) the employees should feel badly
  treated.
h It's strange (that) you should have the same initials as me.

Ex 3

a obvious b essential c pointless d better e aware
f make g important h careful i impossible j vital

Ex 4

a It's best to put on plenty of sun-cream before you go out.
b I was sorry to hear your bad news.
c This bad weather makes me feel miserable.
d It's obvious that something will have to be done.
e I'm busy revising for my exams at the moment.
f It was wonderful to meet David Bowie.
g I felt terrible lying to her.
h I am determined that this should not happen again.
i It's good of you to give me a lift.

Ex 5

a impossible b unusual c surprised d clear
e unwilling f unwise g aware h be able i possible
j hopeful

Unit 27

Ex 1

a soon b particularly c quite / really d hard
e Technically / Apparently f quite / really g completely
h early i truly j Luckily / Fortunately

Ex 2

a really b incredibly c widely d completely, utterly
e completely, perfectly, really f awfully, terribly, very
g entirely h greatly i especially, particularly
j totally, utterly

Ex 3

a I quite understand how you feel.
b Unfortunately, nobody came to the party.
c I found the match rather unexciting.
d The decision was financially disastrous.
e This result was entirely unexpected.
f Mrs Burns has kindly agreed to provide sandwiches.
g This printer is completely useless.
h I can hardly see the end of the road.
i The answer is perfectly obvious.
j Logically, the missing money must be in this room.

Ex 4

a B b A c A d C e B f B g A h B i C j B k A
l C

Unit 28

Ex 1

a the b as c probably d too e too f than
g more and more h every bit i a lot j like
k a lot more l the best

Ex 2

a most b enough c better d as e probably / easily
f about g bit h them i away j lot k as l away

Ex 3

a as b enough c like d too e like f as g enough
h as i like j like k too l enough

Ex 4

a C b B c C d B e B f B g C h C i A j B
k C l C

Unit 29

Ex 1

a at b down c to d towards e on f to g within
h upon i along j at

Ex 2

a Jim put a sheet over his head and pretended to be a ghost.
b Anna walked across the street.
c I wish I were far away from here.
d When do you think Alan will be back?
e The dog was running round and round and barking
  furiously.
f I first visited Moscow over forty years ago.
g The temperature is below average for this time of the year.
h The elephant was coming towards Peter at high speed.
i When he's away from his friends, David stops showing off.
j We paid under €200,000 for this flat.

Ex 3

a out b through c away d abroad e by f ashore
g Among h backwards

Ex 4

a in b on c Under / In d in e at f on g in
h under i at j On

Ex 5

a down b through / above c over / across d through
e down f between g along h in i backwards
j under k between l ahead

Ex 6

a into b through c On d along e to f ahead g on
h at i through j in k through l between m far

Ex 7

a out b fro c up d round e on f far g backwards
h abroad

Ex 8

a in India b in danger c through the region
d on the plains e below average f under construction
g on the island h along the western side i between
j along the route

Unit 30

Ex 1

a already b later c by d on time e once f until
g Once h during i At the end j next Saturday

Ex 2

a until 5.30 b During the night c for weeks d at last
e in half an hour f by now g In the end h ever since
i in time j at once

Ex 3

a ago b before c already d at last / finally e For
f During g by h Since i in / during j until

Ex 4

a for b later c in d already e since f yet g once
h by i finally j since

Ex 5

a C b A c C d B e B f A g A h B i C j B

Unit 31

Ex 1

a of b at c to d in e with f with g from
h between i on

Ex 2

a on b against c with d to e on f on g from
h for i from

Ex 3

a C b A c C d B e A f C g C h B i A j C

Ex 4

a concentrate b provide c boast d blame e tamper
f refer g specialize h benefit i apply j advise

Ex 5

a involved b distinguished c differed d approve
e specialize f insist g resulted h forced
i relied / depended j objected k associated

Unit 32

Ex 1

a from b of c with d about e of f of g for h in
i of j for

Ex 2

a purpose b effect c practice d chance e detail f date
g person h room i time j fault

Ex 3

a In business b aware of c wrong about d by mistake
e different from f annoyed by g an effect on
h at fault i better at j without exception

Ex 4

a I was unaware of the problem.
b The drinks machine is out of order.
c You damaged this chair on purpose!
d David was absorbed in his work.
e Mr Gordon has a good relationship with his employees.
f Many people in the crowd were in tears.
g Send in your application without delay.
h Harry is addicted to computer games.
i We don't have this book in stock, but we can order one.
j Robert is an authority on genetic engineering.

Ex 5

a aware b risk c responsible d faced e control
f addicted g theory h used i room j average

Unit 33

Ex 1

a to kick b worrying c to open d pick up e banging
f appearing g to stand up h cleaning i wondering
j to think

Ex 2

a involve b mind c deny d avoid e risk f imagine
g stop h regret i consider j bear

Ex 3

Suggested answers:

a spent b begin / start c considered d meant / involved
e persuaded / encouraged / advised f continued
g appears / seems h allowed i involved j tried / attempted
k gone

Ex 4

a It appears that the match will be cancelled.
b The burglars jumped out of the window to avoid being
   caught.
c Ulysses is considered to be Joyce's greatest work.
d They are planning to reach the mountains by the end of the
   week.
e I prefer not to waste time watching television.
f Do you fancy going skating on Friday?
g We can't go on ignoring this problem.
h My parents didn't let me stay out late.

Ex 5

a continued to b stopped c decided to d involved
e expected f seemed to g persuade h warned
i urged j forced k regretted l demand

Unit 34

Ex 1

a which b What c who d which e who f I asked for
g what h which i which j who

Ex 2

a whose b whose c who d which e whom f whom
g which / that h which / that i which j where

Ex 3

a which b – c which d who e which f What g –
h which i that j that k which l that m who n where
o they p which

Ex 4

a ...the man who jumped over the counter and took the
   money.
b ... up late, which wasn't unusual.
c ... many people, some of whom gave us good descriptions of
   the robber.
d ... the house where my aunt and uncle live.
e ... who meets Angela likes her.
f ... of whom were half an hour late.
g ... found a shepherd's hut where we sheltered from the rain.
h ... which was extremely crowded, stopped at every station.
i ... isn't the building [that] I thought the bus stopped outside.

Ex 5

a whose b who c whose d which e whom f which
g what h which / that i – j – k who l which
m what n what o – p – q who r whose

Unit 35

Ex 1

a even though b Seeing that c the way d in case
e Much as f The moment g No matter what
h although i Everywhere j Considering that

Ex 2

a Whenever you're in the area, drop in and see us.
b As soon as I saw you, I knew I liked you!
c Fiona started training as a ballet dancer when she was six.
d I won't leave / I'll stay until you come back.
e You can park your car anywhere you like outside.
f Now you're here, you'd better sit down.
g Once the exams are out of the way we can start learning
   something new.
h The memorial shows where the plane crashed.

Ex 3

a Although b Considering c As d until e After / Once
f way g so h When i case

Ex 4

a It sounds as if they are having a good time.
b This isn't the way you are supposed to be doing this.
c He looked as if he was carrying something.
d I took up jogging, as you suggested.
e He behaved as though he owned the place.
f The meat tasted as if it hadn't been cooked properly.
g Peter didn't conduct the experiment the way he was
   instructed to / told to.

Ex 5

a B b C c C d A e A f B g A h C i C j B

Unit 36

Ex 1

Suggested answers:

a √
b After I had left the room, the telephone rang.
c As I had lost my money, the conductor wouldn't give me a
   ticket.
d While I was falling asleep, there was a loud knock at the
   front door.
e √ f √
g When I opened the box, it turned out to be empty.
h √
i After I had been asked for my name, I was taken to meet the
   prime minister.
j When I arrived at the station, the train had already left.

Ex 2

a Although b Being c Without d It e While
f Abandoned g Though h There i If j By

Ex 3

Suggested answers:

a Located b discovered / found c shown / illustrated
d being / becoming e Having f caught / captured
g facing h Visited i being
j Realizing / Discovering / Finding k protected

Ex 4

a It being a public holiday, there was a lot of traffic on the
   roads.
b On opening the letter, I realized it was from Professor Alton.
c Though destroyed by fire during the war, the palace was
   later reconstructed.
d Carol walked from the room, tears streaming from her eyes.
e In trying to remove the memory card, I broke the camera.
f Since using Glosso shampoo, my hair has become soft and
   shining.
g Jan was taken to hospital after being knocked down by a car.
h Having been shown to his room, George lay down on the
   bed and slept.

Ex 5

a A b A c B d A e C f B g A h C i B

Unit 37

Ex 1

a C b A c C d C e A f B g B h C i A j C

Ex 2

a 6 b 10 c 4 d 9 e 3 f 1 g 5 h 8 i 7 j 2

Ex 3

a break out b come off c come about d fall back on
e break off f get off g come into h come out
i do away with j bring round

Ex 4

a It's getting on for 8.00, so you'd better get ready to leave.
b I couldn't really understand what she was getting at.
c I don't think we can count on Johnson to support us.
d There's an important point I think I should bring up.
e In 1939, Jim was called up.
f The director is drawing up a list of suitable candidates for the
   job.
g The statement of the accused was borne out by other
   witnesses.
h Carol has come up with a really good solution to the problem.

i The stranger offered to sell Harry the Eiffel Tower, and Harry fell for it.
j A lack of marketing expertise eventually brought about the downfall of the entire motor industry.

Unit 38

Ex 1

a B b A c C d A e A f C g A h B i C j B

Ex 2

a 6 b 10 c 2 d 4 e 9 f 1 g 8 h 5 i 7 j 3

Ex 3

a look into b go round c give out d play up e pack in
f point out g make up for h keep to i go about j give away

Ex 4

a The government expects the economy to pick up in the later part of the year.
b You've missed out the question mark at the end of the line.
c There are a lot of people hanging around in the street outside our house.
d I think it's time we paid him back for all the awful things he has done!
e Ann was supposed to look after my dog, but she let me down.
f What on earth is going on here?
g Frankie nearly won both races but just missed out.
h I didn't like the film at first, but then it started to grow on me.
i Don't let on that I put that notice on the door!
j Tony made up a story about meeting Bob Dylan in a café.

Unit 39

Ex 1

a A b A c C d C e A f C g A h C i B j C

Ex 2

a 6 b 2 c 10 d 4 e 8 f 1 g 9 h 3 i 7 j 5

Ex 3

a put down b track down c set about d put out e set out
f step up g work out h turn down i stand for j see off

Ex 4

a The local planning office has turned down the company's application to build flats on the site.
b The lawyers made notes as the judge ran through the details of the case.
c The security guard was taken in by the thief's disguise.
d Carol turned up at the party unannounced, much to everyone's surprise.
e Harry has very good ideas, but he put them across to an audience.
f I don't think you should keep running yourself down.
g Someone has to see to the children's lunch at 12.30.
h Mr Johnson will be stepping down as company spokesperson at the end of the month.
i A group of foreign investors has taken over the company.
j Jim was set upon by three muggers in the street.
k €500 for that? I think you've been ripped off.
l The report runs to over five hundred pages.

Ex 5

a I can't seem to shake off this pain in my left leg.
b Tina is really good at taking off the accounts manager.
c We can put you up for a few days.
d I think someone has slipped up, because I'm not owed any money.
e I think this bad weather has set in for the day.

f The foreign minister promised that his country would stand by the agreement.
g David has taken to running up and down the stairs for exercise.
h That really sums her up!

Ex 6

Suggested answers:

a I was worried about the examination and didn't manage to drop off for ages.
b That song is growing on me.
c The prime minister and the finance minister have fallen out again.
d Three young boys carried out the robbery on their way home from school.
e We waited for a bus for ages, and we ended up walking.
f I can't make out how much this is going to cost.
g The Mexican restaurant we tried didn't come up to our expectations.
h The spare parts we have been waiting for have been held up in the post.
i Helen didn't quite understand / couldn't make out what George was getting at.
j I don't like the way he talked to you! I wouldn't put up with it, if I were you.
k When the teacher asked who had broken the desk, two boys owned up.
l Fiona doesn't really go for camping holidays.
m I'm going to try out my French when I'm on holiday.
n I'll try and get round to calling you later on today.

Ex 7

a Make sure you hang on to your ticket, as you'll need it later.
b Nick says he's going to complain, but I don't think he'll actually go through with it.
c I don't think you should impose your beliefs on people.
d I decided to drop in on my old aunt while I was in the area.
e The work we had done on our house was carried out by a firm of local builders.
f The party finally broke up after the neighbours complained about the noise.
g Emily says she'll visit us one day, but I can't pin her down.
h Our luxury cruise holiday didn't live up to our expectations.
i When the food gave out, the two men were forced to eat insects.
j Rita is a strange person, I can't make her out.
k George hit it off with his mother-in-law.
l I don't think the gunmen will give in without a fight.
m I'd like to point out that I'm not in fact English, but Scottish.

Unit 40

Ex 1

a although b at least c on account of d thus
e As a result f Moreover g on the contrary
h Accordingly i due to j Consequently

Ex 2

Suggested answers:

a result b respects c Above d extent e owing f Compared
g However h account i Furthermore / Moreover

Ex 3

a Regular exercise keeps you fit. Furthermore, it gives you a feeling of well-being.
b Henderson suffered a serious leg injury in 2005, but despite this she has come back to dominate the 400 m this season.
c Pets provide lonely people with company, and, what is more, have been proved to have a beneficial effect on many common medical conditions. / What is more, they have been proved …

d There has been lower consumer demand. However, the company has increased profits by 6%.
e Bicycles are pollution-free and silent. As well as this, they take up very little parking space.
f The heater has been tested for safety. Nevertheless, it must be used according to the instructions.
g I don't really like the design of this sofa. Besides, it won't fit into the living room.

Ex 4

a To some extent b However c As well as d in some respects e Above all f as a result of g Furthermore
h However i consequently j as a result

Unit 41

Ex 1

a First of all b As far as snakes are concerned c such as
d Alternatively e utterly f simply g instead h from
i In a way j a kind of

Ex 2

a 10 b 5 c 2 d 6 e 4 f 1 g 3 h 9 i 8 j 7

Ex 3

a concerned b such c kind d so e for f ie g say
h respects / ways i literally j Apart k as l sheer

Ex 4

a sheer b simply c mere d literally e utterly f sheer
g sheer / utter h utter i simply j utterly

Ex 5

a C b A c A d C e B f B g A h B i C j A

Unit 42

Ex 1

a I haven't done it yet b neither do my friends c it
d told her so e if so he is f more so g doing so h so
i this is the most expensive one j hers

Ex 2

a one b very much c it is d ones e hers f did so
g neither / nor can Brian h so i not j so

Ex 3

a C b A c B d C e A f B g A

Ex 4

a I don't have a bike now but I used to <u>have one</u>.
b – c … and <u>he likes</u> playing computer games.
d … but my friends aren't <u>worried about it</u>.
e … but she doesn't <u>make her own clothes</u> any more.
f – g … but Theresa hasn't <u>been there</u>.
h …but he didn't say who <u>he would bring to the party</u>.
i – j I've done the shopping and <u>I've</u> cleaned the house.

Ex 5

a 'Do you think you'll be late tonight?' 'I don't suppose so.'
b Bond started to disconnect the red wire, but as he did so, something told him he had made a mistake.
c If you wanted to stay at home, why didn't you say so?
d Sue tried to reach the top shelf but couldn't do so / it.
e I can't stand folk music, and neither / nor can David.
f Helen left her bike outside the cinema, but she didn't remember doing so.
g The robbery was committed by two people, or so we believe.

Ex 6

a There is no problem as far as money is concerned.
b In a way, I think you're absolutely correct.
c Everyone was there apart from Jim.
d These are my cards and those are yours.
e In conclusion, I would like to thank the organizers of this conference.
f This country has high youth unemployment in comparison with other European countries.
g Tom has been absent from college due to illness.
h Tony thinks it was a terrible film, and so do I.
i United played badly, but at least they won the match.
j The tennis tournament has been postponed owing to bad weather.
k 'Will you be here next year?' 'I don't think so.'
l The scheme has been successful to a certain extent.
m As a result of the earthquake, many roads in the area have been closed.
n The two artists appear to be different but are similar in some respects.
o She was forced to give up driving on account of her poor eyesight.
p Instead of taking the bus, I went on foot.
q First of all, write down a list of your ideas.
r Many animals, such as bears, sleep for much of the winter.
s No artefact which is alien, that is to say not from our planet, has ever been discovered.

Ex 7

a C b A c C d C e B f B g A h B i C j A
k A l A m C

Unit 43

Ex 1

a Rarely b Should c Never have I seen
d What he is talking about e managed
f Strange as it may seem g when h into the room ran
i Had we known j could k Little l Were

Ex 2

a C b B c A d C e A f B g C h B i C j B
k C l A

Ex 3

a Were we to take no action, the situation would only become worse.
b Rarely does a member of the government admit to making a serious mistake.
c Under no circumstances are you to leave this room.
d Only later did the police reveal the true identity of the thief.
e Try as Andrew might, he couldn't pass his driving test.
f Had you consulted me at the outset, I could have given you the right advice.
g Were you to offer me a higher salary, I would take the job.
h Should the weather worsen, the match will probably be cancelled.
i Only after checking the accounts did they realize money was missing.
j In no way has the breach of security affected the examination results.

Ex 4

a seem b little c sooner d Onto e until
f came / walked g Had h Only i could j when
k did l Why

a ... the room ran two armed policemen.
b ... on a clear day like today can you really enjoy the view.
c ... the ship collide with an iceberg, the passengers would be in no danger.
d ... though the case may be, such cases are not completely unheard of.
e ... came / poured the rain.
f ... has a government acted with such blatant dishonesty.
g ... you to ask me again, I would give you the same answer as before.
h ... the matter is I have no idea.
i ... we realized that the hurricane would hit the city, we would have evacuated the residents in advance.
j ... did anybody suspect that the police inspector was the murderer.
k ... when the accounts were checked was the theft discovered.
l ... had Paula shut the door than she realized she had left her key inside.

Ex 6

a do b Only c did d had e have f did g then
h Under i when j but k has l did

Ex 7

a B b A c C d A e C f B g C h A i B j A

Unit 44

Ex 1

a not the slightest bit b nothing whatsoever c do hope you
d the very last moment e who sent f the very thing
g to do h Wherever i who j at all

Ex 2

a A b C c C d B e C f B g B h C i A j B

Ex 3

a The police asked David the same question again and again / over and over.
b There was no chance at all of saving the damaged ship.
c The house I was looking for was at the very end of the street.
d All I want to do is sleep.
e I want my own bike.
f It was when I saw smoke coming from under the door that I became alarmed.
g Thanks very much indeed for your help.
h Whatever can you mean?
i It was what Robert did next that took everyone by surprise.
j It is your own fault.

Ex 4

a own b that c is d own e what f at g more h at
i it j very k Whatever l What

REVIEW

Unit 3

a was sitting b had occupied c stood d had reduced
e had undergone f were raining g had largely evaporated
h had been i looked j had given

Unit 8

a ... was believed to have been stolen.
b ... was thought to have crashed in the mountains.
c ... was known to have rejected the plan.
d ... was reported to have fled to South America.
e ... were thought to have found fingerprints at the scene of the crime.
f ... was believed to have killed over a thousand people.
g ... was known to have visited the murdered man on the afternoon of his death.
h ... was reported to have paid the singer $2 million in damages.

Unit 9

a got b get c is having / is getting d get e had f got
g had his hair / got his hair h get i got j having / getting

Unit 11

Ex 1

a If you happen to have a camera with you at the scene of the accident, you can take some shots of all the vehicles involved.
b Check the weather reports before you leave, otherwise you might take the wrong clothes with you.
c If it were not for the income from advertising, newspapers would not earn enough money.
d Investors will not buy shares unless they have confidence in the market.
e We guarantee to get you talking even if you can't speak a word of English.
f Permanent residents can vote provided they are aged 18 or over.
g Were I to accept the job, would I be able to work from home some of the time?
h Supposing there were a serious outbreak of bird flu in Europe, what would the EU do?
i If we don't do something now, the situation will get worse.

Ex 2

a or b if c had d even e been f wouldn't g were
h provided

Unit 12

a I wouldn't make any hasty decisions, if I were you.
b He behaves as if he were in charge of the office.
c I'd sooner you didn't bring the dog with you.
d I wish I hadn't sold my old car.
e I hope you have a good time at the party!
f I'd rather you didn't call me again.
g I wish you weren't leaving in the morning.
h If I were you I wouldn't drink any more.
i I wish I could find the answer to this problem.

Unit 14

a can't be b must be c might have gone
d should have got here e must have left it
f she's bound to be g can't have recognized h can get
i may as well j might have told

Unit 16

a In the past, surgeons would operate on patients without any kind of anaesthetic.
b They would work as quickly as possible to minimize the patient's suffering.
c Such operations would often take place in the patient's own home.
d In some countries, religious authorities wouldn't allow surgeons to study anatomy using dead bodies.
e Surgeons would often learn about anatomy by treating soldiers in battle.
f Doctors would also be expected to follow the explanations of ancient writers.
g When new medical discoveries were made in the Renaissance, traditional doctors wouldn't believe that the old methods were wrong.
h Some ancient ideas – such as that of removing blood from patients (bleeding) – would survive in medical practice until the late nineteenth century.

Unit 18

a 'Would you like to stay to lunch?'
b 'Don't forget to take your keys.'
c 'Why don't we all meet outside the cinema?'
d 'I didn't have anything to do with the burglary.'
e 'I'm sorry I took so long over the phone call.'
f 'You broke my kitchen window! / It was you who broke my kitchen window!'
g 'No, I won't give you my name!'
h 'Would you like (some) tea and cakes?'
i 'I'll return the money as soon as I can.'
j 'I wish I'd studied harder at university.'

Unit 19

a A b C c C d B e C f A g C

Unit 20
Ex 1

a The b a c the d the e the f the g the h a
i the j The k the l – m The n – o the p the
q – r the s the t the u a v the w the x –

Ex 2

a We use a telescope to view distant objects.
b The rent for this flat is €500 a month.
c I've got a pain in my right arm.
d This is a really wonderful meal.

e Sandy is an Australian.
f The sports utility vehicle (SUV) is becoming less popular.
g The answer seems to be two and two thirds.
h Is there a Steve Jenkins here?
i Do you want to come to the cinema?
j The war ended in 1918.

Unit 21
Ex 1

a A b the c the d a e – f a g a h – i The
j the k a l the m –/ the n – o– p a q a r the
s the t – u the v – w a x the y the z A 1 –
2 – 3 a 4 the 5 the 6 the 7 the 8 the 9 –

Ex 2

a A b an c – d – e a f – g the h the / – i the
j the / – k – l the m – n a o A p an q a r A
s a t a u – v a w – x A y a z an

Unit 23

a Shakespeare was the son of a town official in Stratford on Avon.
b Shakespeare's plays were published in a collected edition after his death.
c He is usually judged to be England's greatest playwright.
d He was a shareholder in an acting company known as the Lord Chamberlain's Men.
e He was also an actor and the author of narrative poems and sonnets.
f He was successful enough to become a property owner.
g He died at the age of fifty-two.
h Theatre audiences have enjoyed his plays for over four hundred years.
i His plays are often changed to suit the interests of modern audiences.
j There are also many famous film versions of the plays.

Unit 24

a Someone b both c there d it e both f himself
g someone h There i there j it k one l there
m Anyone n their o There p It q it r everyone

Unit 26

a It's hard for me to carry all these bags on my own.
b I wasn't aware that I had to hand in my work today.
c It makes me nervous to think / when I think about starting my new job.
d It's easy to miss the turning if you're not careful.
e I was shocked to hear that Kevin was ill.
f You're welcome to stay here whenever you like.
g I'm sure I left my wallet on the table.
h It's not worth going to see the new Larry Jotter film.
i It makes me happy to know you believe me.

Unit 27
Ex 1

a fairly b rather / fairly c quite d rather / fairly e quite
f quite / rather / fairly g quite / rather / fairly
h quite / rather / fairly i rather

Ex 2

a 8 b 1 c 2 d 6 e 3 f 4 g 9 h 11 i 5 j 10 k 12

Unit 28
Ex 1

a … is one of the best books I've read.
b … more interesting to go out dancing than to stay at home watching television.
c … feel so much shocked as horrified.
d … abstract a concept to explain.
e … far the best film this year.
f … about as much as I can.
g … the worst June weather we've ever had.
h … as easy to speak French as I thought.
i … near as good as his last one.
j … you tease the dog, the angrier it will get.

Ex 2

a I liked this film but it isn't nearly as good as the previous films in this series.
b Johnny Depp gives by far the best performance in the film.
c It's one of the longest films on release at the moment.
d It's [getting] harder and harder to understand the plot of films like this.
e The special effects of this film are much more impressive (than those of the last film).
f But I was not so much shocked as scared out of my wits, by some parts.
g This is easily the most entertaining film I've seen this year.
h In some ways it's not as funny as the last film in the series.
i But this film is every bit as worth seeing.
j The more you watch this film the more you enjoy it.

Unit 30

a David hasn't finished his novel yet.
b We waited for a bus for half an hour, but in the end we gave up.
c Nick didn't get to the airport in time to catch his plane home.
d I'll (only) be here until Friday.
e I'll talk to you after the lesson.
f The trains here are very comfortable but they are never on time / they never run on time.
g We'll send you the certificate once we receive / have received the fee.
h I'll be there by 11 00.
i Peter could hear loud howling noises throughout the night.

Unit 31

a Luckily the fire officer succeeded in rescuing the cat from the top of the tree.
b Can I discuss this problem with you?
c My parents don't approve of some of my friends.
d How much you pay depends on the condition of the vehicle.
e My computer has a problem, but someone is coming to see to it tomorrow.
f Are you insured against fire?
g Mr Wilkins has decided to resign from the company.
h Take a seat, and I'll ask someone to attend to you.
i The runaway bus collided with a parked car at the bottom of the hill.
j This ice-cream really tastes of strawberries.

Unit 32

a C b B c A d B e B f C g A h B i A j C

Unit 33

a B b A c B d C e C f A g C h B i C j B

Unit 34

a C b A c A d B e C f A g A h B i B j C

Unit 35

a … I would like to help you, I don't really have the time.
b … how much you offer me for it, I won't sell you the house.
c … house prices continue to rise in most areas, in some areas they have actually started to fall.
d … you have not paid the last six monthly instalments, this contract is at an end.
e … the weather conditions were atrocious, all the runners finished the race.
f … we could have a snack first.
g … case I got cold.
h … it was raining, the match went ahead.
i … it's too late to start the meeting now, I think we should hold it another day.
j … rapidly that the guards were taken by surprise.

Unit 36

a … lost my watch, I had to borrow my brother's.
b … pressing this button, you can change the size of the page.
c … cheap, the bike was in good condition.
d … realizing the meeting was in a different place, Sue went straight home.
e … being interested in the topic, I left the lecture before the end.
f … instructed, write your name.
g … been arrested and charged with theft, Tony phoned his lawyer.
h … receiving their letter, I phoned the company.
i … missed the last bus, I had to take a taxi.
j … coming to this school, I've made a lot of new friends.

Units 37 and 38
Ex 1

a Tim has fallen for the girl he sits next to in maths.
b How are you getting on in your new school?
c I agree that you had a bad time, but you brought it upon yourself!
d You'll have to do without milk in your tea.
e The film didn't come up to my expectations.
f Your explanation just doesn't add up.
g There's a point I'd like to bring up before we finish.

Ex 2

Suggested answers:

a I think it's time you got down to some serious work.
b Sorry, what did you say? I'm dropping off!
c Tina's name kept cropping up / coming up in our conversation.
d In the end, the problem comes down to a lack of proper planning.
e Feelings of resentment between them built up over a long period.
f Alan can't always explain exactly what he is getting at.
g Helen has come up with a really good way to cut the cost of this project.
h We hit upon this hotel completely by chance.
i I think we should push on until we get to the top of the hill.
j Are you going in for the Advanced French Test this year?
k Sorry to be so late, but I was held up in my last meeting.
l Things have certainly been looking up since I was promoted.
m Sue promised to come and help me but she let me down.
n Don't let Helen in on our plans, or she'll be jealous.
o Little Johnny owned up to taking Paula's sweets.

Unit 44

a What b It c at all d very e What f at all g very
h it i What j at all k What l own